Rape, Incest, Murder! The Marquis de Sade on Stage

Volume Three
Asylum Plays Plays

John Franceschina

Rape, Incest, Murder! The Marquis de Sade on Stage
Volume Three
Asylum Plays

Published in the USA by:
BearManor Media
P O Box 71426
Albany, Georgia 31708
www.bearmanormedia.com

ISBN: 978-1-59393-741-6
Printed in the United States of America
Book design by Robbie Adkins

Contents

Introduction

On 2 April 1801 Sade was confined to Sainte-Pélagie prison following his arrest in March because of the furor raised by the publication of his collection of stories, *The Crimes of Love*. Almost immediately upon his arrival, the marquis joined a literary society called *Dîners de Sainte-Pélagie*, for which he wrote a number of verses (included at the end of this volume) and ultimately became its president. Limited to a membership of nine inmates (to correspond to the number of Muses in Greek mythology), the group met every week for dinner and literary recitations. The artistic stimulation the society provided was clearly insufficient to a man of Sade's personality, and around 14 March 1803, when the marquis encountered a group of rowdy young men who had been sent to prison after causing a disturbance at the Théâtre-Français, his indecent propositions and lascivious gestures with a wax dildo created such a turmoil that Sade was transferred, first to Bicêtre prison (on 15 March), and finally to Charenton on 27 April 1803.

With its tree-lined promenades, thirty-acre garden, and scenic panoramas, Charenton Asylum, designed for the treatment of mental disorders, was a far cry from Sade's earlier incarcerations. Instead of a cell, the marquis enjoyed a suite on the third floor of the right wing of the hospital that included a bedroom, a small study, and a library with windows overlooking the Marne River. The apartment was furnished simply with a canopy bed, an old desk, a commode, two straw-stuffed chairs, a mirror, a folding screen, and a fireplace. Sade was at liberty to stroll the grounds and communicate with other prisoners at will, and in August 1804, the director of the asylum, François Simonet de Coulmier, allowed Madame Marie-Constance Quesnet, Sade's mistress, to take room and board at the hospital. From that point on, Marie-Constance occupied the room next to the marquis and was introduced to the other inmates as his illegitimate daughter.

Coulmier believed in a relaxed, almost paternal, method of governing the institution and was continually exploring various methods of therapy to treat and entertain his patients. Shortly after Sade's arrival at the institution, the marquis managed to convince Coulmier that theatrical activities would provide an excellent method of group therapy for the inmates, and the director ordered the building of a real theatre in the Notre-Dame ward, complete with stage, wing space, an orchestra pit, and an auditorium capable of accommodating nearly two hundred spectators. In addition, facing the stage was a box reserved for Coulmier and his guests. On each side of this box were twenty seats reserved (on one side) for male and (on the other side) female patients selected from the least deranged of the inmates, and finally Madame Quesnet had a box reserved for herself and six guests.

Between 1805 when performances began at Charenton and 1813 when the theatre was officially silenced, Sade functioned as the artistic director of the enterprise. Although Coulmier selected the repertoire—conservative, easily accessible plays—Sade took charge of all aspects of production, selecting actors, designing scenery, directing rehearsals, writing publicity notices, selling tickets, and acting as stagehand, prompter, and a kind of master of ceremonies during performances. Although most of the performers were inmates of the asylum, professional actors from the Paris stage appeared in the principal roles, and Sade was graciously assisted in rehearsals by Madame Saint-Aubin from the Opéra-Comique. Once a month, the theatre produced a double-bill drawn from popular dramas, comedies, or musical theatre pieces, and included such plays as *L'Impertinent*, *Le Nouveau doyen de Killerine (The New Dean of Killerine)*, *Le Sourd; ou, l'Auberge pleine (The Deaf Man; or, The Inn Full Up)*, *Le Depit amoureux (The Rebound)*, *Claudine et le chaudronnier (Claudine and the Boilermaker)*, *Les Chasseurs (The Hunters)*, *Les Folies (Lunacies)*, *Ambroise*, *L'Esprit de contradiction (The Spirit of Contradiction)*, *Marton et Frontin*, *Les Fausse Confidences (False Secrets)*, and *Les Deux Savoyards (The Two Savoyards)*. In addition, Sade wrote several original plays for the theatre at Charenton only one of which still exists: *The Festival of Friendship*, an allegorical work written in honor of his patron Coulmier, performed on Coulmier's name day, and translated for the first time in this volume.

News of the performances at Charenton spread quickly and soon watching inmates of an insane asylum perform familiar plays became a popular diversion drawing spectators from all walks of life and locales. Sade's guest list for a performance in 1810 offers a representative sample of the typical audience in attendance:

Mr. Treillard, three seats
Madame Ronchoux, No. 13, Choiseul Street, two seats
Madame Cochelet, lady-in-waiting to the Queen of Holland, eight seats
Madame d'Houdetot, three seats
The Irish doctor, one seat
The Sauvan family, four seats
Mr. Finot, a lawyer in Charenton, and family, two seats
Mr. Deguise, chief surgeon at Charenton, and family, three seats
Madame Lambert, three seats
Madame Gonax, four seats
The parish priest, for Mr. Norvert, four seats
The mayor of Charenton, two seats
The diplomat, one seat
Mr. Millet, one seat
Madame Quesnet, seven seats
Mr. de Sade, seven seats
Mr. du Camp, three seats
Mlle. Adélaïde, three seats
Madame de Huteuil, five seats
Mr. Le Roi, two seats
Madame Urbistandos, mother of one of the inmate actresses, six seats
Mr. Vivet, two seats
Mr. Chapron, three seats
Mr. Veillet, four seats
Madame Marchand, two seats
Mr. Le Couteux, two seats
Mr. Florimond, two seats
The three Nogent women, three seats
Mr. Flandrin, one seat
Employees of the asylum, thirty-six seats
Inmates of the asylum, sixty seats

Often, spectators left eyewitness accounts of the presentations. Some, like the poet Auguste de Labouisse-Rochefort, were highly critical of the marquis's acting and personal appearance, though most were pleasantly surprised at the histrionic abilities of the mental patients who managed to hold their own among the professional actors on stage. The journalist and vaudevillian Armand de Rochefort (not related to the poet) was equally intimidated by Sade's presence at the usual pre-show banquet but found the music played as an overture before the performance "flawlessly performed" even though the musicians were all inmates of the asylum. He was especially impressed by the patient in the starring role—a role that had been made famous by the celebrated actress Mlle. Mars—observing that she exhibited both an ease and flawless memorization that surprised and amazed the audience. He added that even though the inmate playing the romantic leading man managed to say all the right lines, his performance was less successful.

The most extensive account of a performance at Charenton was left by Mlle. Flore, an aspiring young actress who was drawn to Charenton more to meet Madame Saint-Aubin, the "diamond of the Opéra-Comique," than to see the plays: "I couldn't believe that the insane were capable of an art that required so much study and work, especially for those who had use of their reason. But I was told that this method of keeping them busy, of distracting them from their manias by making them focus their attention on entertainment, was a method of therapy often used with success."

In addition to providing a rather detailed account of Sade's personal appearance in her *Mémoirs* (quoted in the introduction to *The Festival of Friendship*), she notes the names and personalities of the actors on hand in the first play, *Le Depit amoureux*. The role of Gros-René was played by Stockleit junior, a young actor who had established his reputation at the Ambigu-Comique theatre; Marinette was played by Madame Quesnet, "an aging actress . . . who was in a relationship with one of the *pensionnaires* of the asylum." The role of Éraste was performed by a young man with a very interesting face, said to have been driven insane after losing his fiancée in a terrible accident. The madwoman playing the part of Lucille was blond, vivacious, and expert in her portrayal of a flirt. Mascarille was played by Laujon's son, a madman who believed that he was a great painter, asking as much as 40,000 francs for his drawings.

Although the first play proceeded without incident, the second piece was less successful:

> A madman was playing the part of a valet, and not performing badly, when the actor who played his master gave him a letter and told him to go and deliver it. The valet looked at him arrogantly and said, "What do you take me for? Am I your servant? Run your own errands!" And he left the stage without anyone being able to make him return. Another actor who was playing the role of a noble father continually refused to wear his wig, and because they insisted, he mischievously allowed them to put it on, but as soon as he walked out on stage, he threw it into the prompter's box. They had to lower the curtain.

Mlle. Flore concluded her recollection of the evening's performance by praising a beautiful young Spanish inmate named Mlle. Urbistandos who played the role of Joset in *Les Deux petits Savoyards*, "to the delight of the entire audience, and afterwards sang beautifully the *couplets* written by the Marquis de Sade in honor of the director of the asylum, the guest of honor." What most amazed Mlle. Flore was not the beauty of the almond-eyed Spanish girl, or her melancholy appearance, or the fact that she could act and sing to the delight of the audience. "What startled me," Mlle. Flore added, "was that the couplets written by that man of hideous morality radiated charm and spoke very highly of virtue!"

The dichotomy between Sade's theatrical impulses and those of his licentious public life continued to haunt the marquis throughout his career. In a life filled with ironies, it is especially ironic that these noble, enlightened, even sentimental creations should be overshadowed by a violent, libidinous lifestyle and the prose works that reflected it. The greatest irony of all, perhaps, is that this "monster," this "Saint of Satan" may have found, in the amateur theatricals at Évry, Mazan, La Coste, and Charenton, his greatest fulfillment as an artist.

Fanny; or, The Effects of Despair

Introduction

Little is known about the creation of Sade's three-act prose drama, *Fanny; or, The Effects of Despair.* Gilbert Lély cites it as one of four plays written during the Revolution or at Charenton while Annetta Foster dates it between 1790 and 1801 "when Citizen Sade was free and in contact with the various Parisian theatres during the Revolution and its aftermath." In his collection of Sade's unpublished letters, Jean-Louis Debauve includes a note written in 1798 to the actor Jean-Baptiste Lavenette, called Corse, one of the five administrators of Ribié's Théâtre d'émulation. Debauve suggests that an unnamed play discussed in the note could be *Fanny*. He also remarks that the Théâtre d'émulation during this period was fond of doing adaptations of English Gothic novels, such as Ann Radcliffe's *The Mysteries of Udolpho*, or M.G. Lewis's *The Monk*. These "dark" Gothic dramas are full of subterranean prisons, caverns, abductions, murders, and highly charged scenes of emotion and terror. It is not unlikely that Sade might have offered his "English" melodrama to Ribié's theatre.

Both Lély and Foster, however, note that in his *Descriptive Catalogue in 1788*, Sade indicated the existence of a one-act drama entitled *The Unfortunate Girl* intended to be part of his five-hour extravaganza, *The Marriage of the Arts*. Though that play is not included in the 1810 version of the extravaganza, and is considered lost, Lély discovered that it was later expanded into a three act drama entitled *Cleontine, or The Unfortunate Girl*, also supposed lost.

Before Sade's plays were published by Pauvert in 1970, Count Xavier de Sade discovered a series of fragments from *Cleontine* which correspond exactly to certain scenes from *Fanny*. While names of some of the characters have been changed (Cleontine becomes Fanny, for example, Lord Nelson becomes Lord Wilson), the editors of Sade's plays maintain that the plots of the two plays are "rigorously identical" with both heroines poisoning themselves in the belief that their lovers have been untrue. More telling, perhaps, are the alterations noted by Sade's editors, which softened *Fanny* and made it more accessible than the earlier versions.

In *Cleontine*, for example, Nelson is actually arrested and carried off by Lord Butler; in *Fanny*, Lord Butler only threatens such violence. In the earlier play, Lord Butler delivers the message of the play in a kind of self-criticism; in *Fanny*, Sir James delivers the line, "Ah! See what happens because of discipline, greed and ambition!" In *Cleontine*, Nelson succeeds in grabbing a sword from Sir James and running himself through; in *Fanny*, Wilson's suicide attempt is prevented, and he simply faints over Fanny's body. Finally in the earlier play, Sir James also considers suicide saying, "Come, my lord, I'm as wretched as you are, and I'll die as well."

While these changes are hardly momentous, they do signify a tendency in Sade's playwriting to moderate the violence as the plays are revised. While we might guess that this was Sade's attempt to please theatre managers, and to make his plays more acceptable to the public in terms of traditional structure and sentiment, it is impossible to know for sure why the Marquis de Sade ultimately "watered down" his plays. Certainly *The Marriage of the Arts*, in its last form did not follow the accepted structure of eighteenth-century French drama, and the repeated indictment of men by the women who have been ruined by them was not an entirely acceptable sentiment in Sade's day (the feminist passages omitted from the original production of *The Marriage of Figaro* in 1784 attest to that fact).

Sade's biographer, Maurice Lever, suggests that after 25 August 1790, when Sade met the woman he would nickname "Sensible," Marie-Constance Quesnet (née Renelle), he became a changed man:

> Between Constance and his books, Donatien aspired to nothing more at the age of fifty-one, than to spend his days peacefully, as a man of letters. His sole occupation was to get his plays produced. His senses, appeased at last, no longer gave him trouble.

A letter written three months earlier on 19 May 1790 to Reinaud the lawyer, indicates Sade's conservative political views, and certainly suggests that his youthful "demons" have mellowed out considerably:

> In any case, do not mistake me for an embittered man. I tell you, I am nothing if not impartial, annoyed to have lost so much, still more annoyed to see my sovereign in irons, and aghast to see what you gentlemen in the provinces have no idea of, that it is impossible for good to be done, and to continue as long as the monarch's sanctions are constrained by thirty thousand armed bastards and twenty pieces of artillery. Though, for that matter, I have few regrets for the Old Regime. It certainly made me too unhappy to shed any tears over it. . . . Valence, Montauban, and Marseilles are theatres of horror where cannibals daily perform dramas in the English manner, such as make a man's hair stand on end. . . . Ah! It's certainly been a long time since I said to myself that this lovely, sweet *nation* . . . was only waiting for the opportunity to be galvanized into action, to show that balanced forever between cruelty and fanaticism, it would return to its natural manner as soon as the occasion permitted.

Sade's criticism of dramas performed in the English manner might certainly account for the tight structure and conservative nature of the play he referred to as his "English drama." Could the play have been rewritten in reaction to what Sade had seen? Speculations notwithstanding, *Fanny; or, The Effects of Despair*, in its final draft, is a fine example of the *genre serieux* with its overblown sentimentality and excessive moralizing. It will surprise readers that this play was written by the author of *Justine*, or *The 120 Days of Sodom*. But Sade's life was changing, and his drama is perhaps an indication of that change.

FANNY
or
THE EFFECTS OF DESPAIR

Prose Drama in three acts

CHARACTERS

Lord Butler, *a member of the Irish aristocracy*
Fanny, *Lord Butler's daughter*
Sarah, *a girl of thirteen or fourteen, Fanny's younger sister*
Sir James, *an old millionaire, Fanny's intended husband*
Lord Wilson, *Fanny's lover*
John, *Fanny's elderly confidential servant and foster-father*
Servants, mute characters

The action occurs at Lord Butler's castle on the coast of Ireland.

The costumes are strictly Irish. Sarah should be dressed very simply. We anticipate that this role, written for a child from twelve to fifteen years of age, would be absolutely amiss performed by a younger or older person.

The setting is a prison. An iron door at the back leads to the inside rooms of the castle. Another, to the right, leads to a small cell adjacent to the prison, which contains FANNY. On the left, there is a table with a water pitcher and a cup; some wooden chairs complete the furnishings of this dismal place.

It is eight o'clock in the morning.

ACT ONE

SARAH. (*Alone; she is seated next to the table in a melancholy frame of mind.*) Unhappy victim of a father's ambition. Poor Fanny, in the springtime of her life, engulfed in the horrors of prison and only able to leave at the expense of her heart! Either to die there or to sacrifice the dearest gift she might have received from heaven! Oh, sister! Sister, how I pity you. Ah! If my affection, if my compassion can soothe the horror of your fate, I offer them, with all the sincerity in my soul. I thank heaven for my father's cruelty. Not wanting to permit any servant to come near you, he entrusted me alone with the responsibility of taking care of you. This is the hour when she awakens. I'll see if she needs anything. (*She quietly goes to unlock the door to the cell.*) She's sleeping. We must respect her sleep, it's the sole comfort of the unfortunate. (*Taking a paper out of her pocket.*) Nevertheless, I'd like to tell her about this letter which her faithful servant John just received on her behalf, from Lord Wilson, the dear and worthy object of her love. Maybe she'll find some consolation in it, if he can leave her behind in the terrible predicament in which my father dares to keep her. Here comes John himself. By what coincidence is he permitted to enter? Let me think about what has to be done.
JOHN. (*Entering, with a serious expression.*) Where is your sister, Sarah?
SARAH. She's sleeping, Mr. John. She hasn't stopped crying all night.
JOHN. (*Wiping from his eyes a few tears that flow involuntarily.*) Unhappy Miss! When my wife used to feed you, when she raised you on your mother's knees, when you used to appreciate that mother who loved you so much! When all the wishes of the family were revolving around you, was it then to be the plaything of so wretched a destiny that the sky seemed to gather over your young head so much kindness and good fortune? Sarah, we have to wake her up. I bring her orders from my Lord Butler.
SARAH. (*With the most tender and naïve concern.*) What? My father still isn't tired of persecuting this poor girl? What's the news?

JOHN. Have you given her that letter which Lord Wilson happened to send me so mysteriously? How inconsiderate to have come . . . to arrive at so critical a moment . . . at the same time as his rival. Well, Sarah, have you given her that letter?
SARAH. Not yet.
JOHN. You have to give it to her, Miss. You must try to get her to read it before the visit that is being prepared for her, so that she might, at least, alleviate her grief. Although, in reality, I tell you, Sarah! I'm carrying out this lie regretfully. It's useless to maintain a passion that can only make her miserable. This is the last time I'm going to do this. I'd give anything in the world to turn her against love.
SARAH. Oh! What is this visit, Mr. John? What is this visit that you're making us afraid of?
JOHN. Sir James! He's coming. He's coming from London. They traveled all night. The messengers had already dismounted when my lord ordered me to come and announce it to his daughter. And to persuade her to receive him properly.
SARAH. (*Completely terrified.*) Ah, my poor sister! She'll die, Mr. John, she'll die! And why does this man want to marry a girl against her wishes? Doesn't he know very well that he's hated? Doesn't he know that she'd prefer death to this marriage and that nothing will change her mind?
JOHN. Sarah, you're young, inexperienced. You know neither men's passions nor their effects. May you not have to learn all of that, like her, one day, at your own expense! Marriage is only an arranged affair, my dear Miss. A father, a settlement. His children hardly trouble him to know if they'll be happy or not, but he expects to be. He's busy finding, in the matches he makes, either the necessary consolidation of domestic affairs, or the help he needs to increase his wealth. That's what makes marriages, Miss. Should you be surprised that there are so many unhappy ones?
SARAH. But doesn't young Wilson have all that is necessary?
JOHN. No. His lineage is worthy of your father's, without a doubt, but he's neither important nor wealthy. He only has expectations, and they can fall through. What Sir James brings is more substantial: a stable age, twelve thousand pounds in revenues. No nobility at all, I admit, he's only a businessman, but Miss Fanny

is noble enough for both of them, and my Lord Butler pays his debts.

SARAH. And the unfortunate girls are born then to satisfy their fathers' ambition and greed?

JOHN. That's only too true! Sarah, if your sister were able to take something upon herself, if she were able to suppress a passion which is dragging her through so much misery! Perhaps afterwards . . . ! Sir James is a rough man, an old colonial merchant, whose manner, I know only too well, is not well-suited to please the daughter of an Irish aristocrat. But he's really a gentleman, sincere, honest. He has qualities in his possession which would be suitable for his exaltation in a country where virtue would count for something and nobility for nothing when it hasn't achieved any honors. Ah! How I would like to overcome Miss Fanny's resistance. Not being able to be with the one she loves, it's still worth more to belong to a man like Sir James than to spend her youth in such a horrid place. For I warn you, her father has decided to leave her here if she doesn't immediately yield to his wishes.

SARAH. Ah! Her aversions are so passionate! My sister has known Sir James for a long time, you know. She respects him but she cannot love him. This unyielding dislike has been growing since she was a little girl. He was the bogeyman during her childhood. He has remained the object of her displeasure throughout her youth, and I know that she never looks at him without shuddering all over, the cruel indication of the feelings he instills in her. Besides, how do you suppose she might ever give up the feelings she has for Wilson? They were in school together, intended for one another by their mothers. Ah! Mr. John, those feelings might never end. That's what my sister told me.

JOHN. Sarah, wake up Miss Fanny. I can't wait any longer.

SARAH. There she is. There she is. Her heart, I think, anticipated both of us. The poor girl. She knows very well that, in the entire world, she only has the two of us who are still risking our lives to serve her.

(Fanny is wearing a black crepe dress. Her hair is disheveled. There is the greatest carelessness in her behavior and attire.)

SARAH. (*Running to her and hugging her, with tears in her eyes.*) Hello, my beloved sister.

FANNY. (*Embracing her very tenderly. To JOHN, with surprise.*) Ah, Mr. John, who could have sent you to me? It seems that I am less miserable when I have the pleasure of seeing you. You remind me of the first years of my life. What years, my friend, and how different they were from these. (*She cries, leaning on JOHN.*)

JOHN. (*Sobbing.*) Miss, don't cry. No longer tug at the heartstrings of the wretched servant who stays with you. Today you need courage . . . strength and not tears. Sarah is going to give you a letter. Read it quickly. It's from someone who interests you, but someone I advise you to forget. Look at the state you're in, the loathsome slavery in which you are held by a father who's cruel, I know, but a tyrant who must be obeyed. Look, be sensible, and convince yourself that your fatal bonds with Lord Wilson are the only things that prolong your disgrace. What good does this stubbornness do now? Forgive the words of an old servant who raised you, but what good is this fidelity when it's the day before the sacrifice?

FANNY. Heavens, what are you saying?

SARAH. (*Weeping, and kissing FANNY's hands.*) Oh, my sweet little sister, here is the moment when heaven must confirm all your plans.

FANNY. Oh! What's going on, then? What's going on? You're frightening me.

JOHN. (*Continuing quickly.*) No, Miss, no. He's an honest man. He likes you. He loves you dearly as if you were his own child.

FANNY. (*Trembling.*) Ah! Don't remind me of paternal tenderness when you want to give me the notion of a kind heart. But I'm anticipating you. Sir James . . .

SARAH. (*Weeping.*) Oh, sister.

JOHN. (*Quickly.*) He's here.

FANNY. (*Pretending to be courageous.*) I'll see him. Have someone send him to me, John. I'll see him. A first misfortune unlocks the soul and makes it vulnerable. The second time, more violent still, a person only trembles on account of adversity because she's unaware of it. Nothing frightens me today, father. Yes. Yes, you're right. When you've seen a dagger pointed at your breast for a long time, the moment when it strikes at least makes an end of the terror.

SARAH. Wait. Let this letter, if possible, completely soften the horror of the upsetting news we've just given you.

FANNY. (*Reading the letter that SARAH just handed to her.*) Ah! What new distress! He's coming too, Mr. John. You didn't tell me. He's coming, he's coming, he says, to break my chains or to lose his life. What rashness! What an undertaking! With a father like mine on the coast of Ireland where, for more than fifteen leagues, people recognize Lord Butler as their master or sovereign lord. He'll have him arrested. He'll treat him despicably. Don't let him come here. Mr. John, Sarah, prevent him from coming here. Oh, Wilson, you whom I'll adore my entire life, I'd rather deprive myself of the happiness you promise me, than to cause you to lose your honor or your life.

SARAH. If he has taken it upon himself, don't expect us to be able to discourage him.

JOHN. Is that an order, Miss? I'll do all that I can, and as I labor only in behalf of your happiness, it alone will guide my every step. Leave it to me, Miss. Leave it to me.

FANNY. My friend, I don't know how to answer you. Nevertheless, if it were successful in getting me out of this cruel situation . . . forbidding him to see me when he's exposing himself to everything for me! What do you advise me to do, Mr. John?

JOHN. (*Firmly.*) Immediately break the ties that can only make your life miserable.

FANNY. (*Passionately.*) Give up Wilson! Me? Break the sweetest bonds of my life? You should tear him from me a thousand times rather than hope I would authorize it.

JOHN. Very well, Miss. You no longer need to discuss this. It's up to the others to work on your behalf (*To himself.*) without letting you know about it.

FANNY. Ah, my friend, don't leave me.

SARAH. (*Quickly to FANNY, tearing the letter out of her hands.*) Hide that letter. Hide that letter. Here comes our father. Oh, heaven protect her!

LORD BUTLER. Get out, John. It's taking you a long time to carry out my orders!
JOHN. If my integrity were less known to you, my lord, I could take your accusation to heart.
LORD BUTLER. Get out. (*To SARAH.*) Leave us. (*Both of them comply.*) After having given you time to think, Miss, I've finally come to be informed of the results. To see if you want to win back the heart of a father whom you've made angry. Speak. Explain yourself. My designs are known to you. You know who I want you to marry, that man so horrible who, nevertheless, adores you. That man you hate with so little reason. In a word, Sir James, my friend, the one I intend for you to marry. He's here and I've come to make sure of the way you're going to receive him. Will Miss Fanny always forget what she owes her father? Will she always be a rebellious daughter? Speak, I'm listening to you. Remember that your fate is in your hands.
FANNY. Good heavens, is this intended to relieve the situation of a miserable wretch, to offer her clemency at the price of that which you know would be impossible for her to do?
LORD BUTLER. Miss, you're questioning me when I want an answer from you; and you're complaining about a treatment that your stubbornness alone prolongs. If you accept what I propose, your complaints would be useless. Their cause is abolished. If you refuse, then, which of the two of us has the right to complain: you who would disobey me when you owe everything to me, or myself who finds only a rebellious child in a daughter who ought to be more submissive?
FANNY. My lord, I owe you my life. I will never forget that I received it from you. But if that life is only a burden for me, if I'd rather lose it than prolong it to be so unhappy, in imploring you to seize it from me, in begging you to tear it away from me yourself, I return your kindness. From that moment, you no longer have the right to torment me.
LORD BUTLER. Miss, I want neither to take away your life, nor to make you unhappy. You're not at the age to understand what's good for you. Marrying off children has always been the father's responsibility. Only fathers can and must take care of it, and your clever reasoning will not upset the established order. A

terrible passion is blinding you. Nip it in the bud. Discard everything in your imagination that stands in the way of recognizing your real interests. Then you'll understand that we only endeavor to serve them. Or if this disastrous delusion is too strong to be destroyed, then in no way oppose the measures which those who love you, and who know better than you what's good for you, try to use to lead you back to the path of happiness from which you're being distracted by your imagination.

FANNY. I thought, my lord, that no one better than oneself was in the position of choosing what was best for her.

LORD BUTLER. You're wrong, Miss. A choice can only be made with sound judgment. It's no longer sound when blinded by passion.

FANNY. But, father, the motives that incline you to force me to marry a man that I hate, and that make me refuse . . . aren't they passions too?

LORD BUTLER. Granted . . . for the moment. But mine would have the advantage over yours, being governed by wisdom.

FANNY. (*Spiritedly.*) Ah, father, aren't the impulses of the heart preferable to those of the mind? When the hand of God created us, our soul was his masterpiece and its instincts should be the best.

LORD BUTLER. Cunning creature!

FANNY. (*Even more passionately.*) Besides, isn't the arrangement of marriage you're offering me newer than the one my mother wanted? You know, seeing as I was brought up with Wilson since we were children, she intended us for one another. She also used to say that she was trying to make me happy. I believed her. How is it, my lord, that today you can imagine that the same happiness which my mother assured me ought to be found with Wilson must no longer exist now, except with Sir James? If my heart has already found happiness in the first engagement, how can you expect it to find joy in the second?

LORD BUTLER. You mother was talking to you like you were a child. She didn't realize that little family jokes must someday become serious things. She had hardly even seen the one she was talking about. But I who know him . . . I assure you that's he not at all right for you . . . that he has nothing that deserves your affections . . . and you must either forget him or accept the full effect of my anger.

FANNY. (*With a noble courage.*) Your anger will move me less than your indifference. A heart like mine is frightened with being no longer loved. It is less terrified of being hated.

LORD BUTLER. Ungrateful daughter!

FANNY. (*Continuing with the greatest passion.*) Either you shouldn't have created a sensitive soul within me, or, having done so, you cannot punish me for surrendering to its power. Must I learn from you how to repel its sweetest impulses? Take it away from me, my lord. Take away this life which displeases you. You would trouble me much less in tearing it away from me than in tyrannically depriving me of that which can do it kindness.

LORD BUTLER. Deluded girl! Even if your indiscreet passion is destroying everything inside you, down to your natural feelings, at least do not be disrespectful.

FANNY. (*Throwing herself at her father's knees.*) Oh father, I will forget neither the respect I owe you nor the feelings I have for Wilson . . . both imprinted upon my heart by the same hand. Do not destroy the one or the other . . . both are too mutually intertwined. Let me die here. You put me here. Here I'll stay. But do not demand a sacrifice from your daughter that is impossible for her to make.

LORD BUTLER. (*Furious.*) Get away from me, miserable wretch.

FANNY. (*Bending almost to the ground and hugging LORD BUTLER's knees.*) Good God, if some tenderness remains at the bottom of your heart, don't take advantage of the hideous state to which you've reduced me.

LORD BUTLER. Get away, I tell you. Get away from me, cursed daughter.

(*He pushes her, and as the gesture is made with great force and passion, she falls backwards completely, supported by one of her hands.*)

FANNY. (*Raising her other hand toward the sky.*) Cruel man! May the father of mercy not push you away from his feet, one day, like you just drove me away from yours!

LORD BUTLER. (*Going out, and with the greatest authority.*) May my curse become the price of your rebellion! I will never see you again during my lifetime. I'll forget that I had a daughter. I'll even forget your name.

FANNY. (*Darting from one end of the stage to the other, into her father's arms.*) Ah! Forgive me. Forgive my losing my senses. Heap all your anger upon me, but don't threaten me with the loss of your heart. (*Melting into tears.*) What do you want me to do, father?

LORD BUTLER. See Sir James.

FANNY. (*Stuttering.*) I'll obey.

LORD BUTLER. I want him to see you here.

FANNY. (*Lowering her eyes, and blushing.*) Here, father?

LORD BUTLER. Yes, I want him to see you in the midst of this humiliation. I expect from him what I cannot obtain myself. He will return you to my arms if your delirium has vanished, or he will let you die in this prison if nothing can overcome the desires you ought to blush to admit. (*He exits.*)

FANNY. (*Alone.*) The desires I ought to blush to admit! I am far from placing shame on the admission of my love. Oh, Wilson! This heart where you reign will never know the painful impulse which exists only to accompany crime. Yes, I promised to see Sir James. But, oh, comfort of my miserable life, I didn't promise to forget you. Ah, could I? I'll die if I have to . . . but, dying for you, I'll carry to the grave the feelings people will try to make me smother. What's he doing? Where is he? I'll see him. What's John doing? Maybe he won't be allowed to reach me? Or he won't dare? Oh heaven, what a predicament! Waiting for the result of this horrible business. Let me go write a few lines that I want to leave inside the tomb. *(She indicates the cell where she exits.)*

END OF ACT ONE

ACT TWO

(Two servants carrying in a tea table and then going out.)
JOHN. (*To the servants.*) Put it here. (*To JAMES.*) Oh, Sir James, there's the sad sanctuary where virtue dwells.
SIR JAMES. Make her come out, John. Tell her that I beg her to come and have a cup of tea with me!
JOHN. (*Entering the cell.*) Humor her, sir. Humor her, I beg you.
SIR JAMES. (*Alone.*) What a dwelling place for her whom nature has made most perfectly! (*FANNY appears.*) Come, lovely child, come into your father's breast. I'm the one trying to guide you there.
FANNY. Generous man, earn that favor by a sacrifice.
SIR JAMES. Very well, tell me what you want. You've known all your claims upon my heart for some time now. Sit down, and let us discuss this comfortably.
FANNY. (*Sitting down.*) What do I want? I want you to forget me. I want you swear to me that you'll give up your intentions regarding me. I want you to assure my father immediately that you're no longer thinking of marrying me, and that you'll never consider it again.
SIR JAMES. (*Who was already beginning to sip his tea; he puts down his cup.*) Listen, my child. I love you and I have always loved you. Don't think that I'm the cause of the harshness that your father uses with you. I condemn it. Yes, I repeat, I love you. Your power over me is great and if it takes all that I have . . . three times all I have, it all belongs to you, just say the word. But don't think that I can give up my own happiness, for there is no happiness dearer to me than possessing you. There's nothing about me that can offend you. I know myself. I'm blunt, but I'm honest. The sweetness of your personality should inevitably combine with the frankness of mine, and whatever you may say about it, we'll be happy. There's a great difference between our ages, I know, but that's all the better for you. With the head that I know you have, you need a prudent man. I'll guard you from all the misfortunes to which your effervescent mind would lead you. I'll moderate your fiery youth; you'll revive my frosty old age. Come on, my

child. Providence certainly provides for its own. You can be certain that it created us for each other.
FANNY. In affirming that, you're only taking the advice of your heart. Don't you think that mine ought to be consulted, likewise?
SIR JAMES. Ah, what objection can it come up with against me? Is it an attachment? That doesn't frighten me. I know about young girls' fantasies. From kindness, from patience, from good behavior, a fellow soon wins back through respect what he couldn't get from love. Little by little, the heart comes to its senses. You lose sight of all those misfortunes of youth, but a husband's good behavior is not forgotten. You find yourself bound by gratitude. There it is! Already the heart is softened. Ah, my child, with a girl who possesses all the qualities I know you possess, the heart is soon won over when virtue ensnares it. I will not conquer you, Fanny, but I will earn you. You will not love me, but you will not refuse me tenderness, and that's all I need at my age.
FANNY. (*To herself.*) An honest man. Ah! I must deceive him less than another. (*Aloud.*) Sir James, in a heart like mine, the impulses are linked together; they all connect to the ability to love. Since another entirely possesses the results of this ability, over which I have no control, nothing would be left for you except insignificant feelings which I'd be ashamed to offer you. They wouldn't make you happy, and I would consider myself the most wretched of wives if, destined to spend my life with you, I wasn't making you completely happy. Those feelings that you consider trivial aren't as frivolous as you think. They are childhood affections, and nothing will ever be able to destroy them. Oh, James, do you think that I value you highly after the confession I've just made?
SIR JAMES. (*In the most regretful tone of voice.*) What I think is that you don't love me, and that you're making a mistake, Fanny. You'll never find a man more prepared than I to make you happy. (*He stops drinking tea and wipes a few tears from his eyes.*) Fanny, you distress me. You're making me cry. These are the first tears I've shed in my life . . . me, who'd try to pay with his blood for all the tears that I'd see flowing from your eyes. (*With a voice, interrupted by sobs.*) My only ambition was to make you happy. You're depriving me of my life's sweetest hope. (*Looking at her tenderly.*)

Tell me that wasn't your final word. Fanny, tell me that was only to soften the cruelty of your confession.

FANNY. Heaven, to what have you reduced me! Between two unavoidable evils, I must spare you the cruelest. Without a doubt, it would be being married to you without being able to love you. Oh, James, yield a moment longer to the nobility within your heart. Here are the two of us, entirely divided by different interests: I can't give up mine without despair, you can't relinquish yours without sadness. Which of the two must yield to the other? Let your tenderness decide!

SIR JAMES. Unjust girl! Why don't you think that I might love you as much as you love the cruel object that is robbing my life of happiness?

FANNY. (*Spiritedly.*) Sensitive and virtuous man, why don't you believe that there can be no one in the world like the one who makes me completely happy?

(*SIR JAMES rises with a gesture of sadness. FANNY does likewise. Both of them are thinking.*)

SIR JAMES. (*Looking very dejected.*) Is that your final word, Fanny? Is that all I'll get from the creature in the universe for whom I had felt the greatest tenderness?

FANNY. (*The greatest outpouring of heartfelt emotion.*) Oh, Sir James, she'll always pay you back with her esteem. I'll consider you my benefactor. I'll cherish you as a second father. All of my heart's affections, except for love, will be yours without restraint. I will not have a greater delight than to prove it to you all the days of my life.

SIR JAMES. (*Holding her against his breast, in tears.*) Ah, then stop using the same pleasing tone of voice, which would certainly be appropriate for depicting love, to swear your hatred for me. My dear girl, a few years will perhaps extinguish that passion which stands in the way of the one I'd like to inspire in you. I'll wait.

FANNY. (*Quickly.*) My entire life spent beneath the chains of misfortune would only confirm further this passion which devours me. I'll die, Sir James. What's worse, I'll spend the rest of my life here, if I have to. But I will never give up the one I've loved since my childhood.

SIR JAMES. So then, will the proof of the esteem be to break, in cold blood, the heart of the man who loves us more?
FANNY. No, but it will consist in not wanting to deceive that man. It will consist in preferring to cause him a moment of sadness rather than the cruel obligation of making him unhappy for life.
SIR JAMES. (*Very touched.*) Incomparable girl, tell me then that you don't hate me.
FANNY. I'll tell you more. I promise you the fondest friendship, if you give up your pursuits and don't try to coerce me.
SIR JAMES. You don't want to assure me, then, that you don't hate me.
FANNY. Oh, Sir James, you want a reply from me which you can dictate yourself.
SIR JAMES. (*Very touched.*) Goodbye. (*He goes out and returns.*) Fanny, you'll lament me one day, perhaps. I was worthy of your heart, and you didn't realize it. (*He exits in tears.*)
FANNY. What's he going to do? Ah, God! Perhaps I should have been evasive, but how do you deceive a man like that? Oh, John my dear, you see me more miserable than ever.
JOHN. (*With the most serious expression.*) I know, Miss, and I'm coming against my will to crown the horror of your fate.
FANNY. (*Terrified.*) Heavens, what's going on? Tell me, tell me, Mr. John. I'm in a position to hear everything.
JOHN. My lord Wilson.
FANNY. (*Quickly.*) Yes?
JOHN. He's gone.
FANNY. Without seeing me?
JOHN. He wasn't able to, Miss, but here's a letter. (*She tries to take it from him; he withholds it from her.*) Swear to me, Miss Fanny, that you'll read it calmly. That you'll control yourself.
FANNY. (*Trembling.*) Yes, yes, I'll control myself. You see I'm very calm.
JOHN. No, Miss, you're not.
FANNY. (*Not controlling herself.*) Ah, give it to me, give it to me, cruel man. Can't you see that my heart is exposed? Finish the job. Make it bleed!

JOHN. (*Giving her the letter.*) Read it, Miss, read it. You're right. The occasion is horrible, but what choice is there!
FANNY. (*She takes the note and reads it aloud. Her voice gradually weakens; she can scarcely speak the last words. As soon as she's finished, she falls into a kind of immobility. Her eyes are vacant, and tears flow over her cheeks.*) "I was coming to sever your restraints. There's no longer time. You've been, they tell me, Sir James's bride for the past two hours. Enjoy in peace the fruit of your treachery. Is this, then, the price of the most tender love? I will imitate you, Fanny. In fifteen hours, I'm off to London and tomorrow, Miss Volmar's husband. You know my refusal to form such an alliance got me into trouble with my whole family. It's no longer time for sacrifices. Treachery doesn't deserve any. Goodbye, Miss. Be happy. Yes, be happy, at least as happy as I'm going to be." (*After a pause; gradually returning to her senses, and with the most contained emotion.*) Do you know who gave him this news?
JOHN. (*Lowering his eyes.*) I don't know, Miss.
FANNY. (*Hurriedly, with madness in her eyes.*) Did he see James? Did he see my father? Did he see Sarah?
JOHN. (*As before.*) No, Miss.
FANNY. (*With a vacant look, going from excitement to calm.*) You haven't seen him?
JOHN. He had already left when I arrived at his dwelling. I wanted to warn him. He had gone and left that letter for me in the care of the innkeeper's son, Thompson.
FANNY. (*Still calm on the outside, but horribly disturbed internally. To herself.*) The cruel man. He had already gone. (*To JOHN, after a pause.*) John, I'd like to write a letter. Leave me for a moment. Tell Sarah to come get my letter in a quarter of an hour. Yes. In a quarter of an hour it will be done. And Sir James?
JOHN. He's talking to my lord.
FANNY. (*She completely loses control and goes from being calm to the most vehement outpouring of emotions.*) Listen, John, you've always liked me. Here's the time to prove how dear to you I am. (*Suddenly going from this outburst to the most apparent calm.*) You'll tell my lord . . . (*She falls back into madness.*) To London, tomorrow, Volmar's husband. I'll never see him again. I'll never see him again. (*She becomes calm again.*) Yes, my friend, you'll tell James

that, if by chance he wanted to come in here, I'm resting and that I beg him to leave me in peace for a moment, so that I can finish what I have to do. Do you promise to say that?
JOHN. Miss, you're disturbed. I shouldn't leave you.
FANNY. (*Angrily.*) Oh, you really have to leave me, John. You really have to leave me. I need to be alone. You certainly see that I am calm enough to be left alone. (*With the greatest restlessness, looking around, going from rage to pity, and taking JOHN's two hands.*) My friend, couldn't I escape from here?
JOHN. Oh! Miss, I'd risk my life, and we wouldn't succeed.
FANNY. (*Giving way to the depths of despair, in tears, falling into the chair which is next to the table.*) Ah! This is the first time I've completely felt the horror of my chains. (*She gets up after a pause.*) Go away, John, go away. Either you've never loved me, or you'll obey me immediately.
JOHN. But, Miss Fanny, don't you miss him?
FANNY. (*Completely distracted.*) Who? My mother? (*Recovering, and dissolving into tears.*) Oh, John, John, you remember my mother. How she used to like you.
JOHN. Good heavens, she's losing her mind! I was talking about Wilson, Miss Fanny and asking if you miss him?
FANNY. (*She laughs. All the muscles of her face contract mysteriously. Tears run down her cheeks.*) Wilson? Who, me? Miss him? Oh, no, no. I'm happy. I don't regret anything, John. I don't regret a thing.
JOHN. Ah! Miss, my dear Miss, come back to your senses. Think . . . to have left like that, he certainly had to love you a little.
FANNY. (*The gesture that she makes here should be the same shudder that would come from her during a violent shock of physical pain.*) Ah, leave me, you barbarian! (*She becomes delirious.*) The villains! I know very well that they'll end up killing me. (*She runs around the stage. In her frenzy, her hair falls over her face and breast and covers her.*) Whoever you may be, defend me. They're attacking me. They're surrounding me. Tigers, quench your thirst with my blood. (*She throws herself into JOHN's arms.*) Oh! John, John, why have you abandoned me to scoundrels? (*She becomes motionless once again. Her tears flow in abundance.*)
JOHN. Miss, it is absolutely impossible to leave you in the state you're in.

FANNY. (*Completely calm.*) My friend, it's your presence that disturbs me. I've the greatest need to be alone. In the name of all that is dearest to you, leave me alone for a moment.
JOHN. All right, I'm going. I'm going, but are you calm at least?
FANNY. (*Contained.*) You certainly see me that way, my friend.
JOHN. (*Going out.*) Goodbye, Miss. (*Returning.*) Ah! Listen to me. Seize the opportunity. Heaven has allowed this mistake to bring peace to your life. (*He exits.*)
FANNY. (*Alone, and calm.*) Yes, heaven has allowed it, not to bring peace to my life, but to destroy it. It's all over and my time has come. (*She sits next to the table.*) Oh, Wilson, Wilson, did you have to believe that I was unfaithful? Let me gaze once again upon his picture. (*She takes a box out of her pocket.*) With eyes so sweet, tomorrow you'll be Volmar's husband? Will you love her, Wilson? Will you love her like your Fanny? Oh, no, no, never! I have to write him. The picture of his deceitful face must be returned to him only with the last strokes of my hand. (*She takes writing paper out of her pocket and writes on it with a pencil. She reads aloud each phrase as she writes it.*) You've misunderstood me. Between death and infidelity, I wouldn't have hesitated a minute. I'm sending you back your picture. Keep mine at the bottom of your heart since in two days it will be disfigured by the horrors of the violent death I will indulge in because of you. Yes, that's how I want you to see me forever, so I can be avenged. When your eyes are reading these words, mine will be closed. Perhaps they will have already been devoured. Goodbye, Wilson. (*She wraps the box in the writing paper; then taking a bottle out of her pocket.*) Here's what's going to shorten the course of my life. What I've saved for this horrible moment, which I've foreseen for a long time. (*She pours the liquid into a glass.*) Hurry. When a person is as miserable as I am, it's cowardly not to throw off the chains that connect us to life. And what in the world would I have to regret? Betrayed by my lover, sacrificed to a man I don't love, treated cruelly by my father. For whom, almighty God! For whom should I preserve such a miserable life! (*She raises the glass to her lips, then quickly puts it on the table. She hastily unwraps the package and takes out the picture, setting it in front of her.*) Come, Wilson, I want to be able to look at you while I'm dying for you. I want to

draw the disgust for life from the same features where formerly I inhaled the need to love and to live. (*She throws herself upon the picture, kisses it passionately, and, after a pause, swallows the poison.*) Heavens, how a moment just changed everything for me! *(She gets up.)* Haven't I committed a crime? Forgive me, God, forgive me. I thought I saw you trace my death sentence with the sharp point of a dagger that would tear my life to pieces. I thought I'd anticipate your command. Don't punish me for a single mistake. Open your heart to innocence betrayed and persecuted. I'm certainly resolved to die unhappy, but don't let me die unhappy and guilty. Let me hide the action I've just taken. Ah! It's not life that I regret. I only mourn for the crime I'm afraid I've committed in breaking away from it. *(She goes into the cell.)*

END OF ACT TWO

ACT THREE

SARAH. Sister. Where in the world is she? (*She goes toward the cell. FANNY appears. Aside.*) She isn't aware of the good news I'm going to tell her. Ah, sister, reclaim hope and courage. Wilson is behind me, in there. He's waiting for me to go and open the secret door that connects the tunnels.

FANNY. (*Looking vacantly at her sister without hearing her, and like a madwoman.*) What are you saying? What name did you just speak? Is the entire universe let loose against poor Fanny? What did you say, Sarah? What did you say? I can no longer make out the sound of your voice.

SARAH. I'm telling you that Wilson is right behind me, in there. He's escaped John's watchful eyes. John absolutely refused to let him see you. Don't hold it against him, sister. He was doing it for your own good. He thought he could succeed in making you forget him, but Wilson desperately threw himself at my knees. He called me his dear little sister. Ah! Good heavens! (*She runs to help FANNY who staggers and falls overwhelmed on the chair close to the table, speaking the following words with a weak and smothered voice.*)

FANNY. Ah, good God, what have I done!

SARAH. Ah, my dear friend! What is it? When I'm coming to tell you the good news! Is that the effect it has on you? Come back to your senses. Wilson is in there. Take advantage of seeing him the only time you can risk it without fear. Maybe our father . . .

FANNY. (*In the greatest depression.*) Oh, well, yes, go get him, Sarah. Go tell him I'm waiting. These moments are more precious than you know. Ah! Don't waste a single one. (*SARAH goes out. She calls her back.*) Sarah! Listen, kitten, listen . . . (*SARAH hastens to throw herself at her sister's feet.*) This is perhaps the last chance I'll have to speak to him.

SARAH. (*Crying and kissing her sister's hands.*) Oh, why? Why?

FANNY. (*Hugging her with tears in her eyes.*) You see, my child, you see what the cruelty of fate has reduced me to! Here you are, ready to come into the age of strong emotions. Ah! May you be

able to protect yourself from the one that has been the torment of my life. (*She hugs her.*) Sarah, I repeat: we will perhaps never see one another again.
SARAH. (*Tearfully.*) Oh, God!
FANNY. (*Quickly, and without waiting for a reply.*) Be wiser, Sarah, than my example teaches you, and if ever love tries to work its way into your heart, remember Fanny's misfortunes, and don't forget me as time passes. (*She hugs her again, pouring out a flood of tears.*) Go, find him, Sarah. Go tell him that I'm waiting.
SARAH. (*Sobbing.*) Ah! How you've grieved me. He's going to ask me why I've been crying like this.
FANNY. (*Thinking that she is already feeling the effects of the poison.*) Run, Sarah. Time is short. Good heavens! (*SARAH exits.*)
FANNY. (*Alone, and still seated at the table.*) God almighty, you allowed this to complete my destruction. It was decided in your eternal decrees that poor Fanny wouldn't have a moment's peace on earth. John, I see what you've done. (*Casting her eyes on the letter.*) Never, never would Wilson have written these words! John, John, you thought you were helping me and you've cost me my life. Is there a fate more hideous than mine! (*She is overwhelmed with despair.*) I've found happiness only to lose it immediately! Wilson, Wilson, I will see you only to bid you an eternal farewell. I hear him. Don't let me dishearten him. He'll find out about my misfortunes soon enough.
(Sarah enters, bringing along WILSON.)
SARAH. Here he is. Here he is, sister. (*Continuing, and taking from the table the package FANNY wrapped for WILSON.*) Look here. She was writing to you. Such a dear sister! She's always thinking only about you.
WILSON. (*Trying to take the package.*) Ah, my beloved Fanny! Let me devour those lines.
FANNY. (*Spiritedly holding on to the package.*) Stop, Wilson. Respect for a few moments more that horrible secret. You'll find out about it only too soon.
WILSON. A secret, a secret from me, Fanny? Heavens! Everything I see, everything I hear makes me tremble. This distressing place, your despair, that letter, the product of your sadness. Oh, my beloved, explain yourself.

FANNY. (*Negative gestures, and still seated, engulfed in her suffering.*)
SARAH. (*Quickly.*) John deceived her. He told her that you had gone away without seeing her. That news hurt her, but your presence should bring her back to life. Wilson, Wilson, console her. Such a dear sister! All her happiness depends on you.
FANNY. (*Getting up and going to WILSON.*) Oh, my friend, how charming it is to see you again. But under what circumstance do we meet again?
WILSON. It's horrible without a doubt! But your chains are broken. Come, Fanny. Your misfortunes are over. I've put an end to them all by coming to take you away from this place. Come, follow me.
FANNY. Follow you . . . and what would you do with me, Wilson? In three days, all your feelings would be destroyed. Love vanishes like a shadow, and we ourselves pass on the earth like waves the ocean carries up from its depths. You can expect to live for a long time yet, you, my beloved, and toward the end of your life, our marriage will have made only a dent in the confusion of your life's events. Hardly at all, then, will you remember me. To you, it won't even seem that I existed. (*She weeps.*)
WILSON. Oh, Fanny, you're breaking my heart when you should be consoling it.
FANNY. (*Beginning again, and firmly.*) Oh, well, it's the only grief I'll cause you . . . and the last. But you must accept it completely. I changed my plans. Stop, my beloved, stop thinking that true happiness is in the marriage you offer me, and prepare yourself for pain.
WILSON. (*Quickly.*) What is it?
FANNY. (*Quickly.*) Giving me up forever.
SARAH. Giving you up?
WILSON. Oh, God, can I do it?
SARAH. (*To FANNY.*) Sister, what are you thinking of? (*To WILSON.*) Oh, Wilson, console her. Love her and blame only the turmoil into which she has been plunged by so much injustice and unkindness.
FANNY. (*In despair.*) Wilson, we must part. Oh, my friend, doesn't everything in this world have to die? The earth is a field

of slaughter where bloody nature is situated between birth and death. Let us part, Wilson, let us part.

WILSON. (*Full of energy, and rage.*) Cruel woman, what are you saying? Rather rip this heart to pieces, this heart from which you will never escape. Every drop of blood that gives it life is enkindled only by your love. My blood would flow beneath your barbarous hands so that my love for you would still exist. It's not my life that creates it. It's you alone who are the essence of my existence. It's not up to you to take it away from me. Oh, spirit of her mother, I implore you: it was from your hands that promises were made, promises that we would love one another forever. Come punish her for breaking them. Come restore her to the sanctity of our bonds, or unite me with your ashes so that some part of me might be joined to that which was dear to her.

FANNY. (*Having given way to the frenzy of madness, sadness, and passion.*) I welcome the invitation. Come, follow me. We'll be married in her bosom.

WILSON. Ah, Fanny, misfortune is weakening your voice. Explain yourself, I implore you. What do your ominous words mean?

FANNY. (*Suddenly stricken with faint attacks from the poison which, through the desire she has to hide them, force her to become confused in what she says.*) They mean you're losing me, at the moment you think you're finding me again. They inform you that fate is disposing of us in another way . . . that someone has lied to me. (*She faints into the chair next to the table. WILSON hastening to her side, holds her in his arms.*)

SARAH. (*Very frightened.*) Oh, heavens! I don't like the state I see her in. (*Investigating a sound she hears.*) Someone's coming. It's James. No matter. He's big hearted. He's incapable of betraying us. (*To JAMES.*) My lord, my lord. Quickly, come see my sister's despair. Here's her lover. Protect him! Don't betray us. Oh, my lord, my lord! (*Throwing herself at JAMES's feet.*) You're sensitive. You wouldn't want to cause us any harm.

JAMES. (*Lifting SARAH up, and to FANNY who has arisen.*) Cruel woman, this is the man you prefer to me!

FANNY. Yes, such was the object of my affection. I once loved him, I admit it. (*Throwing herself into WILSON's arms.*) I still adore him, even at the moment when all the powers of my soul are about to be annihilated forever. James, forgive Wilson. Don't hate him.

JAMES. Wilson? Why, sir, could you be the son of Admiral Wilson who used to command the English navy?

WILSON. Yes, sir. (*Here, SARAH stands next to her sister and looks after her. Lord Butler enters, followed by four servants.)*

LORD BUTLER. Worthless pervert! So you dare to show your face in spite of me, finding your way into the most secret passageways of my house. Even into the hiding place where I'm trying to shelter my daughter's innocence from your dangerous temptations! (*To his men.*) Seize him, my friends, or I won't be responsible for the consequences of my rage. (*His servants approach. JAMES disperses them.*)

JAMES. (*To the servants.*) Get out of here. (*They exit.*) Butler, you were going to commit an injustice. Fanny, here is your sweetheart. I want you to accept him from my hand. Listen to me, my lord. This gentleman is the son of my benefactor. I owe everything I have to Lord Wilson. I was returning from Jamaica . . . I was hauling to London all the riches I had acquired. A French vessel attacked me; it was about to seize my ship. His father, who commanded the English fleet, flew to my rescue and freed me. I will not repay such a favor by carrying off his son's wife. It's not my personality that attracted you, my lord, it was my money. Here, you take it, Wilson. That fortune I owe your father, it's yours. I'm an old man. I have no children, no heirs who can haggle over it. Take it all, and let me have enough to live on. It won't be long. Oh, Fanny, at least, I will have earned your respect. If I couldn't make myself worthy of your love, I will have contributed in some way to your happiness, and I'll be happy since I'll know you're happy.

FANNY. *(In tears, and throwing herself into SIR JAMES's arms.)* Oh, most generous of men. (*Taking her lover's hands; WILSON looking at LORD BUTLER.*) Oh you who've given me life, your wretched daughter . . .

SIR JAMES and WILSON. What has she done? God almighty, what do I hear?

FANNY. (*Quickly, and with a flood of tears.*) There's no more time, father. I was deceived. I thought I had been betrayed . . . that's what I was told. I could have borne anything except his leaving.
ALL. Oh, misery!
FANNY. (*To LORD BUTLER.*) You no longer have a daughter. Poison is flowing through my veins. (*The remainder of her speech is interrupted by convulsions.*) Oh, you who deign to love me still, (*She falls to her knees.*) forgive me for my offense. Pray that heaven may consent to forgive me for it too. (*She grows weaker.*)
SARAH. (*With a cry of despair, and falling into the chair which is next to the table.*) Oh, sister, sister, I'm losing my senses, and my grief is destroying me.
WILSON. (*Continuing quickly.*) Sir James, your generosity touches me, but you certainly didn't think that I'll survive such great misfortunes. I have to follow her. (*He tries to stab himself.*)
SIR JAMES. (*Disarming him, and throwing away the dagger.*) Have courage, young man. Did you think that God put you on the earth to be happy? (*Turning towards FANNY.*) Oh, unhappy child!
FANNY. James, all my feelings are gone. (*She stretches her arms toward her sister.*) Sarah, come get your sister's last kisses. (*SARAH throws herself into FANNY's arms.*) Oh, father. (*She presents her sister to LORD BUTLER.*) Here is the only child you've got left. Don't sacrifice her to the prejudices that are directing, before your very eyes, your wretched Fanny to the grave. May this child make up to you for my loss. Her features will remind you of mine. Sarah! May this beloved father always be your best friend! Love her, take care of her, father. May her affection console you. And never forget that nature has rights that are more sacred over man than the delusions that deceive him, or the passions that debase him. Farewell. (*She reaches out to WILSON who has remained immersed in his grief and who, at this last farewell, falls faint at the feet of his dying FANNY.*)
JAMES. Ah! This is what happens because of greed or ambition!
LORD BUTLER. (*Throwing himself into SARAH's arms.*) Only hope of my old age, come soften the misfortunes of my life. Come, Sarah, come wipe my tears. And may this horrid sight

be eternally engraved upon my heart with the blood my cruelty caused to be shed.

END OF THE THIRD AND FINAL ACT

Introduction

Although *The Antique Dealers* might have been written as early as 1790, the manuscript copy of the play is dated 1807 and bears a note that it was revised by the author the following year. The French editors of Sade's plays believe that the work was one of many the Marquis de Sade had copied while he was incarcerated at Charenton and appears to be in the same hand as the manuscript of *Truth and Treason*.

There is no evidence that the play was ever produced. In fact, there are only two references to the play in all of Sade's correspondence: a rejection notice Sade received from De la Beaume, Gaillard's deputy at the Théâtre du Palais-Royal, and an unsigned critique of the play attributed by Sade to the manager of the Théâtre de Bondi.

In De la Beaume's reply, the author's knowledge and imagination were praised, but the play was thought to be too serious, too scicntific, and too undramatic "at a time when the public is so hard to please." The second note suggested "obvious" similarities between Sade's farce and Molière's *Learned Ladies*, a five-act verse comedy, produced in 1672 and Regnard's *The Follies of Love*, a three-act verse comedy, produced in 1704. It condemned Sade's play for having too much intelligence and not enough laughter and concluded that overall, Sade's "highly worthy work, was unfortunately not theatrical enough. In plots like this, broad comic business should constantly propel and heat up the action."

It is not surprising that theatre managers were concerned about maintaining their audience's interest. In his *Literary Correspondence* XV, January 1789, theatre critic Baron de Grimm writes:

> The fate of plays at the Théâtre-Français has been most unhappy for some time. The impatience of the audience is such that it has become impossible not only to perform more than one or two acts at a time, but to even hiss them comfortably. . . . The play's fate was settled thus, arbitrarily, or precipitously in any event, on Wednesday, 7 January. We cannot give so much as an outline of it, for although the audience allowed a little over two acts to be performed, it was really possible to hear only the opening scene. . . . In the second, the dialogue was found to drag on so tediously, there were so many boring and tasteless details, and the ill humor of the audience was expressed with such turbulence, that with the closest attention in the world it was impossible to make any reasonable judgment either of the play itself, or even of the author's intentions.

Whether or not Sade's farce deserved its condemnation at the hands of theatre managers, it does provide us with an interesting glimpse of fin-de-siècle French society with its continued emphasis on arranged marriages, intellectual obsessions, and social prejudice (this time in the person of Mr. Larabesque, the ignominious English Jew). Sade also follows the ancient tradition of giving "ticket names" to his characters, but with a twist. Here, it is apparently not the author but Mr. Girasole, the antique dealer, who has given pet names to his entourage, in an obsessive attempt to surround himself with things classical. He names his servant Capitolin, in honor of the ancient temple to Jupiter in Rome; his maid is dubbed Cornaline, after cornaline, a precious stone and Cornelia, Julius Caesar's first wife; his daughter is named Agatha (or agate), in honor of the fifth century B.C. Greek poet and playwright, Agathon. In addition, Sade draws upon many contemporary and classical artistic allusions to add to the absurdity of the situation.

Sade has clearly produced a farce that would place heavy intellectual demands on an audience, and for this reason perhaps, it was not produced at the Théâtre du Palais-Royal or the Théâtre de Bondi. A marginal note written by the author on the edge of one of the rejection notices reads, "Théâtre de Variétés." As this theatre was one of the few theatres licensed by Napoleon after 1807 to produce short plays, parodies and vaudevilles, it is not unlikely that the Marquis would have earmarked this theatre for his farce and had intended to submit it there.

Whether or not the play is completely viable beyond its historical interest is clearly up to a modern audience to decide. But, even a quick perusal of Sade's clever dialogue and character drawing should yield some delight if not entirely support Annetta Foster's conclusion that "played at a smart tempo in an intimate theatre before a knowledgeable audience, this comedy could win its quota of laughs."

THE ANTIQUE DEALERS

Prose comedy in one act

CHARACTERS

Mr. Girasole, *an antique dealer*
Mr. Colonnes, *Mr. Girasole's friend and an antique dealer*
Mr. Lémeraude, *Mr. Girasole's friend who stutters*
Agatha, *Mr. Girasole's daughter*
Cornaline, *maid to the Girasole household*
Capitolin, *Mr. Girasole's valet, a Gascon*
Delcour, Agatha's *lover, using the name "Mr. Alabaster"*
Mr. Larabesque, *an adventurer, trading in antiques, an English Jew*

The action takes place at Mr. Girasole's country estate, near Paris.

COSTUMES

MR. GIRASOLE, MR. COLONNES, and MR. LÉMERAUDE should be dressed like fathers are usually dressed in plays, with cloaks, wigs, canes, and clothing in brown or black.
AGATHA is wearing a negligee befitting a middle-class young lady at her father's country house.
CORNALINE, a typical soubrette costume.
LARABESQUE, the English Jew: a red wig, a short beard of the same color, an English frock-coat, a vest, leather breeches, ankle-boots, and a round hat.
CAPITOLIN must be dressed entirely in strips of printing paper. It must be sewn on to his clothing, his jacket, his breeches and his stockings so that his entire costume would be covered with it. You must be careful not to use manuscript paper: the

mistake would be evident. It must be printing paper. He will never wear a hat on his head: he is in his master's house, and always in the living room.
DELCOUR will have a short English frock-coat, sufficiently shabby; a round hat.

The asbestos curtain should be quite simply a piece of two or three lengths of canvas creating the impression of color between green and white, or gray, seeing that there are asbestos curtains in one or the other of these colors.

(An antique shop, where all kinds of antiques are seen on tables and shelves. To the actor's right an asbestos drape is casually thrown over two chairs, and next to the door at the back is an Egyptian mummy case. This same back door leads to Mr. Girasole's apartment. All the members of the household will enter through that door. Strangers will enter from the opposite side. It is six o'clock at night.)

GIRASOLE. (*Coming from his apartment and going to organize some of the antiques on one of the tables or shelves, he says absent-mindedly.*) Cornaline . . . Cornaline.
CORNALINE. Actually, sir, you really ought to change that name for me . . . I'm neither precious nor stone . . . and it's carrying the antique craze a little too far, for you to try and give everyone around you the names of the works of art that infatuate you.
GIRASOLE. (*Distracted because he is more interested in what he is doing than in what CORNALINE is saying.*) Did you say something, Cornaline?
CORNALINE. (*Shouting in his ears.*) Yes, sir, I said something.
GIRASOLE. I'm not deaf, my child.
CORNALINE. No . . . but you're often so distracted that to see you, a person would think you were a hypochondriac.
GIRASOLE. Ah, Cornaline! If you knew the delights of our profession . . . if you were capable of feeling those vigorous surges of the soul at the sight of an antique piece, at the discovery of a ruin, a dilapidated house, a vase, a statue whose style, whose manner gives us an idea of the blessed ages when art was triumphant . . . a little distraction would be allowed, my child, in the

midst of the enjoyment of these pure pleasures . . . unknown to your provincial mind.

CORNALINE. Provincial as long as it pleases you . . . well, sir, I'll be a hick all my life then! For I swear to you that I will never share your delights. The most frivolous of all the novelties of the century will always please me a hundred times more (*Indicating the shop.*) than all these dusty treasures for which I really wouldn't give a nickel.

GIRASOLE. Poor devil. Incidentally, did you unpack those three crates that came for me from Italy?

CORNALINE. No, sir. You've forbidden anyone to touch them without your being there. You're afraid that someone's going to disturb, mix up, or break those matchless wonders. We await your orders.

GIRASOLE. Well, I'm going there. Come, follow me, Cornaline.

CORNALINE. (*Detaining him.*) Sir, a word, I beg you.

GIRASOLE. What do you want, my child?

CORNALINE. Capitolin, your faithful servant . . . Capitolin who, God help us, you named in such a way because you were told that the rarest antiques are found at the Capitol in Rome . . . Capitolin, in short, informed me last night about something very odd.

GIRASOLE. I'll bet he told you about my antique vases.

CORNALINE. No, sir.

GIRASOLE. Ah, I know what it is . . . he informed you of my plans to visit Calabria once again.

CORNALINE. Ah, no, no . . . forget about your Calabria and your antiques for a moment, if it's possible. I want to speak to you about our beloved Agatha.

GIRASOLE. About my daughter?

CORNALINE. Yes, sir, about your daughter, since it would still be easy to make a mistake thanks to the artistic names you give to everyone. This Agatha, born of your blood and who, out of respect for antiquity, you wanted your wife to deliver in the ruins of Herculaneum . . . this Agatha would easily be taken by you for one of the agate stones in your museum, unless it was explained to you. I have to speak to you about Miss Agatha, your daughter, sir. Will so interesting a subject to a father win me a moment of your attention?

GIRASOLE. Certainly, and what do you have to tell me about her?

CORNALINE. That you're trying to bring about this dear child's unhappiness by sacrificing her, like you're doing, to your old Mr. Colonnes, the most annoying man, and the least qualified to make a girl happy. Look, sir, I'm crying out of aggravation, (*Stamping her foot.*) but even if it's the death of me, that marriage will not take place . . . or I'll leave the house instead . . . if you persist in this bizarre fantasy.

GIRASOLE. Are you crazy, Cornaline? What individual on the earth is better suited to make my daughter happy than my friend Mr. Colonnes? And besides, don't you know very well that he's one of the best antique dealers in Europe . . . he's gone to Greece ten times! Cornaline, he's the only man from whom we might have reliable reports about the real location of Troy.

CORNALINE. And what the devil does that mean to your daughter? Is it conceivable that she takes the same interest as you do in all the nonsense that excites you? Your daughter is very concerned about the Trojans and the city they lived in! What she needs is a good husband, sir. A good husband . . . and what you're giving her is an impotent old man who'll make her die of frustration!

GIRASOLE. Impotent?

CORNALINE. He's got the gout.

GIRASOLE. He's educated.

CORNALINE. He only lives by the rules.

GIRASOLE. He discovered Horace's tomb, my child, Horace's tomb!

CORNALINE. Yes . . . and soon he'll make your daughter enter hers.

GIRASOLE. Really, you surprise me . . . but she greets my friend pleasantly when she sees him.

CORNALINE. Purely out of politeness.

GIRASOLE. Oh! Daughters! How cunning they are! And do you think her heart might be predisposed toward another?

CORNALINE. I know nothing about it, sir. What I'm absolutely certain of is that, without a doubt, Mr. Colonnes doesn't suit her. Ah! Here she comes. Chat with her on this subject and you'll see if I'm mistaken.

AGATHA. (*Enters.*) I've come to tell you, father, that we're waiting for you to unpack your crates. (*Trembling as she walks in front of the mummy case.*) Oh, my God! I thought the mummy was still in its case. That ugly face used to always give me a fright. Father, how can you keep such things in the house? It's gloomy. It gives me dark and dismal thoughts.

GIRASOLE. This mummy was Cleopatra. Daughter, look what becomes of greatness. Let us transport ourselves through the mists of time. Let's dig up ancient ruins. Let's deprive the monarchs of the world of their sovereign dignity; we'll see them become dust again like the lowliest of men. We'll see them . . .

CORNALINE. (*Interrupting quickly.*) Really, this is a cheerful conversation for a young girl. Ah! For heaven's sake, sir, be more concerned with her than with your moral contemplations!

GIRASOLE. Well, for example, I'll tell her that I find her hair very poorly combed today. My dear Agatha, why didn't you model if after that magnificent bust of Agrippina which I put here yesterday, deliberately on your dressing table?

AGATHA. Father, it's just that I didn't think that someone my age today wore her hair like Nero's mother.

GIRASOLE. (*Firmly and slightly irritated.*) Ah! To be sure, those styles, conceived in the midst of luxury, taste, and the fine arts, are worth more than those which we slavishly imitate in our own day.

CORNALINE. Sir, we excuse you from those bitter critics . . . it seems to me we were talking about a marriage for the young lady, your daughter. Would you allow us to take up the thread of the conversation?

GIRASOLE. By all means. Agatha, Cornaline maintains that Mr. Colonnes is not the husband who can lay claim to the good fortune of attracting you? What's wrong with him? What's missing?

AGATHA. I don't know where Cornaline could have gotten that idea. Can you doubt that your desires are the only laws of my heart? You raised me too well, father, for me to be able to think

differently. Your decision will rule my behavior . . . and I'll never take a husband other than the one it will please you to give me.
GIRASOLE. (*Triumphantly.*) Well, Cornaline?
CORNALINE. Ah, well, sir! I congratulate you on having so submissive a daughter; such a creature's a treasure! (*Softly to AGATHA.*) Courage, Miss. You're promoting my work for the best! (*Aside.*) A person can be so insincere!
GIRASOLE. (*To his daughter, then to himself, joyfully.*) What is it she's saying to you, Agatha? I bet she's giving you bad advice. What a dear child! How glad I am to see her in such a frame of mind. But it's just that there's not one man in the world who could make this fine girl happy like my friend Colonnes. She takes a liking to our art . . . she's so perfect. Farewell, dear daughter, farewell. Always maintain these fine sentiments, I pray you. (*To CORNALINE, pointing to her.*) And you, snake, if I find out that you're trying to turn her away from her duty, I'll have you wrapped like a mummy! (*To AGATHA, still joyfully.*) I'm going to unwrap my crates, dear girl, and to reward your gentleness, I promise you a bust of Agamemnon, sculpted by Phidias. Farewell, charming child, I hardly know how to thank you for your obedience. Yes, you'll be happy, Agatha, you'll be happy. People are only happy when they use good judgment. (*He goes out.*)
CORNALINE. So give me an explanation for this bizarre behavior, Miss. Really, I don't understand anything. Indeed! This morning you were still burning, you said, for Delcour. For Delcour who adores you, and who you swore, since childhood, to love and marry . . . and now, he's no longer the one? I hear nothing on behalf of this inconsistency. Explain it to me, I beg of you.
AGATHA. Oh, Cornaline! How poorly you know the mind and heart of a young girl. Don't you know that the only way to reach her goal is to attain it through tricks and evasions? Do you want me to rob my lover of the possibility of talking with me by suddenly irritating my father? You must not be very shrewd not to guess my plans. Mr. Girasole doesn't know Delcour, the young man having only seen me at boarding school where he used to visit one of his relatives. Never has he shown himself in our house. I'm aware that he's in town. My plan is to see him here, and ultimately settle the means of bringing the two of us

together . . . and above all, of ridding ourselves of that dreary Mr. Colonnes's unwelcomed attentions. Come on, you'll soon see, my dear, what I've already devised on that score. Is this the time to make Mr. Girasole angry by openly resisting his plans for me? Cornaline, love is more intelligent than friendship; the latter sentiment used to direct your steps, the former guides mine . . . and I'll arrive faster and safer than you.

CORNALINE. Ah! I'm panting! Really, you worried me. I couldn't understand this whim, but I hear you now, Miss. Yes, I hear you. It's only a matter of planning together.

AGATHA. Oh, without a doubt! Planning together . . . doing it . . . and it's in this that your services will be a great help to me.

CORNALINE. It's an awkward affair. Have you considered the methods you're planing to use to open this house to Delcour? You know that Mr. Girasole sees no one. Except for the people he works with, Mr. Lémeraude, the stutterer, and tiresome Mr. Colonnes, not a creature thinks to come and console our weariness.

AGATHA. (*Mysteriously.*) Ah, Cornaline!

CORNALINE. (*After thinking a bit.*) Wait a moment longer, Miss. What do you think of that Jewish swindler they call Mr. Larabesque?

AGATHA. Who, that escapee from a London synagogue who's coming to sell us the remains of old pots for antique vases and pebbles from the Thames for mosaics from Herculaneum?

CORNALINE. Exactly. You know, Miss, he's a professional manipulator. I'm convinced that in no time at all he'll find a way to get your lover in here. He'll make him his student, his associate. Sound him out on this business and be certain that he'll remove all the obstacles.

AGATHA. Yes, but he'll need some money and we barely have any.

CORNALINE. We'll promise it to him. Besides, Delcour will give all he can get his hands on. He'd sacrifice his life to see you for a moment. A moment, Miss! Ah! Don't you know what a moment is when you're in love? (*She hears CAPITOLIN coming.*) What does Capitolin want? (*Softly to AGATHA.*) Don't tell him our secret. I'm not sure enough of him.

CAPITOLIN. (*From backstage: this role must be spoken in a Gascon accent*[1] *from beginning to end.*) No, I say what's on my mind . . . I'd rather serve the devil than an idiot like that man there.
AGATHA. What's the matter, Capitolin? You seem upset.
CAPITOLIN. I am, damn it! If I knew what he was going to make me do, I wouldn't have taken the post.
CORNALINE. Let me ask again . . . who are you mad at?
CAPITOLIN. Oh, Sandix[2] . . . everybody . . . me whose fortune would have been made if I had stayed in the wine country. I dreamt one night that I'd be better off in Paris . . . I'm hurrying . . . thank God, I'm not lacking in looks . . . I was born a handsome enough guy . . . nice figure . . . good looking . . . intelligent . . . with all these advantages, I should have found a Duchess and I only come up with an antique dealer who pays me with medals, who clothes me with the works of Homer, and who feeds me with Etruscan vases.
CORNALINE. Courage, my son . . . go, don't grieve. Let Miss Agatha get married. She'll take you into her service and your fortune will soon be made!
CAPITOLIN. Me . . . I'm more than happy just to eat a piece of bread beside you, Miss . . . if only he didn't make me handle dead bodies, like this morning, making me carry that mummy to the house of a Mr. Lémeraude, the man he was sending it to. If only he'd dress me a little more reasonably. I'm not asking for more. (*Looking over the tables.*) Let's see if I'll find what he wants. Help me, please, both of you.
AGATHA. What does my father want?
CAPITOLIN. He asked me for a bust of Nero.
CORNALINE. (*Finding it.*) Look, here it is! How ugly that monster was!
CAPITOLIN. Ah! Really, I think the tyrant's bust appears a hundred times more frightening when man, freed from his chains, breathes at last under the protection of a good master. Gotta go. I'm in a hurry 'cause I'm afraid he might call me. (*To CORNALINE.*) Farewell, my lovely angel . . . if you can find love in your heart, remember that it'll be my image in there. (*He exits.*)

---

[1] The Gascon dialect is spoken in south-western France and is influenced by Basque and Spanish languages. Parisians generally ridiculed the dialect as being unsophisticated.

[2] Sandix is a kind of red lead, made by calcining carbonate of lead.

AGATHA. Really, my dear, I do believe that servant is making eyes at you. Could it be then that you love him as well? If that's the case, tell me so that I might convert into cash, as soon as I'm able, whatever you promised him as a dowry.
CORNALINE. Me, Miss? Me fall in love with a Gascon?! Oh! My sights are higher than that.
AGATHA. What do you mean?
CORNALINE. That Mr. Lémeraude, that friend of your father's . . . do you believe that he's romancing me, Miss . . . and that I don't mind paying attention to him? He has a yearly income of a hundred pistoles,[3] and that's a fortune to a poor orphan like me. Shh! I hear someone. Of course! It's Mr. Larabesque in person. He couldn't have come at a better time. We're going to throw ourselves at him . . . we'll see if he retaliates.
CORNALINE. Mr. Larabesque, your most humble servant. (*Aside.*) The nice thing about him is that he never comes empty-handed!
LARABESQUE. (*Carrying two busts, puts them on a table; he should have an English accent.*) These are two busts at a ridiculous price. Really, people will never pay me what they're worth. I'm quite sure that Mr. Girasole won't take them, but it costs nothing to look, and it gives me pleasure to have the honor of showing him these masterpieces.
AGATHA. (*Looking at the busts.*) What are these figures, Mr. Larabesque? It seems to me that I don't know them.
CORNALINE. And how would you know them, Miss? They're two antiques that Mr. Larabesque just created a few minutes ago.
LARABESQUE. God damn me, I'm not capable of such a trick. That one is Philoctetes, Hercules's companion; and this one is Antinous. These originals are priceless!
CORNALINE. You ought to make quite a profit selling such pretty things.
LARABESQUE. Ah! If this were my only business, I'd be dying of hunger forever . . . but thank heavens, I know how to make a living.
CORNALINE. I think that there are few occupations you haven't tried, Mr. Larabesque, from the honest ones to the . . .

[3] In French currency, one *pistole* was worth approximately ten *livres*.

LARABESQUE. Dishonest ones. Is that what you were going to say? Not entirely . . . as yet, Miss.
CORNALINE. No, no, I wanted to say . . . intriguing ones.
LARABESQUE. At the right time. In this business, it's true that I'm involved with them a little . . . but, what do you want, Miss? When fortune doesn't smile at a man, he has to know how to speed it along.
CORNALINE. (*Shrewdly.*) Is it true, Mr. Larabesque, that a few days ago you performed a most important service for a young lady living in this neighborhood, by reuniting her with a lover who adored her, but who couldn't succeed in possessing her?
LARABESQUE. It pleases me to make people happy, and when, while I'm working for others, someone also wants to labor on my behalf, that encourages me to continue.
CORNALINE. (*Taking him aside, and mysteriously.*) Listen, Mr. Larabesque. Would you be the man to do for us what you did for that nice young girl I was just talking about?
LARABESQUE. (*Puffing himself up.*) Ah! What does it involve, Miss?
CORNALINE. Not to put the lady into the lover's arms. Oh, no, that's too gigantic a favor; we won't ask that much of you. We'll be happy just to ask you if you'd be willing to reestablish a lover at the feet of his mistress.
LARABESQUE. I notice, m'lady, that there's not that great a difference. No matter. Give me an explanation. Is it in this house that these things must be done?
CORNALINE. Yes, absolutely, here!
LARABESQUE. (*Puffing himself up.*) This is an exceedingly difficult task.
AGATHA. Really, Cornaline, you're asking for things that . . .
CORNALINE. Well, Miss, if they shock you, don't listen to them. The gentleman, your father, is waiting for you to unpack his crates. We'll handle your interests here a lot better without you.
AGATHA. (*While going out, but feebly.*) I tell you, Mr. Larabesque, don't listen to this temptress. She'd lead the most virtuous of daughters astray.
CORNALINE. Leave it to me. Go, go, harsh Lucretia. Everything will be fine.

CORNALINE. You see, my dear . . . a fortune for you is at stake here.
LARABESQUE. Look here, Miss. I think I understand what you're trying to say, but whatever need I might have to make my fortune, I have a still greater need not to hang myself!
CORNALINE. Ah, shame on you, my friend. Must you look so closely when it's a question of becoming famous? Should a hero be afraid of death?
LARABESQUE. It's not at all heroic to hang yourself, Miss Cornaline.
CORNALINE. But you wouldn't be treated so roughly. I'm convinced that you wouldn't find in all the synagogues of Europe two examples of Jews who might have died like you say.
LARABESQUE. I'm not curious to begin with.
CORNALINE. Well, at least listen. Haven't you seen a young man hanging around here just waiting for the moment to see and meet Miss Agatha?
LARABESQUE. Yes, I think I've seen him. Twenty to twenty-two years old, right?
CORNALINE. Exactly.
LARABESQUE. Chestnut hair?
CORNALINE. Yes, chestnut hair.
LARABESQUE. Well-built, thin, and handsome?
CORNALINE. Oh, charming.
LARABESQUE. A little absent-minded . . . distracted?
CORNALINE. Like all lovers.
LARABESQUE. Well, what am I supposed to do with this young man?
CORNALINE. Put him in your charge to get him into the house . . . in a word, to lead him to us.
LARABESQUE. Under what pretense?
CORNALINE. The simplest in the world: make him carry, with you, some antiques to Mr. Girasole. Delcour has spirit and intelligence. Merely acquaint him with the role he's supposed to play and leave the rest to him.
LARABESQUE. And who'll pay me for all my trouble, Miss?
CORNALINE. Delcour. Delcour will reward you generously, depend on it. No sooner will you have offered him your services,

that he'll leap for joy and cover you with gold to repay you. Go quickly where I send you, my friend. There's not a moment to lose. Leave your busts with us. (*Indicating them.*) They'll be the reasons for your return. I'll give them to Mr. Girasole on your behalf, and you'll return with Delcour to complete the sale.
LARABESQUE. Miss Cornaline, won't you take the responsibility for part of the reward?
CORNALINE. What do you mean?
LARABESQUE. Not even a little kiss?
CORNALINE. Come now! Come now! Don't you know what a girl from my country risks in granting something to a man from yours? Believe me, that alone is holding me back, my dear Larabesque, for I'm naturally attracted to you . . . you're built in such an attractive way. Such a cute little beard. (*She passes her hand over it.*) Ah! Leave me alone! Just be successful and you'll see how I'll reward you for your trouble! (*She leads him out.*)
LARABESQUE. Ah, then, I'll have to see! (*He exits.*)
CORNALINE. Thank heavens! There now, the matter is off to a good enough start. Pulling the wool over Mr. Girasole's eyes is not what troubles me. Aren't the shrewdest fellows always taken in, when love and women join forces to attack them? Ah! My poor master! You're so often mistaken about one of the copies, we have to try to deceive you with the original. (*Seeing MR. LÉMERAUDE.*) Good. I'm talking about originals, and here, without question, is one of the most famous in the entire country, coming to bore me in the usual way, with his tedious love-making and his stuttering. No matter. I have to be nice to him. We need everybody in the world today, and we mustn't offend anyone!
LÉMERAUDE. (*Stuttering.*) Ah, good day my cha . . . cha . . . charming Corn . . . Corn . . . Cornaline. You know how I feel about you?
CORNALINE. You're very kind, sir, really . . . but I'm not worthy of a scholar such as you. What would you do with a poor idiot like me?
LÉMERAUDE. (*Stuttering.*) Good gracious, what idiot? A gi . . . gi . . . girl like you is a tre . . . tre . . . treasure in an of . . . of . . . office. While the husband is w . . . w . . . working, the wife is doing research . . . she d . . . d . . . digs through authors from

antiquity and fr . . . fr . . . frees her husband fr . . . fr . . . from all the dreariness of w . . . w . . . work. (*Squeezing her intimately.*) Oh, da . . . da . . . darling, let me kiss those little wh . . . wh . . . white hands.

CORNALINE. How impulsive . . . how anxious, and at your age! You know very well Mr. Lémeraude that they wouldn't give you twenty-five years to live!

LÉMERAUDE. (*Stuttering.*) Isn't a fellow always young close to the ones he loves, my dear Cornaline! Aurora is m . . . m . . . much less a . . . a . . . attractive than you and hasn't she re . . . re . . . rejuvenated, s . . . s . . . so they s . . . s . . . say, many a lot older than m . . . m . . . me!

CORNALINE. Always about nice things, sir. You're accustomed to praising me . . . it's so sweet that I permit it. Be that as it may, why are you coming to see Mr. Girasole today?

LÉMERAUDE. (*Stuttering.*) That's a . . . a . . . asking the sun wh . . . wh . . . why it's pu . . . pu . . . pulling the earth, at every mo . . . mo . . . moment, towards its or . . . or . . . orbit. Those beautiful eyes that I ad . . . ad . . . adore . . . are they n . . . n . . . not for me, my mis . . .mis . . . mistress, the star that illuminates for us all the sph . . . sph . . . spheres that surround it?

CORNALINE. Here's something thoughtful for once, but doesn't the metaphor belong to an astronomer rather than an antique dealer?

LÉMERAUDE. (*Stuttering.*) That me . . . me . . . metaphor, da . . . da . . . darling, is the w . . . w . . . work of your ch . . . ch . . . charms, and your ch . . . ch . . . charms teach me everything.

CORNALINE. These pretty speeches aside, once again, Mr. Lémeraude, tell me what brings you here?

LÉMERAUDE. (*Stuttering.*) I go . . . go . . . got it into my h . . . h . . . head, these last few d . . . d . . . days, to settle up with Mr. Girasole about that Egyptian mum . . . mum . . . mummy, he used to have there in that case. I paid him for it; his valet, Cap . . . Cap . . . Capitolin, promp . . . promp . . . promptly delivered it to me. No sooner had it arrived when I was seized with certain q . . . q . . . qualms of conscience. I cannot explain what I fe . . . fe . . . felt, but I don't think it's right to keep such things in your h . . . h . . . house, and I'm coming be . . . be . . . because of this to ask Mr. Girasole to k . . .k . . . kindly consent to t . . . t . . . take it ba . . . ba . . . back.

CORNALINE. Really, sir, your qualms are enlightening; the more I know you, the more I like you. I've never wanted anything more than having a scrupulous husband, so that if I unfortunately happened to become corrupted, he'd repent for me, and that would be very convenient.

LÉMERAUDE. (*Stuttering.*) Always ch . . . ch . . . cheerful, Co . . . Co . . . Cornaline. Always cr . . . cr . . . crazy! It su . . . su . . . suits you well, you charming girl. It sh . . . sh . . . should at your age.

CORNALINE. Look, believe me, sir, hide that childish qualm from my master. Here he is now, coming in with Mr. Colonnes, his future son-in-law. Don't give him any evidence of these fears; they'd make you look like a fool.

GIRASOLE. (*As if in the midst of a conversation with MR. COLONNES.*) No, my friend, I'll never yield to you on that point. The greatest difference we notice between Egyptian statues and the masterpieces of Zeuxis and Praxiteles comes, by no means from the superiority of these later artists over the first, but only from a particular style in the studios of Thebes and Memphis. I'll prove what I'm telling you, my friend. (*Coming on stage.*) Ah, of course! Here's Mr. Lémeraude. I trust he'll resolve the issue.

LÉMERAUDE. Gentlemen, kindly remember that I've only just come into the profession. I'm still your student, and as a result, very far removed from being able to choose between Rome and Carthage.

CORNALINE. (*To MR. GIRASOLE.*) By the way, sir, here are two busts your English Jew just delivered. Unable to wait, he left them and will return, he told me, shortly, with one of his associates newly arrived from Sicily with some treasures.

GIRASOLE. (*Energetically.*) Ah, what a happy coincidence! And is this associate educated? Did he tell you that we could take advantage of his conversation?

COLONNES. You'll see. It'll be some malicious vender of engraved stones, whose only objective will be to cheat us.

CORNALINE. Ah, no, no, sir. That's not the way Mr. Larabesque talks. The young man he wants to introduce to you is full of courage and intelligence. He's traveled through a great many countries and singularly profited from his trips.

LÉMERAUDE. (*Stuttering.*) If this is true, we must listen to him.

COLONNES. Certainly. We should try to record with him some of the precious lines which even the rarest books deny us.

GIRASOLE. Nicely argued, well thought-out, my friends. Ah, this occurrence fills me with joy. Wait for us, Colonnes; as a matter of fact, here's my daughter. (*AGATHA enters.*) She'll accompany you. Lémeraude and I are going to look in my large showcase for all the most magnificent antiques it contains to show to this young man. Follow us, Cornaline. Agatha, I leave you with my friend. (*Returning to MR. COLONNES, mysteriously.*) You must agree, Colonnes, that there are some moments in life when my Agatha is worth more than a medal.

COLONNES. (*Sneering grossly, taking AGATHA's hand and leading her on stage.*) Better than a Flora . . . better than a Venus. The charming little child.

COLONNES. Ah! How glad I am to find myself alone with you for a moment here . . . how pleasing it is to me, at last to be able to express my passion for you. Look, my beloved, I must admit to you that I'm putting all my happiness in your possession: wealth, honor, peace of mind. I'll sacrifice everything up to my antiques to possess you, lovely Agatha. Would you be so barbarous as to refuse me?

AGATHA. I know to what extent I'm indebted to the value of your gifts, sir, and I would answer, "depend on it," if, rather than adding to your happiness, as you say, I wasn't afraid of making you miserable by giving myself to you. If you only knew, sir!

COLONNES. Of course, Miss! Is it that you've already made some choice? Would I be so unfortunate that another . . . ?

AGATHA. (*Continuing quickly.*) Ah! No, no, sir. Think nothing of the kind. I've submitted to my father's wishes ever since I was a child. His wishes are my commands. And his commands are all the more precious . . . which is difficult . . . because they better correspond with my heart when the goal is to give me to you.

COLONNES. (*Enraptured.*) Ah! What tender words have just been spoken. Agatha, you enrapture me. The famous column that the Romans erected in honor of Trajan's victories, and which is still admired in the capital of the world, would have stroked the pride of that emperor less than it just stroked mine, through an acknowledgment so innocent and filled with charms.

AGATHA. Gently, sir. Let's not proceed so quickly, I beg you. What good are the feelings I've expressed to either of us, when horrible circumstances have created insurmountable barriers between us forever?

COLONNES. Oh heavens! Suddenly, in an instant, you make my heart go from ecstasy to despair. Those terrible words were for me what that flaming lava from Vesuvius was to the Greek cities of old, destroying them in a few hours. Barriers, Miss? Barriers? Who can remove them? God Almighty! When your father . . . when your feelings . . . when my own . . . when everything is coming together for our mutual happiness.

AGATHA. (*Grieved and with embarrassment.*) Ah, sir, it's something we can't talk about . . . that we're forced to hide . . . which doesn't make it any easier.

COLONNES. Tell me about it, I implore you, or you'll reduce me to despair.

AGATHA. (*As above.*) You wouldn't keep it a secret, and you would lose me if you tell.

COLONNES. I swear to you on all I hold dear, that nothing will tear out of me what you agree to divulge to your best friend.

AGATHA. (*As above.*) Well, I cannot get married, sir. I'm unable to.

COLONNES. (*Still urging her more vigorously.*) For heaven's sake, explain yourself!

AGATHA. Good. I will have no sooner done that when you'll betray me. You'll tell my father and he'll never forgive me.

COLONNES. (*Very quickly.*) I swear to you the most eternal silence! Speak, dearest Agatha, and you can be as sure of my discretion as of the impossibility that a single cause might ever stand in the way of my passionate desire to possess you.

AGATHA. (*Plaintively, mysteriously, and portraying everything she's about to say.*) Oh! Sir, what a cruel admission you're demanding of me. Never . . . never! You want it, in a word, sir? Just imagine that I'm subject to attacks of hydrophobia.

COLONNES. (*Trembling.*) What? Have you been bitten?
AGATHA. In my childhood, a wolf attacked me, and since then I occasionally fall into fits of madness. I think I'd devour you, sir, if you dared to come near me when I was suffering. Now see . . . see if, with such an illness, I'm in a proper condition to be your wife.
COLONNES. (*As cold as he is amazed, and having trembled throughout the previous declaration.*) These attacks . . . do you get them often?
AGATHA. Regularly, every night when I go to bed, sir, and nearly every morning when I awake.
COLONNES. (*Going away.*) How sorry I feel for you, Miss . . . so beautiful, so fresh . . . to be subject to such an illness. Ah! That's too bad . . . it's really too bad. But how could your father want to marry you off in that condition?
AGATHA. (*Recomposed, but appearing weak.*) He was told that marriage was the only real cure for my condition.
COLONNES. He's mistaken, Miss, he's mistaken. Be that as it may, Agatha, you can be certain of my discretion. I won't say a word. But let's both change our behavior immediately. I'll gradually grow cold in my feelings for you. I'll use my travels as an excuse. Have a lot of concerns, show more than ever your unwillingness to get married, and little by little the plans will be forgotten, and everything will work out by itself.
AGATHA. Oh! Sir, how sorry I am about the bonds which would have made me so happy.
COLONNES. What! Indeed, my angel, you feel an attraction for me.
AGATHA. (*Becoming enflamed to the point of making him believe that she's about to have an attack.*) Attraction, sir . . . attraction . . . Ah! The most tender affection . . . frenzy. . . madness! (*Hurling herself at him, each time, he manages to escape.*) Oh! My beloved Colonnes, I have to give you up then. I'll die. Yes, I'll die of despair!
COLONNES. (*Shaking her off as much as he can.*) Just a moment, Miss! Hold on . . . not so much love . . . not so much feeling, I beg of you. Good heavens, what passion! What energy! Compose

yourself. Calm down. The overindulgence of your love frightens me to a point . . . Perhaps you'll recover one day, and then . . .

AGATHA. (*Crying.*) Ah! Monster, you're not as sensitive as I am. I know it well. (*Recovering herself.*) Your coldness diminishes my regret. Go. With less sadness, now, I'll see you as someone else's husband. But keep quiet, or you'll never have a deadlier enemy than I.

COLONNES. (*Escaping.*) Yes, yes, calm down.

AGATHA. (*Alone at first.*) Thank heavens, I'm rid of him! Delcour, you see all that I do for you. (*Noticing her lover.*) Oh, heavens, it's him!

CORNALINE. Here he is, Miss, here he is! Here's the one who adores you.

DELCOUR. (*At AGATHA's feet.*) And who wishes to die at your knees.

AGATHA. Oh, heavens, get up, Delcour. I'm sympathetic to this behavior, but if my father were to come and see it . . .

DELCOUR. As far as I'm concerned, I've nothing to answer for.

CORNALINE. And me, I answer for everything . . . but follow my advice. First of all, the gentleman must not be taken for a scholar.

DELCOUR. Ah, really, it would be very hard for me to be accepted as such. I've been able to acquire all the accomplishments of a man in my position without, however, having studied the sciences which the gentleman your father and his friends have cultivated for so long.

CORNALINE. Though you might be as intelligent as they are, I don't want you to look it. Make some blunders . . . use anachronisms . . . gradually they'll mistrust you . . . they'll suspect some secret, and from there will spring both the moment to unveil you, and the necessity to no longer pretend. Bear in mind that it's only a question of getting you into this house . . . and here you are . . . the main goal is achieved!

DELCOUR. Incidentally, I much prefer this method, than trying to pass for an antique dealer. If I attempted it, how wouldn't I be discovered by such learned men?

CORNALINE. Come on, now! Take courage! Someone's coming. Remember to play your role well.

LARABESQUE. Nevertheless, I'm still supposed to introduce him as a great man.
CORNALINE. Yes, but exaggerating his praises so as to deceive them only for the little time we have to pretend.
LARABESQUE. Good, good. I understand.
AGATHA. Ah, Delcour, this intrigue makes me tremble so.
LARABESQUE. (*To MR. GIRASOLE.*) Here, sir, is an antique treasure which I'm introducing to you. Never did Horace, Virgil, Aristotle, and the famous Strabon[4] have in their heads what this young man possesses on the tips of his fingers. He's a walking museum, sir . . . I thought I'd give you a great big present just by introducing this man to you. He has traveled all the known parts of the world. He has gone a lot farther into the bowels of the earth than many travelers have gone on the surface. Would you believe, sir, that this man . . . this man spent fourteen days in the waters of the Tiber looking for antiques . . . and lived for three weeks inside Mount Etna.
GIRASOLE. (*To DELCOUR.*) Ah! Sir, what a pleasure it is for my friends and I to entertain a man like you. What is this learned man's name, Mr. Larabesque?
LARABESQUE. This young man is called Mr. Alabaster, and I expect you'll reward me for having obtained for you an acquaintance like him.
LÉMERAUDE. (*Stuttering. During this line and the one preceding it, the young man, trying not to be idle, examines the rare objects in the case, like an expert.*) No do . . . do . . . doubt about it, my dear Larab . . . Larab . . . Larabesque, my colleagues and I will gi . . . gi . . . give you a rewa . . . rewa . . . reward equal to your efforts ri . . . ri . . . right now. You are doing a gr . . . gr . . . great and impo . . . impo . . . important ser . . . ser . . . service for our ac . . . ac . . . academy.
DELCOUR. (*Using the name of Mr. Alabaster.*) I would be too happy, gentlemen, if my feeble lights could, for a moment, add to your satisfaction, but how can I hope to shine in the midst of a company like yours, where learning is at its center, so to speak, and talent is in its temple.

[4] Strabon (also known as Strabo, 64/63 B.C. – 24 A.D.) was a Greek geographer, historian, and philosopher.

GIRASOLE. (*Softly, to MR. COLONNES.*) He expresses himself well, like an artistic man.

LARABESQUE. Can you imagine, sir, I led an ignoramus here to have the honor of conversing with you? I told you, sir, this gentleman has traveled the whole world . . . he's been in the oceans . . . he's been in the clouds . . . he's been everywhere. You won't find his equal in the entire universe.

CORNALINE. It's enough to look at the gentleman's appearance to judge his abilities.

AGATHA. It's certain that the gentleman conveys a sweetness in his face . . . a good humor.

DELCOUR. You're too kind, Miss. You'll excuse me if I don't reply as I should to the courteous words you're kindly trying to address to me. We studious types are different . . . we know nothing of society's good manners. Our studies absorb us entirely, and we prefer the laurels of Apollo to the often dangerous myrtle trees, plucked for Cythera.[5]

CAPITOLIN. (*To DELCOUR.*) Sir, did you see Homer in your travels?

GIRASOLE. Imbecile!

CAPITOLIN. And Sandix. I'm certainly allowed to speak of those whose works I'm wearing as clothing.

GIRASOLE. Leave that valet's tittle-tattle and tell us, I pray you, sir, if his highness, the Grand Duke of Tuscanny, has finally finished putting into his superb gallery in Florence all the precious pieces that used to be contained in his palace in Rome?

DELCOUR. Yes, sir. When I passed through that Tuscan capital, someone had just carried in the Apis bull.[6]

GIRASOLE. Sir, I don't at all remember having seen this Apis bull. If you please, in what medium was it realized?

DELCOUR. (*Like someone who is not sure of his business.*) Sir, that bull . . . is an alabaster bull, made by Pigalle.[7]

GIRASOLE. By Pigalle? An antique bull?

DELCOUR. Yes, sir. An antique bull by Pigalle.

---

[5] In Greek mythology, Cythera was the island dedicated to Aphrodite, the goddess of love.

[6] Apis was a bull deity worshiped in Egypt. The statue of the Aphis bull in the Louvre dates from the 4th century B.C.

[7] Jean-Baptiste Pigalle (26 January 1714 – 20 August 1785) was a French sculptor.

LÉMERAUDE. Why, Mr. Pi . . . Pi . . . Pigalle is one of our most skillful sculptors, without a doubt . . . bu . . . bu . . . but the most modern and up to da . . . da . . . date of the age.
DELCOUR. (*Mimicking him for a moment, only on the word indicated.*) Sir, I'm talking about Pi . . . Pi . . . Pigalle the Greek. (*The rest quickly.*) Pigalles, in Greek, who used to live in the year 52 from the founding of Troy, which corresponds according to the Ptolemian tables to the year 10, 200 of the Chinese Hegira.[8] Is it my fault, sir, if you're unaware of the existence of that famous artist whose masterpieces cram both Sicily and Italy.
GIRASOLE. Pigalles? Ah, yes, Pigalles, perhaps that's the one. A person doesn't always commit to memory the names of all the artists in the world who have become famous.
CAPITOLIN. Sir, you stopped at the bull's horns. Finish the description, please.
GIRASOLE. Didn't I tell you to shut up, Capitolin? If you interrupt us again, you'll be expelled from the Academy.
CAPITOLIN. (*Aside.*) And, yet, seeing what it is, if I had spoken of an ass, you would have said that I was one!
GIRASOLE. (*To DELCOUR.*) Before leaving the subject of Italy, sir, give us, I implore you, the news about Naples and especially Salerno.
DELCOUR. Oh, sir, that Salerno was a very great man. You wouldn't imagine the pleasure I've gotten from reading his books.
LÉMERAUDE. (*Stuttering.*) You're mis . . . mis . . . mistaken, sir. Sa . . . Sa . . . Salerno wasn't a man, it was a ci . . . ci . . . city.
DELCOUR. And who questions it, sir? A city . . . a city that was once superb.
GIRASOLE. And particularly famous for its school of medicine.
DELCOUR. Ah, well, exactly . . . it's what I was telling you, sir . . . and the doctor of Salerno of whom I have the honor of talking about, Salernus, Salerna, Salernum, great-grandson of the German cousin of Hippocrates's sister, was one of the greatest authors of his day. We have from him, in Syrian, two treatises on the pubis bone that will immortalize him forever.
CORNALINE. (*To MR. GIRASOLE.*) Well, sir, isn't he a scholar? You're talking about educating your daughter, Agatha.

---

[8] Typically, the word is used in reference to Muhammad's flight from Mecca to Medina. It's usage here is clever doubletalk.

Isn't this the man you need to initiate her into the deep, dark mysteries of antiquity?

COLONNES. Let's move on to Sicily, sir, I beseech you. I'm most anxious to see you describe the famous Etna, which I was prevented from going near, due an unforeseen illness that kept me at Messina. According to what people say, you went down into its bowels, sir?

DELCOUR. (*Embarrassed.*) Yes, sir, into its bowels. Ah, sir, the bowels of that mountain are quite a spectacle!

GIRASOLE. Beforehand, settle my doubts, I beg you, sir, about the famous round tower they found close to that mountain. Some (and my friend Colonnes belongs to this group) claim that it is a monument that Empedocles[9] had built at the foot of Mount Etna, to be within an arm's reach of knowing the nature and causes of its volcanic phenomena. The others (and dour Mr. Lémeraude is among this group) maintain that it's an ancient temple to Vulcan. Settle our notions, sir, and resolve our dispute through your knowledge.

DELCOUR. (*Dogmatically.*) I observe with reluctance, gentlemen, that you're all wrong about the monument that interests you. The tower about which you do me the honor of speaking is a monument of Incan splendor. Among the Incan princes, one of them named Asperjos, a contemporary of Clovis, had that tower built to watch the movement of the stars.

LÉMERAUDE. (*Stuttering.*) But sir, the In . . . In . . . Incas were the lords of Peru. They didn't know about our hemi . . . hemi . . . hemisphere. What con . . . con . . . connection could there be between them and Mo . . . Mo . . . Mount Etna?

DELCOUR. Excuse me? What connection, sir? (*To the Jew.*) My friend, it seems to me you had said that you brought me here to confer with learned men, but I see clearly that you've deceived me, and that I'd be better off going where my work calls me, than to waste time here with people . . . with people who are not at all informed. (*He pretends to leave.*)

GIRASOLE. (*Stopping him.*) Excuse us, sir, excuse us. Consent to make known your ideas to us, and we'll always become worthy of yielding to them.

[9] Empedocles (490–430 B.C.) was a Greek philosopher who threw himself into Mount Etna in the belief that he would return as a god after being consumed by the volcano's fire.

DELCOUR. Very good, sir. I'll converse with you as long as you like, but I beg you not to engage me in conversation with that stutterer who always wants to talk about everything and never knows a word about what he's saying. Through one of the mouths of Etna, formerly, people used to correspond with one another, by means of a subterranean corridor, as far as the middle of America, and the first discoveries of that continent were only ever made that way. The lords of Peru were able then to go to Sicily, and the Sicilians to Peru. How could you be unaware of such a fact, sir? There isn't an antique dealer in Sicily who doesn't still show you the remains of this underground route that extends more than two thousand leagues under the sea.
COLONNES. Then it was a monument almost like the one in the grotto of Mount Pausilippus that you encounter leaving Naples?
DELCOUR. Precisely, sir, and I don't know how scholars like you cannot be familiar with this situation.
AGATHA. Father, this young man is a walking encyclopedia. Really, he's providing you there with a very valuable idea!
COLONNES. Sir, sir, I implore, let's get on to that description of Etna which I await so impatiently.
DELCOUR. ((*By the way in which he is standing, he has only MR. GIRASOLE, AGATHA, and MR. COLONNES on his right. It is to them that he delivers his speech. When he is about to begin his dissertation, CAPITOLIN crosses to his left, very close to him. After CAPITOLIN, MR. LÉMERAUDE, then the Jew and CORNALINE. These last four do not form a semi-circle. The desire to hear makes them stand naturally one in front of the other like what we call a "house of cards." They have their mouths open and are listening with the greatest attention.*) First, picture for yourself, sir, a mountain whose circumference is equal to that of the largest cities, and whose height is three thousand fathoms. As soon as you come near it, the appalling noise of its insides takes away your ability to hear your own voice. Are you seeking to climb it? The noise gets louder. Scarcely have you reached the top when the lava that comes out continuously makes you regret your recklessness. There, the clouds of flames which appear suspended above your head, sulfurous vapors inflicting the air you breathe!

Here, columns of fire spew from the mouth of the volcano; bituminous material exploding from its spouts surrounds you. Finally, everything, sir, everything is the picture of hell. And on this perilous course, whether you go forward, or retreat, beneath each of your steps, desolation and death are found in tracks of fire. (*Speaking the word "retreat," he collided with CAPITOLIN who was standing next to him, listening like a fool. CAPITOLIN fell against MR. LÉMERAUDE who knocked down the Jew, and the Jew knocked over CORNALINE. After a moment, the four get to their feet.*)

LÉMERAUDE. (*Stuttering.*) Ah, si . . . si . . . sir, what a description! (*Speaking of CAPITOLIN.*) That oa . . . oa . . . oaf has su . . . su . . . such fear . . . I thought he'd overpower us all with the disgusting we . . . we . . . weight of his clumsy stupi . . . stupi . . . stupidity.

CAPITOLIN. (*Stretching out, like someone checking to see if he has broken any limbs.*) Oh, Sandix, when someone falls on me, I really have to fall on someone else. The gentleman put a lot of passion into his description. He spoke about flames, about I don't know what that's burning; and since I'm dressed with combustible materials, I was afraid that my jacket would catch fire.

COLONNES. I wouldn't know how to thank you enough, sir, for all the wonderful things you've just taught me.

CAPITOLIN. (*To MR. GIRASOLE, after having permitted the previous line to make its effect.*) Sir, are you not dining tonight? The roast will burn . . . the spit's been turning for over three hours now.

GIRASOLE. No, tell them to delay it. (*CAPITOLIN exits.*) I promised my son-in-law and Mr. Lémeraude that I'd let them see the experiment of the incombustible curtain.

DELCOUR. Which we call asbestos, isn't that right, sir?

GIRASOLE. Precisely, sir, and I invite you to witness the proceedings. (*Indicating the curtain.*) Here's a piece that I brought back from one of my travels. We'll try to set it on fire. If it's all right with you, I'm going to settle some accounts with our friend Larabesque. I'll be with you in a moment. Son-in-law, Mr. Colonnes, follow me, I beg you. Mr. Larabesque is sometimes a little expensive . . . you'll help me make him listen to reason.

LARABESQUE. Ah, sir, my conscience!
GIRASOLE. (*Leaving with his two friends and LARABESQUE, laughing.*) Ah! Ah! The conscience of a Jew!
AGATHA. (*Quickly.*) Oh, heavens! How is he going to take all of this?
CORNALINE. The best in the world! Don't worry about a thing, Miss.
DELCOUR. That damned stutterer is the one who worked up my blood the most!
CORNALINE. He's my boyfriend. We've got that one wrapped around our little finger!
DELCOUR. Then it's the other one, Agatha . . . it's the other one who's intended for you.
AGATHA. Ah! If you knew how I got rid of him! Come on now! I tell you he no longer wants me.
CORNALINE. And what did you tell him?
AGATHA. I convinced him that I was subject to attacks of hydrophobia.
DELCOUR. What nice eccentricity! But maybe your father will contradict you? A lover is always worried. Ah! My dear Agatha, I still see a thousand clouds over the happy days you promise me. At least will your heart remain mine in this constant flux of events, which I anticipate only too well?
AGATHA. (*Looking at him tenderly.*) I don't forgive you for doubting it. God, what's that I hear?
CAPITOLIN. (*Running. Shouting from backstage.*) Watch out! Look out! Beware! (*To DELCOUR.*) Ah! Really, Mr. Scoundrel, you're coming here to trick us. Oh! Oh! You're not clever enough for that yet. You're discovered! Go on! Go on! Clear out as fast as you can. I'm giving you your notice.
DELCOUR. Oh, heavens!
AGATHA. (*Speaking at the same time as DELCOUR.*) Why, what's going on? Tell us. You're making me tremble.
CAPITOLIN. It's that . . . it's that your father had some suspicions. He said that the gentleman had employed a few chro . . . chro . . . what the devil do you call them? (*Looking at his sleeve.*) Let's see if I don't find it on my clothes . . . no, wait. Ah! Chromisms!

CORNALINE. Anachronisms.
CAPITOLIN. Yes, anachronisms . . . the manner which Mr. Colonnes and Mr. Lémeraude urged your father to use to frighten that rascal, Mr. Larabesque a little, ended up pulling the truth out of him. They offered to beat him, and very satisfied with the offer, he didn't care to accept the gift. He admitted that this young man was only an adventurer whom he took along with him for personal gain.
AGATHA. (*Quickly.*) Is that all? Did he saying anything about me?
CAPITOLIN. No. (*He studies AGATHA, then, after a pause.*) Is there by chance something between this young man and you? Let me in on this affair. You know the Gascons: honest, loyal, incapable of betraying a secret, when a person does them the honor of letting them in on it.
CORNALINE. (*Quickly.*) Well, yes. Here, help these two lovers get out of this mess. Just be cleverer . . . and more successful . . . than that cursed Jew, and your fortune is made!
CAPITOLIN. (*Carrying his head high.*) Eh, Sandix, why didn't you say something? If you would have spoken to me at first, you would have already been engaged for six weeks. You don't know my skill in handling romantic intrigues. If I were to tell you all that I've accomplished in this category! You were going to appeal to the devil? To a Jewish antique dealer! Come on, tell me all about it. The gentleman, then, is the young lady's lover?
CORNALINE. Yes, and the young lady is the gentleman's lover.
AGATHA. Hurry, then, Capitolin. Hurry and find a way to keep Delcour in this house, and . . .
DELCOUR. (*Interrupting, quickly.*) And I'll take care of you.
CAPITOLIN. That's the easiest thing in the world. (*To DELCOUR.*) Didn't you say that you wanted to live here? (*To AGATHA.*) And you, Miss, didn't you want the gentleman never to leave this house?
AGATHA. Without a doubt, that's what we want.
CAPITOLIN. (*Taking them both by their hands, and holding on to them.*) Very well! All you need is that neither of you go away and your goal will be reached!
CORNALINE. Oh, the insufferable beast!

CAPITOLIN. No abuse, Miss Cornaline, or I'm certainly not getting involved with any of this.
CORNALINE. Really, for what you're doing, for what you're contriving, it would be worth everything if you just disappeared!
CAPITOLIN. Don't you need to think about it? There's a method in everything.
AGATHA. (*Hearing footsteps.*) Oh heavens, here's my father.
CAPITOLIN. (*Seizing DELCOUR and leading him into the wings.*) Nothing is lost. Come quickly. Go hide in that big chest where they keep the asbestos cloth, and don't move.
DELCOUR. (*To his mistress, while being dragged away.*) Agatha, my beloved Agatha, at least don't forsake me.
CAPITOLIN. (*Hurrying him.*) Ah, hell! You'll make love tomorrow. We don't have time today.
(*DELCOUR is hidden in the chest through the efforts of CAPITOLIN and CORNALINE.*)
CAPITOLIN. (*Returning onstage, and speaking loudly with the intention of being heard by those who are entering.*) The villain! Ah! How I've entertained him. I doubt he'll come back here again!
GIRASOLE. (*Angrily.*) Abusing people's good faith to that degree! I certainly would have beaten that scoundrel to death! Well, Capitolin, did you get rid of him?
CAPITOLIN. You clearly see, sir, he's not here. I tell you he has no desire to return here. Ask, ask Cornaline how I thrashed him.
GIRASOLE. Agatha, do you understand this indiscretion?
CAPITOLIN. Who knows what that rogue's hidden objectives could have been.
COLONNES. I suspect debauchery. Only debauchery would have brought that character into your house.
AGATHA. (*Arrogantly to MR. COLONNES.*) And who do you think he could debauch here, sir?
GIRASOLE. Oh, no, no. Don't be offended, my dear child. We know quite well that your chastity shelters you from all temptations; but that doesn't make it any less shameless for that rogue of a Jew to bring an adventurer here to us.
LÉMERAUDE. (*Stuttering.*) From the first words out of this cha . . . cha . . . character's mouth, I would have to . . .to . . . told you that he was a sco . . . sco . . . scoundrel . . . with his ro . . . ro . . .

road going from Si . . . Si . . . Sicility to America, and his Sa . . . Sa . . .Salerno who's a gre . . . gre . . . great man.

CAPITOLIN. Those guys aren't educated.

GIRASOLE. Come on! Gentlemen, let this not make us forget the intention we had of experimenting with the asbestos cloth, little known to our colleague, Mr. Colonnes.

LÉMERAUDE. (*Stuttering and putting on his glasses.*) Before we devote ourselves to that experiment, gentlemen, I expect that you'll really want to listen to the reading of this short dissertation on the subject in question. Isn't it true, Mr. Girasole, that it is good to establish at the outset that, what among us learned folk is called asbestos cloth, is nothing but the *labertus* of the ancients, the *spartapolios* of the Greeks, and the *cosroi* of the Hebrews.

GIRASOLE. (*Interrupting him.*) My friend, I'd be afraid that the reading of this treatise would take us too far from the subject. Wouldn't it be better for us to perform the experiment? Capitolin, go fetch us the chest that contains that precious miracle.

CAPITOLIN. It's too heavy, sir. I can't carry it all by myself.

GIRASOLE. Get yourself some help. (*CAPITOLIN exits.*)

AGATHA. Father, I'm afraid to watch this experiment.

GIRASOLE. Why, my daughter?

AGATHA. I don't know. I feel a kind of reluctance. Maybe there's even danger in it . . . and besides, you're talking about dead bodies. All that suggests sadness to me. Father, instead, show these gentlemen all the museum pieces that arrived for you from Naples.

COLONNES. Everything in its time, Miss. Why do you want to deprive him of the pleasure of seeing an experiment which has been unknown to me until now?

CAPITOLIN. (*In a hurry, frightened. Shouting.*) Ah, sir, hurry! That cursed Jew is over there. He's making a horrible noise. He's saying that you beat him, that you didn't pay him, and that he's going to prosecute you in court.

GIRASOLE. (*Going out with his companions.*) Damn the scoundrel! Come, my friends, come lend me your assistance in talking some sense into that wretch!

CAPITOLIN. (*Fanning himself with his hat.*) Oh! I think that was managed pretty well. (*To AGATHA.*) Well, another time you'll put your trust in a Gascon! I knew very well that the Jew mustn't be very far away. I ran after him. I hired him to act nasty. I saw that, in this way, we would gain some time.

(*Here, the three ANTIQUE DEALERS reappear, preceded by two valets who carry the chest and put it down in the middle of the stage.*)

GIRASOLE. That cursed Jew is gone . . . we're finally rid of him! We'll attend to nothing but our experiment. Open that trunk, Capitolin.

CAPITOLIN. (*Opening it, trembling.*) Sir, it's as if it was going to catch on fire all of a sudden.

(*The chest is opened, DELCOUR comes out, frightens everyone, and this scene of terror remains for a few moments in the eyes of the spectators.*)

EVERYONE. What do I see?

DELCOUR. (*Proceeding to throw himself at MR. GIRASOLE's feet.*) You're looking at your daughter's lover, sir, the same one who was trying to pull the wool over your eyes a little while ago.

GIRASOLE. Who are you, sir?

DELCOUR. My name is Delcour, sir. For the past three years, I've been in love with Miss Agatha, your daughter, and you see me ready to die at your feet if you refuse me the privilege of joining your family.

AGATHA. (*Hugging her father's knees from the opposite side.*) Oh, father, don't renounce your daughter . . . don't let the kindness she's received from you inflict upon you the cruel duty of making her the most unfortunate of creatures.

COLONNES. One moment, my friends. There is something in all of this that would be good to clear up before going any farther. (*To the young man.*) I believe I know your name, sir. Consent to repeat it, if you please. (*The two lovers rise.*)

DELCOUR. My name is Delcour, sir.

COLONNES. Would your father, sir, be the one who occupies Drome's department?

DELCOUR. That's my father.

COLONNES. Oh, beloved son of the most tenderly loved brother. Delcour, throw yourself into your uncle's arms. My friend, make up for the sadness of having been separated from my brother for twenty years because of the most unforeseen circumstances. (*To MR. GIRASOLE.*) My friend, in giving up the claims to a marriage which didn't at all suit me, allow me to introduce you to the only man who appears to me worthy of your Agatha's hand. You know his family . . . he was born to be exceedingly rich one day, and to his wealth, I add my fortune!

GIRASOLE. (*To MR. COLONNES.*) All of this surprises me . . . but that trick . . . that method of getting into my house . . .

DELCOUR. (*Quickly.*) Ah! Sir . . .

COLONNES. Forgive love's mistakes. It's the most tyrannical of passions. Let's be fair, my friend, and remember our youth. (*To AGATHA.*) Ah! You little rascal, is that, then, the cause of that peculiar disease?

GIRASOLE. (*With animation.*) Very nice, very nice, my girl. Well done for a first intrigue! I hope, at least, that it will be your last.

AGATHA. Grant me the one I love, father, and beside him, I'll no longer pay attention to anything but virtue.

CAPITOLIN. (*Falling to his knees.*) Sir, I beg of you, don't offer any more opposition. Look. I'll work for you for two years for nothing, if you try and make your daughter happy.

GIRASOLE. Keep quiet, keep quiet, you devil. By right, I should fire you for being mixed up in all of these tricks. (*To the young man.*) Sir, you want Agatha. Mr. Colonnes, you agree to it. Well, my friends, get married! I'm willing since it suits you . . . but on one condition: will you concede that to me?

DELCOUR. Give the order, sir. Give the order.

GIRASOLE. (*To the young man.*) That you'll educate yourself, sir, and learn Greek.

DELCOUR. (*With ecstasy.*) Syrian, Hebrew, Chinese, and Turkish if you like, sir.

GIRASOLE. And that you'll acquire the knowledge that can make a good antique dealer. Above all, that you won't use those revolting anachronisms in our company. I'll never swallow your Salerno, or the road from Sicily to America.

CORNALINE. Indeed, sir, he'll learn all you want. Won't he be trying to please the one he loves? Ah! Love, then, will take charge of his instruction . . . and the progress under such a master will be as quick as it is certain.

THE END

Truth and Treason

Introduction

Little is known about Sade's three-act melodrama, *Truth and Treason*. Not included in the *Descriptive Catalogue of 1788*, the manuscript is dated 1807, with a marginal note indicating that final revisions were completed in August 1808. Gilbert Lély suggests that the play was probably the melodrama in "three prose acts" referred to in a letter dated 6 March 1791 as *The Virtuous Criminal* and accepted for performance at the Théâtre du Palais Royal. There is no evidence to support this claim. The recent discovery of the manuscript of a play called *The Madness of Misfortune*, which Lély believed to be lost, reveals an annotation in Sade's handwriting indicating that play, and not *Truth and Treason*, had been "revised for the Théâtre du Palais Royal."

Given the dates on the manuscript, we can only assume that the Marquis de Sade completed his melodrama about incarceration, greed, lust, and deception, while an inmate of the Charenton Asylum, the third jail in which he had been confined since April 1801. Following the publication of his novel, *The Crimes of Love*, Sade had been imprisoned without the benefit of a trial in Sainte-Pélagie, a convent turned political prison. After he attempted to sodomize a young prisoner, the Marquis was transferred to Bicêtre Prison, popularly known as "the mob's Bastille." In his *Souvenirs, Episodes and Portraits of the Revolution and the Empire*, Charles Nodier described Sade on the day of his transfer:

> All I first noticed was a monstrous obesity which hampered his movements to such a point that he was unable to move with the same vestiges of charm and elegance which one could detect traces of in his general deportment. Yet his eyes still retain a hint

> of brilliancy and exquisiteness which glowed from time to time for a moment like the last spark of a dying ember. . . . All I recall is that he was courteous to the point of being obsequious, affable to the point of unctuousness, and spoke with respect of all that is accorded respect.

A month after the Marquis was transferred to Bicêtre Prison, his family persuaded the Prefect of Police to consign him to the more comfortable regimen of the Charenton Asylum. Charenton had been established as a hospice for the insane and by this time, having spent twenty-seven years of his life in eleven different prisons, Sade was considered "incorrigible" and in a state of "incessant licentious insanity." Both the police and the Marquis's family were satisfied with Sade's incarceration in the lunatic asylum, but many of the doctors at Charenton were not. In a letter to the Minister of Police, dated 2 August 1808 (the same month in which Sade completed his play), Dr. Royer Collard argued that the Marquis was not mentally ill:

> His one delirium is that of vice—and this cannot be aided in an insane asylum. He has to be placed in the severest isolation to protect others from his outbreaks and to separate him from all circumstances that might increase his horrible passion. Our place at Charenton does not fulfill any of these conditions. De Sade enjoys too great freedom here. He can have intercourse with a great number of patients and convalescents either in his or their rooms. He has the right to walk in the park and often meets patients there. He preaches to them his criminal theories and lends them books. Finally, we received a report that he is living with a woman whom he claimed was his daughter.

Collard went on to complain that Sade's theatrical activities at the asylum produced "harmful effects . . . upon the mind" and ought to be discontinued. This view was in opposition to the opinion held by Coulmier, the director of the asylum for whom Sade, as "asylum poet" had written allegories and occasional panegyrics. Coulmier stated to the Minister of Police, on 2 September 1808, that "seeing in light drama a curative method for the mentally deranged" he considered himself fortunate to have "in the hospice a man capable of giving a stage training" to those whom he sought to treat by this therapy. However, he admitted, upon reflection, that Charenton might not be the proper environment for a man "who has corrupted public morals by his impious, lascivious writings and committed so many crimes." This was a typical reaction to the Marquis's creative work. On 5 June 1807, a number of Sade's manuscripts were seized by the police and destroyed including *Florbelle's Days; or, Nature Unveiled* which had just been completed a month earlier after "thirteen months and twenty days' work." Either *Truth and Treason* was considered acceptable by the police and not burned among what they referred to as a "succession of obscenities, blasphemy and foulness beyond description" or written later, sometime between 6 June 1807 and August 1808. There is no record of the play ever having been performed.

TRUTH AND TREASON

Prose Drama in Three Acts

Whoever only pays attention to goodness, and does nothing but good deeds, his reward is in his heart. For him, that's enough.[10]

CHARACTERS

Count Verneuil, *owner of the castle where the action occurs*
Countess Verneuil, *his wife*
Madame de Valbelle, *a friend of the Countess*
Adeline, *Valbelle's daughter*
Félix, *son of the Countess, in love with Adeline*
Chevalier de Faublan, *longtime inhabitant of the castle*
Delcour, *Verneuil's protégé*
A Servant
A Messenger
A Police Officer and Four Bailiffs, *characters dressed to appear in an official position*

(*The action takes place in a room in Count Verneuil's castle during the reign of Louis XV.*)[11]

---

[10] Sade erroneously attributed the epigraph to *Truth and Treason*, Act 4.
[11] Sade erased the note, "In Paris, 1807."

ACT ONE

FAUBLAN. It seems to me, my dear Delcour, that you haven't made much progress in your pursuit of Miss Adeline's heart. That lovely daughter of Madame de Valbelle is far from renouncing, in your favor, the long-standing feelings of affection she has toward Countess Verneuil's son.
DELCOUR. Chevalier, don't you know that it isn't easy to get possession of a heart already seduced by a handsome young man? Adeline loves Félix. He thinks of no one but her. They write one another constantly. As soon as the Count returns, his son will urge his father to consent to the match. While I am the most unfortunate of men; for, in spite of all that opposes my happiness, in spite of all the laws of duty and honor that thrust themselves upon me, I am unable to conquer the love that I feel for that too seductive Adeline.
FAUBLAN. You're a fool, my friend. You're getting too worked up over this pretty girl. Remember that the heart always has to obey the mind. Whoever disregards this rule is asking for trouble.
DELCOUR. Ah! My dear Faublan, look at Adeline. Gaze into her eyes and tell me if it's possible to know her without loving her . . . and loving her, to be false to her.
FAUBLAN. What you're saying, my friend, is the story of every lover and every woman. It never stopped a man from betraying a woman every time the situation presented itself. The fair sex so vigorously make that claim against us, that it would be ungrateful, on our part, not to give them their due.
DELCOUR. What about this passion that you seem to have for Countess Verneuil, a woman so sweet, so open, so friendly? Is it nothing but deception on your part?
FAUBLAN. My boy, you need me to take you under my wing.
DELCOUR. I should think that I'd turn out to be a bad student.
FAUBLAN. (*After looking around on all sides.*) It's time, my dear Delcour, that I tell you my plans. I know what goes on in your head, and the intimacy we've been sharing for some time now makes me believe that I can speak freely, without hesitation.
DELCOUR. Ah! You can count on my discretion.

FAUBLAN. Then learn some things that will perhaps encourage you regarding Adeline. I have no property, but thanks to my abilities, I'm now enjoying an income of over forty thousand francs a year. The inheritance of hard work is more valuable than inheriting a fortune, my friend. Adversity takes the one away from us, our skill creates the other. And if you know how to go about it, you can ruin a lot of other people without the slightest risk of being ruined yourself.
DELCOUR. Ah, Chevalier, those are principles that . . .
FAUBLAN. That you need more than any other, since just like me, you can only count on wealth that comes from your hard work.
DELCOUR. In that case, I'll die poor. But, go on, sir. I am uniquely curious about what you're going to teach me.
FAUBLAN. For some time now, I've been considered Count Verneuil's friend. I was only a friend of his wealth. It tempted me. And to take possession of it, I found nothing simpler than getting rid of him. I imagined that in ruining him, both his wife and his wealth would quickly be in my possession. And to succeed in my plans, three months ago, I stirred up trouble against the Count. I hired an assassin to attack him, but, unfortunately, he was killed in the scuffle. It didn't much matter. I was still confident of getting Verneuil out of the way. Through my efforts, the matter was made public. Louis XV had just passed a very strict law against duels. The Count went to Lausanne. As soon as he was gone, I spread the news. I presented the story so emphatically to his disadvantage that he himself was thought of as a murderer. The French court, wanting to preserve the honor of this gentleman, thought it was doing the greatest service to him and his family by getting the judge in Lausanne to lock him behind bars for the rest of his life. That's where he is now, and that's where he's going to stay.
DELCOUR. (*Shaking with horror.*) Oh, what a dreadful conspiracy.
FAUBLAN. You're young, Delcour, still with all the frankness of youth. A trifle astonishes you. You still don't know what is possible when a fortune is a stake.

DELCOUR. Do you need to commit new crimes to become rich? Aren't you rich enough already?
FAUBLAN. One is never rich enough, Delcour, but I'm going to keep quiet if you're going to be shocked over nothing.
DELCOUR. Very well. Go on, sir, continue.
FAUBLAN. Now I have to perfect my work. Félix, moved by filial devotion to help the Count, has to be caught in the same trap. Here our interests combine, my friend, for if that young man is harmful to my designs, he is also a hindrance to your love. His ruin makes me certain that the countess will grant you Adeline. No more fear or childishness, my dear Delcour. Let's unite our forces, far away from those who hinder our success.
DELCOUR. You very dangerous man, you're trying to seduce me!
FAUBLAN. (*Coldly.*) I do not seek to seduce you. I'm simply opening your eyes to good fortune. I pity you if you deny the friend who's unlocking the doors to your future.
DELCOUR. (*Desperately.*) Isn't there a middle ground between losing the woman I adore and crime?
FAUBLAN. Crime is imaginary; misfortune is inevitable. Think about it, Delcour. Think about it. In freeing Adeline from the lover who possesses her, you will become the master of her heart. In the entire world, she will only have eyes for you. At that moment, you will take possession of her mother's mind. Madame de Valbelle is a very clever woman, capable of unraveling and foiling our plans. We must be in complete control of the situation. A few tricks will be necessary to reach our different goals. I am unhappy with the man I'm using. You will replace him. Here's the plan: I'll write the necessary letters; your skillful hand will copy the handwriting. While I proceed in the field of battle, you will hover on the sidelines. You will carry my appointed letters to the ministers of state. They will spread the news through the capital. Our cannons will burst simultaneously, and success will crown our efforts.
DELCOUR. Ah! What do you want from me, Faublan?
FAUBLAN. (*Quickly.*) Your happiness. It's certain if you stick with me; lost if we cease to understand one another.

DELCOUR. (*Nearly exhausted.*) Ah! If love is a virtue, why does it involve us in crime?
FAUBLAN. (*Taking his hand.*) That's just the way it is. I'm counting on you. Let's change the subject for a minute, to talk about something that's of a personal interest to you.
DELCOUR. What are you talking about?
FAUBLAN. I've got some money to give you, Delcour. I was a friend of your father. I was close to him when he died. "My dear Chevalier," he said to me, "you will find my son attached to the Count Verneuil. Please give him this wallet. It contains sixty-thousand francs, the sad remains of an old fortune. I charge you, at the same time, old friend, to give my son the final embraces of a father who never ceased to love him." Allow me to discharge my precious duty out of fondness for you. (*He gives DELCOUR the wallet and embraces him.*)
DELCOUR. (*With difficulty.*) I am singularly touched, sir, but I cannot accept my father's gift right now.
FAUBLAN. Why not?
DELCOUR. No, no, sir. It would seem too much like payment for services rendered. I shouldn't receive anything at this time.
FAUBLAN. These qualms . . .
DELCOUR. (*Quickly.*) Counterbalance, a little, my unwilling association with you.
FAUBLAN. (*Replacing the wallet in his pocket.*) Hush! Madame de Valbelle is coming. Go away. We'll see each other again. Above all, be as careful as you are clever. All that you hold dearest depends on it.
DELCOUR. (*Going off, aside.*) Ah! I hold nothing dearer than virtue, and I will not destroy it.
VALBELLE. (*Entering.*) Well, sir, what do you think about Félix's long absence? It's beginning to disturb us.
FAUBLAN. (*Tactfully.*) What have you heard about his trip?
VALBELLE. Both Madame de Verneuil and I were of the opinion that he had obtained either the release of the poor Count, his father, or a great reduction of the sentence. The last letter he wrote before leaving for Lausanne was very positive.
FAUBLAN. I'm afraid that someone has led the young man into error and forced him to take a trip for nothing. The latest news

contradicts what you've just said. One is easily deceived when he's unhappy.

VALBELLE. (*Very distressed.*) Heavens! What could have happened? You're making me tremble, sir.

FAUBLAN. I can tell you nothing. You are so linked with Madame de Verneuil that whatever breaks the heart of one of you will inevitably break the other's as well. It would be necessary, anyway, to keep it quiet, for if the news got around before the matter came to an end, it could put the estate in danger. My friendship for the Count is such that I would hate to increase his suffering because of an indiscretion.

VALBELLE. (*As before.*) Ah! My God, sir, you chill me to the bone. Out with it, I beg of you.

FAUBLAN. Very well, Madame, it has to do with a transfer . . . to a maximum security prison. Some stolen papers . . . communications broken down over a situation, in a word, infinitely more serious than what we thought. They say they're trying to get Verneuil off easy with life imprisonment.

VALBELLE. And you've heard nothing about his son?

FAUBLAN. No, but I expect to hear from Baron Pressing today without fail. My friend, the Baron, is in a position to know all there is to know concerning Count de Verneuil. He will certainly make me aware of everything that happens. Besides, I doubt that anything bad has happened to Félix. We just have to hope that all the bad luck doesn't hit us at once, and that soon we'll see the object of your daughter's affection.

VALBELLE. You'll pardon me, sir, if at the moment I can think of nothing but the hideous news you've just told me. What seems impossible to me is that it contradicts the news the countess received from her husband just a few days ago.

FAUBLAN. (*Very surprised.*) Madame Verneuil received news from her husband a few days ago?

VALBELLE. Yes, and I assure that it was quite different from what you've just told me.

FAUBLAN. It only takes a moment for things like that to change.

VALBELLE. (*Slyly.*) It takes longer when you invent them.

FAUBLAN. What do you mean, Madame?

VALBELLE. What do you want, sir? There are a lot of people here who do not consider you to be an honest man.
FAUBLAN. Ah! Madame, frankness and honesty are the principal virtues of my soul. Are you suspicious of me?
VALBELLE. Me? I suspect nothing. I see a lot of things. I suppose even more. But I'll hold my tongue. The fear of guessing badly restrains me and fills me with skepticism, which I much prefer to certainty. That's why I've always preferred being in doubt, rather than knowing the truth.
FAUBLAN. Perhaps I should offer you an explanation.
VALBELLE. I tell you, I ask for none.
FAUBLAN. But, Madame, I feel obliged to offer you . . .
VALBELLE. Ah! Not a word. The countess is coming. Let me prepare her for the bad news you've just told me. Don't mention a word of it, I beg of you.
FAUBLAN. (*Going off.*) I'll hold my tongue, Madame. You can be certain of that.
(MADAME VERNEUIL enters.)
VALBELLE. The man who just left is very attached to you, my dear countess.
VERNEUIL. Yes, I really believe that he has a fondness for me.
VALBELLE. (*Slyly.*) Is that the only sentiment you've discovered in him?
VERNEUIL. I think he's incapable of showing feelings that would offend me. Faublan knows how much I love my husband and my son. Why would he want to make trouble?
VALBELLE. Of course. But a man in love isn't always aware of his motives. Your husband's situation could provide him with a little hope . . . hard to extinguish now. Come on, let's be honest, my dear. I'm only asking as a friend. You only have to answer in kind. If only you were aware of all the reasons I have for knowing the truth, and how important it is that I know it, to shed light on your affairs.
VERNEUIL. (*With abandon.*) Very well, I will not keep it a secret from you, my dear Valbelle. Under the guise of friendship, of the purest and most unselfish kind, Faublan revealed to me certain offensive feelings, which I immediately repelled. But he bathed me in them with such eagerness and honesty . . .

VALBELLE. That you believed them, isn't that right?
VERNEUIL. Not at all. Moreover, I couldn't. I have always loved my husband, especially now when he's facing misfortune. Other women might have repelled Faublan out of duty, but I rejected him out of the single fear of offending Verneuil by listening to such talk.
VALBELLE. That way of thinking is a credit to you. Of course, I knew well in advance that you would tell me about it. This passionate and clever man has doubtlessly renewed his declarations, hasn't he?
VERNEUIL. He certainly tried, as vigorously as he could, and still I sought to extinguish his less than holy flame.
VALBELLE. Perhaps you should find out what makes him act this way?
VERNEUIL. (*Smiling.*) That question could terrify my self-esteem.
VALBELLE. God knows that wasn't my intention, but, my dear countess, given the situation we're in, trampled by misfortune, we must be terrified of everything. It's times like these when con men and swindlers are laying their traps, and since you possess such an honest disposition, I'm frightened of all their disgusting schemes.
VERNEUIL. You're frightening me.
VALBELLE. Yet, I only want to enlighten you. (*With interest.*) Have you received a satisfactory letter from your son?
VERNEUIL. I read you part of it yesterday. Félix wrote me that, although the Count was terribly upset by the situation, he was nevertheless in excellent health. He had been greatly encouraged by the Minister of State who led him to believe that his misfortunes would soon be at an end. Oh, yes! I shall soon have the pleasure of seeing my husband again and of holding both him and my son in my arms. What happiness that is for a tender mother, for a loving wife. Ah! You can forgive good fortune for passing us by, again and again, when it provides us with such a sweet reunion. Oh, my dear Valbelle, that will be the greatest moment of my life. Not a cloud in the sky. Nothing can go wrong because Verneuil and I will be together. How I look forward, with ecstasy, to the day that will reunite us!

VALBELLE. Ah, how I will share in your joy!
VERNEUIL. My dear friend, give me your trust. Be as honest with me as I've been with you. I feel as if you're concealing something from me. Has something happened that you don't want to tell me about? The suspense I feel is worse than death.
VALBELLE. You'll pardon me, my dear, if I cannot reveal anything to you as yet. I need to consider the matter. I need some explanations. I think I hear my daughter. I don't dare say anything in front of her. But be assured that your interests are dearer to me than my own, and I will not forsake them as long as I live.
VERNEUIL. (*Going out.*) I'm counting on your help and your friendship.
(ADELINE enters opposite from VERNEUIL's exit.)
VALBELLE. Come here, girl, come here. I notice you've been looking troubled and gloomy lately. I want to know the reason why.
ADELINE. Could I keep a secret from such a tender and beloved mother?
VALBELLE. You can be sure that I'm only concerned about your happiness. (*Tenderly.*) I notice that you don't talk to me about Félix like you used to.
ADELINE. I'm afraid to talk. I've heard some things about him that disturb me.
VALBELLE. And what's been feeding your fear?
ADELINE. Certain things that Mr. Faublan has been repeating so often, that I'm almost convinced of them.
VALBELLE. What sort of things has he been telling you?
ADELINE. (*Quickly.*) The worst sort . . . things that break my heart and wound my pride.
VALBELLE. This troubles me. Explain yourself, dear girl. Lay your sorrows in the lap of a mother who loves you, and she will make them her own. She'll either cause them to disappear, or convince you that there's nothing to worry about.
ADELINE. I'm convinced that Félix will never return to France, and that some new object of his affection keeps him in Lausanne.
VALBELLE. What lies! Ah. It's easy to see how you'd jump to that conclusion. Believe me, daughter. Félix still loves you. We

will soon see him again, and he has no other love but his dear Adeline!

ADELINE. Ah! How precious are the consolations I receive from you.

VALBELLE. Continue to be honest, Adeline. For some time now, you've shown a great deal of interest in the Count's protégé. Is that because you suspected Félix of being unfaithful?

ADELINE. I won't lie to you. Delcour seemed to be the only one who could have comforted me in my loss. Spite and revenge made him appear attractive to me, though perhaps, only in my imagination.

VALBELLE. Your fears concerning Félix excuse your behavior. But Delcour never should have interested you. He's not well-off.

ADELINE. (*Very quickly.*) What does money matter when you're talking about revenge?

VALBELLE. Oh, my dear Adeline, what weapons people use to deceive you! That Faublan is very clever. He's completely two-faced! He has a great interest in all of this. Soon perhaps, you will know more about it. While waiting, dear girl, put some sense into young Delcour's head. Make him aware that you know more about what's happening to Félix than he does, and that nothing has occurred that would cause you to break your engagement; that the ties which you have formed, in accordance with your heart, and approved by both families, are not likely to be broken. That you will make amends for any misunderstanding by offering him your respect, and your friendship, a sentiment you have yet to offer any other.

ADELINE. Since you completely assure me that the first object of my affection doesn't deserve to be cast aside, I will take it upon myself to notify Delcour of a truth which will certainly distress him a great deal.

VALBELLE. Then you believe he's sincerely interested in you?

ADELINE. I don't believe that he's tried to deceive me.

VALBELLE. Let me say it again. The young man has nothing. You need to have a rich husband.

ADELINE. Ah! I only want and desire Félix, since he's saving his heart for me alone.

VALBELLE. Stop by Madame Verneuil's house, my dear. I'll join you there later. From her you'll get solid evidence of her son's speedy return, and as a result, proof of the continuance of his love for you. A person is easily seduced at your age, when she has your honesty and tenderness.
ADELINE. (*Going off.*) Ah! A mother like you is precious in these baneful perils of life!
MADAME DE VALBELLE. (*Alone.*) There are some frightening details in all of this. I'm going to have to unravel them. That Faublan is a villain. There's no doubt about it. Delcour is his accomplice. But the young man's soul is still so naïve and honest that perhaps he will reveal everything to me. I'll leave no stone unturned. At the same time, I must serve friendship, virtue, and nature. Ah! If it costs me a few scruples, won't my heart comfort me?

END OF ACT ONE

ACT TWO

DELCOUR. Is it true, Madame, that we will never see Count Verneuil again?
VALBELLE. Where did you hear that, Delcour?
DELCOUR. The whole castle is talking about it. Mr. Faublan tells me what's going on every day.
VALBELLE. Does this talk give you cause for concern?
DELCOUR. As the Count's protégé, raised by him in this house, I ought to miss him, and feel sorry for him, even more so, since it seems to me that someone is trying to blacken his reputation beyond belief in this affair.
VALBELLE. Nevertheless, the matter is quite simple. A duel is forbidden by law. I admit that, but precedent demands it. Between two unavoidable wrongs, the Count chose the one that satisfied his honor. Has anyone told you anything more certain about the fate of that unfortunate man?
DELCOUR. Mr. Faublan thinks that he'll be imprisoned for life. He has Swiss relatives who seemed certain about this.
VALBELLE. Is Mr. Faublan always the one who tells you things?
DELCOUR. Yes, Madame.
VALBELLE. Ah, you unfortunate young man! How that fraud abuses your trust. They're undoubtedly rumors that justify your expectations regarding my daughter.
DELCOUR. Not expecting Félix to ever return, I've been able to surrender to feelings, Madame, emotions that I feel acutely, and which Mr. Faublan nourishes every day by offering me hope.
VALBELLE. And did you receive encouragement likewise from Adeline?
DELCOUR. If she encouraged me, she never let me see it.
VALBELLE. You are very fond of Mr. Faublan.
DELCOUR. He's always been kind to me, and I feel I owe him kindness in return. However, a few days ago, he said some things that disturbed me. (*Close to tears.*) I cannot hide it from you, Madame.

VALBELLE. Confide in me, my dear Delcour. You've always known how much I like you. Defend yourself from the traps and snares of a man who, sooner or later, will destroy you.
DELCOUR. (*As above.*) Very well, Madame. He seems to want to take advantage of my penmanship for some very important letters he says he wants to send to the Prime Minister.
VALBELLE. Heavens! What's in those letters?
DELCOUR. With these letters, he's trying to establish that Count Verneuil maliciously killed his opponent during the duel in question. The letter containing depositions from six eyewitnesses is the one that Mr. Faublan wants to send to the court without delay.
VALBELLE. And the other letters?
DELCOUR. Testimonials from some of the dead man's relatives, all calling for Count Verneuil to be severely punished.
VALBELLE. And you would have lent your hand to such horrors!
DELCOUR. No. That's the truth. The man, in his dishonesty, did not conceal his plots from me. From that point on, I hated him.
VALBELLE. Now you're absolutely certain that Faublan is a scoundrel.
DELCOUR. Ah! There's no longer any doubt in my mind.
VALBELLE. Why didn't you come to me and inform against him immediately?
DELCOUR. He held me against my will; just now he offered me sixty thousand francs that my father, he says, entrusted to him.
VALBELLE. How can that be?
DELCOUR. I lost my father before I reached the age of reason. You know all about it, Madame. Certain matters kept him away from France. At the time, Faublan was close to my father. On his deathbed, my father entrusted him with sixty thousand francs. He wanted to give me the money today, but as it was mixed up with everything that offends me most in the world, I wanted nothing to do with it.
VALBELLE. What deception! Unfortunate young man! You've been deceived about everything. Your father died in London, the victim of a fraudulent bankruptcy, in which he was innocently

involved. He died penniless. It is unlikely that he left any money, unless he put it in the hands of Count Verneuil, your guardian, and your father's friend. Faublan never even knew your father. That villain has taken advantage of you at every turn, I tell you, and those sixty thousand francs were nothing but payment for a crime.

DELCOUR. Ah! I'm thoroughly convinced. How I repent having ever listened to that man! Why does vice borrow all the attractions of virtue? Ah! My blindness leads me to despair!

VALBELLE. Calm yourself, calm yourself, Delcour. You're only the one who was tricked. The man who tricked you is the one we'll punish. Swear to me that you'll reveal everything when the time comes, and I promise that I will restore your reputation, which would inevitably have been destroyed by your behavior, if the plot were not made known.

DELCOUR. You can believe that I'll always be worthy of those who protect me.

(MADAME VERNEUIL appears.)

VALBELLE. Come here, come here, my dear countess. The deception has at last been uncovered, and the villain is in our own house.

DELCOUR. (*To MADAME VERNEUIL.*) Ah! How close I was to committing a crime!

VERNEUIL. Who? You? Good Lord!

VALBELLE. (*Quickly.*) He was only tricked. Listen to me. Faublan is the one who's guilty. He loves you, and to possess you, he ruined your husband. He has committed the most atrocious crimes of deception. Bribery, graft, perjured witnesses, forged signatures: all these things are the work of that villain. In a word, Faublan has done everything to ruin you and, unfortunately, we must continue to treat him kindly. Such is the great art of the criminal. He knows how to manipulate truth so well that he often forces it to tremble before his very eyes. Let's put up a front, and stay on the defensive. Heaven will help us. Ah! How innocence would become oppressed if virtue didn't dry its tears.

VERNEUIL. Never has it wept more bitter tears. I put myself in your hands, dear friend. I'm eternally grateful for all you have

done. Just let me be reunited with my husband, and perhaps I will pardon his enemies out of the goodness of my heart.
DELCOUR. Ah! Don't include me among them!
VERNEUIL. You couldn't possibly be mixed up with them.
DELCOUR. The rest of my life will make amends for a moment's weakness. May I never have another like it.
(FAUBLAN enters.)
FAUBLAN. (*To MADAME VERNEUIL,*) How sad it is to approach you, Madame, when I am the bearer of bad news.
VERNEUIL. (*Alarmed.*) Bad news? What is it? Speak. Speak, sir. My unfortunate soul is ready to receive every wound you seek to inflict upon me.
FAUBLAN. (*Giving a letter and papers to MADAME VALBELLE.*) Look these over, Madame. The voice of friendship perhaps will moderate the horror of this hideous news.
VALBELLE. (*Before reading, she casts an accusatory glance at FAUBLAN; he lowers his eyes. She reads the papers.*) The Baron de Pressing to the Chevalier de Faublan. "It grieves me as much as it saddens me to tell you, my dear Chevalier, that Count de Verneuil, unable to bear his misfortunes, has just killed himself. It occurred just as someone came to transfer him to another prison, as ordered by your Prime Minister. I . . ."
(*MADAME VERNEUIL falls into a chair. ADELINE runs in when she hears her cry out. She attends to her on the right. DELCOUR looks after her on the left. MADAME DE VALBELLE continues to read. FAUBLAN moves to the left corner of the stage.*)
VERNEUIL. (*Frenzied.*) Continue, my dear Valbelle. I need to hear everything.
VALBELLE. (*Continuing in the most serious and somber tone.*) "I am sending you the obituary of this unfortunate man." (*She stops reading.*) Here it is.
FAUBLAN. Madame, please read the third piece attached to this parcel, the one addressed to me from the prime minister.
VALBELLE. (*Continuing to read.*) "His majesty, sir, aware of Count Verneuil's misfortunes, and knowing the affection you have toward his family, has chosen you to be of assistance to his widow, and tutor to his son until he comes of age, in the event

that he resurfaces, since the misfortunes of his father have made him lose his mind."

(*MADAME VERNEUIL faints in the arms of ADELINE and DELCOUR who revive her.*)

VALBELLE. (*Quickly, to DELCOUR in a low voice.*) What do you think of these new horrors?

DELCOUR. (*In a low voice.*) I fear they may be true. Nobody told me anything about them.

VALBELLE. (*Flying to MADAME VERNEUIL.*) Cheer up, cheer up, dear friend. We must verify everything. Don't believe a word of it without proof.

FAUBLAN. Alas! Can I offer you stronger proof than this?

(*MADAME DE VALBELLE casts another withering glance at FAUBLAN. He never returns her gaze.*)

DELCOUR. (*To MADAME VERNEUIL, in a low voice.*) You can believe that he is capable of committing such crimes.

VERNEUIL. (*Coming to her senses.*) Very well, my dear Valbelle. Is it possible to be unhappier than I? (*Desperately.*) Now who will support me out in the world? Who will love me as much as this tender friend? (*She removes the picture of her husband which she carried in a locket around her neck. She cries out from the depths of her soul.*) Eh! Here is all that is left for me!!! Face, which I have always adored, let me cover you with these tender kisses. Carry them to the beloved mortal you portray, who was stolen from me by my fatal destiny. Tell him that I will follow right behind him, and that the monsters who robbed me of him will not triumph for long in their wickedness. (*Coldly to FAUBLAN.*) Finish the duties you have been given, sir. First of all, inquire about my son.

ADELINE. (*Throwing herself at FAUBLAN's feet, very poignantly.*) Ah! Sir, you see me in tears, on my knees. I beg you to hasten his return, and to shed light on all that concerns him.

VALBELLE. (*Briskly to ADELINE*). Get up, get up, girl. Such behavior is allowed only before God. That man can't do anything for you. God can do everything. Don't pray to anyone but Him.

ADELINE. Ah! I hope my tears at least might move him.

FAUBLAN. You can believe that I will neglect nothing to soften the sadness that I was forced to bring to you.

VERNEUIL. (*Getting up, and taking the arms of MADAME DE VALBELLE and ADELINE.*) Don't leave me, dear friends. This moment is frightening for me. Ah! Let me not survive a single day!
VALBELLE. (*Going off with MADAME VERNEUIL and her daughter.*) Let us not as yet surrender to despair. You're often very close to happiness when misfortune weighs you down. (*The three women exit.*)
DELCOUR. (*Alone, while FAUBLAN escorts the women out.*) I'll dissemble and unravel this plot. I've little experience with falsehood, but, unfortunately, it's necessary when dealing with scoundrels.
FAUBLAN. (*Returning.*) Well, Delcour, what do you think of my story?
DELCOUR. (*Faking throughout the scene.*) What? What you said wasn't true?
FAUBLAN. It will happen, I hope. But the news is premature.
DELCOUR. How can you invent such atrocities?
FAUBLAN. You must understand that, in a plan like mine, the ends justify the means.
DELCOUR. But I don't see how the means will lead to the end. After all, you're not going to marry the Count's widow the day after his death, are you?
FAUBLAN. Oh! I'm less interested in that than in his property. Sooner or later, that delightful creature will be my wife. Look at me, the appointed guardian! And you have to abide by what I say. I pride myself on the unselfish way I'm going to manage Madame Verneuil's estate.
DELCOUR. Yes, but she has a very dangerous custodian. That Madame de Valbelle makes me nervous. Madame Verneuil's steadfast friend has a keen mind. She'll figure out our plans and spoil everything.
FAUBLAN. (*Interrupting quickly.*) Hush! (*Showing him papers.*) Here I have all I need to be master of the situation.
DELCOUR. What's in that document?
FAUBLAN. I've exposed her to the Prime Minister as the instigator of the duel. Here's the warrant that banishes her forever.

DELCOUR. What about her daughter, the sacred object of my desires?
FAUBLAN. She's yours for certain. She will be forbidden to follow her mother. She enters a convent. I become her tutor, just like I am for Félix, and in a year the girl and the estate will all belong to you.
DELCOUR. Certainly this is one of your best schemes.
FAUBLAN. I've never had one so secure.
DELCOUR. And when will we deliver the warrant that will rid us of Madame de Valbelle?
FAUBLAN. I'm waiting for the man who'll take it to her.
DELCOUR. The separation will break the already aching heart of that poor countess.
FAUBLAN. What does it matter? If you had to pay attention to all those useless thoughts, you'd never finish anything. You have to see the big picture, my friend, and not get caught up in the details. They make you narrow minded, they freeze your imagination, and often become obstacles that get in your way. You'll be better off not noticing them.
DELCOUR. But should Madame Verneuil happen to see through your tricks, should she catch on to one of your hellish schemes, aren't you afraid of being ruined? The state to which you've reduced her will give her strength. There are certain circumstances when despair makes a person try anything.
FAUBLAN. My friend, haven't you heard of a certain Arabian doctor who has remedies for every illness? He is my model. Leave it to the infinite resources in my head, and you can be sure that our victims will not escape us.
DELCOUR. What about Adeline?
FAUBLAN. Consider her already your wife.
DELCOUR. (*In a very false tone.*) For that prize, you can count on me forever, in life and death.
FAUBLAN. I will make use of your offer as your services are still very useful to me. You need to persuade Madame Verneuil that, surrounded by overwhelming misfortune, she is very lucky to have a man like me to alleviate her grief; that she could be robbed of her fortune and her freedom, and that I am becoming the guardian, so to speak, of all of that. You will prevail upon her,

little by little, to yield to me without reservation. You will place grave doubts in her mind concerning Madame de Valbelle so that she'll miss her even less. You will tell her, besides, that the Prime Minister is well informed about everything, and that he is extremely merciful in not pursuing the letter of the law in so dangerous a matter. A cleverly sown suspicion will incline a person's mind however you want. It prepares it for ideas which would be hard to swallow without it. When you know how to spread suspicion around skillfully, you succeed at everything you do.
DELCOUR. Are you sure that the Count's transfer has taken place?
FAUBLAN. No. But it can't be long. Nothing I've done would prevent it, and the exchange should be taking place as we speak.
DELCOUR. Aren't you a little ahead of yourself in telling everyone he's dead?
FAUBLAN. Won't it happen sooner or later? I've got friends in the right places.
DELCOUR. And who says that Madame Verneuil won't succeed in doing something about it?
FAUBLAN. My money, my skill, and my resources. Remember, Delcour, she'll never beat me at my own game. Where will she get money now that I'm in charge of her estate? How will she out-maneuver my skill, after the extraordinary performance you've just seen? And who will furnish her with resources now that she's in my care? Nothing concerns me, you can be sure of that. At the moment, I'm only worried about the man I'm waiting for. I can't imagine what could be holding him up.
(A SERVANT appears.)
SERVANT. (*To FAUBLAN.*) A man from the village asks to speak to you, sir.
FAUBLAN. Good. Make sure the women don't see him, and bring him here under cover. (*The SERVANT exits.*)
FAUBLAN. Here I am, at the summit of my hopes. Our most deadly enemy is about to disappear forever.
DELCOUR. I'm afraid of the sadness that this scene will cause her daughter.
FAUBLAN. Don't you have enough strength and love to console her?

DELCOUR. Her grief will become my own. I will certainly share in it, but I will never alleviate it.

(Enter MESSENGER.)

MESSENGER. A person of importance, sir, who came down from the inn fifteen minutes ago, would appreciate a few minutes of your time.

FAUBLAN. (*Interested.*) What's this person's name?

MESSENGER. He didn't give me his name, sir. He says you'll know him.

FAUBLAN. How old is this person?

MESSENGER. He's a young man, around twenty to twenty-two years old.

FAUBLAN. What kind of mood is he in?

MESSENGER. He seems nervous . . . anxious . . .

FAUBLAN. And he came down from the inn?

MESSENGER. Yes, sir.

FAUBLAN. Is he alone?

MESSENGER. That's what I don't know. I don't live at the inn, myself, sir. I'm the grave-digger for the parish. The young man was looking for a messenger to send word to you. Hurry. He seemed very anxious to have the pleasure of your company. He told me quite clearly to request that you not keep him waiting.

FAUBLAN. In a hurry? (*To DELCOUR.*) That's our man. (*To the MESSENGER.*) Tell him he can come up. I know who he is, and I await him impatiently.

MESSENGER. I've already asked him to come to the castle but he absolutely refused.

DELCOUR. These people are making a mystery out of everything.

FAUBLAN. My dear Delcour, you should do me the favor of seeing if I'm not mistaken.

DELCOUR. (*To FAUBLAN in a low voice.*) How can you expect me to go myself and find the man who's supposed to arrest the mother of the woman I love?

FAUBLAN. Ah! You have now, and will have for the rest of your life, these childish ideas without the shadow of good sense. All right. I'll go see him myself. Somebody's got to put an end to this business. (*He exits.*)

MESSENGER. Aren't you going to carry your sword, sir?
FAUBLAN. (*Retracing his steps, somewhat concerned.*) My sword? What for? Do people carry their swords in the country? Don't go too far, Delcour. I'll be back in five minutes. It's good that you'll get to witness the scene. (*They go out.*)
DELCOUR. God grant that innocence will triumph in the end. I must run and warn my friends.

END OF THE SECOND ACT

ACT THREE

(*Night. Servants put candles on the tables.*)

DELCOUR. (*Mysteriously.*) Stay in this room. It might be dangerous for you to come out right now. Don't worry about a thing. Above all, don't say anything to the servants.
VERNEUIL. (*With distress.*) You don't know the identity of the stranger who was asking for him?
DELCOUR. No.
VALBELLE. (*Quickly.*) Nor of the nature of his business with him?
DELCOUR. No.
ADELINE. Ah, God! All of this makes me tremble!
DELCOUR. His intentions are shocking, that's certain. Nevertheless, nothing has happened as yet. It seemed to me that in every case, he was relying on hope rather than certainty. He wasn't telling the truth, he was speaking the lie that he wanted to make happen.
VERNEUIL. Ah, then, I can yield again to the hope of embracing my husband!
DELCOUR. Let us be careful not to expect too much. Let's be satisfied with protecting ourselves against anything that could happen. (*To MADAME DE VALBELLE.*) One thing is certain. In his pocket he carries a warrant for your arrest, and now I think he's with the man who's going to carry out the order.
VALBELLE. But you said that he was told to carry his sword. That would look more like a duel than anything else.
VERNEUIL. And who could be challenging him to a duel?
ADELINE. Ah! When you're a man like him, you have a lot of enemies.
DELCOUR. If that's what it is, he won't fight. He is much too base to participate in anything so honorable. Courage was never the companion of deceit. A villain is always a coward.
VALBELLE. We ought to send someone to find out what's going on.

DELCOUR. Don't do that. If these atrocities succeed, we would be playing right into his hands. We must wait quietly for what heaven has to offer us. You can't imagine what tricks he has up his sleeve. You have no idea how resourceful that wicked man can be. But no matter what he might be capable of doing, I'm going stand here and wait. If I don't have the talent to create destruction, at least I have the courage to guard against it. What's that noise?

ADELINE. (*Frightened.*) Ah! Lightning is ready to strike us down!

(*Four men, under the command of a police officer, arrest MADAME DE VALBELLE. ADELINE runs into her mother's arms. She is also arrested. MADAME VERNEUIL falls senseless into a chair. DELCOUR grabs the arm of the police officer stationed at the front of the stage. All of this happens with the greatest speed.*)

DELCOUR. (*To the POLICEMAN.*) See to your orders, sir. The sooner they're obeyed, if they truly exist, the sooner you can look forward to contempt and punishment, if your actions are only the result of wickedness.

POLICEMAN. The Chevalier de Faublan is right behind us. He's the one responsible for the warrant.

FÉLIX. (*Running in very quickly with a sword in his hand.*) Oh, mother!

VERNEUIL. My son, my dear son!

FÉLIX. (*Breaking away from his mother's arms; to the BAILIFFS.*) Get out of here, you cowards, unless you want to be treated like the villain who hired you. I see through your scheme. You have no right to prosecute. You're nothing but the scoundrel's henchmen. Get them out of here, Delcour. (*DELCOUR threatens them with sword in hand. They flee in confusion. Everyone onstage composes himself. FÉLIX returns to his mother.*)

FÉLIX. Oh, my adorable mother, your misfortunes have ended. (*Pointing to the side of the stage where the fighting occurred.*) The monster who caused them has been defeated.

VERNEUIL. (*With the keenest tenderness.*) And my husband, Félix?

FÉLIX. He's right behind me. He'll soon be in your arms.

(COUNT VERNEUIL appears.)

COUNT. (*With ecstasy.*) At last, we meet again, my beloved!
VERNEUIL. Oh, unexpected joy! Unforeseen happiness!
COUNT. Heaven has restored me to you forever!
VALBELLE. How little we expected it!
COUNT. (*Taking MADAME DE VALBELLE's hand with his left hand and his wife's hand with his right.*) Beloved wife, and you my worthy friend, I very nearly died in the snares of that dangerous man who came into our house as a friend. He alone set up the duel that drove me from France. He alone, through I don't know what kind of influence, made me look like a murderer, when I had only obeyed the laws of honor. Finally, he alone had me arrested at Lausanne where I thought I was safe. I was dying of sadness and despair under the weight of these new misfortunes when suddenly my prison unlocked its doors. This happy change was brought about by my son. To him alone do I owe my freedom, my return to France, my life, and the happiness of seeing you again. (*Embracing FÉLIX.*) Ah! My beloved son, what a wonderful way to repay me for having given you life.
FÉLIX. Nothing is dearer to my life than making yours happy. I spied on the activities of the man who sought to ruin us. He had been betrayed the day before his last act of treachery. Then the more he worked at it, the more he was swallowed up in the abyss. I hastened to rescue my father. The speed of my return was so much the more essential because of the power of Faublan's tricks. Perhaps he could have ruined you. I met him in time and forced him to fight. Honor forbade me to allow anyone else to take up my revenge. They carried him away. See how crime, sooner or later, succumbs to virtue.
ADELINE. Oh! My beloved, you risked your life!
FÉLIX. I avenged my parents. (*To ADELINE.*) I became worthy of the woman I love.
ADELINE. Oh! How you add to all that would honor you in my eyes!
COUNT. (*To MADAME DE VALBELLE.*) I want this alliance to be contracted on the spot. It should crown our happy reunion. I would not enjoy my new-found happiness if I didn't make my son happy.

VALBELLE. (*To COUNT VERNEUIL.*) These ties which bring us closer together, my dear Count, are too precious for me not to hasten the moment that would perpetuate them. (*Tenderly to DELCOUR.*) Delcour, you will always be our friend.
DELCOUR. (*To MADAME DE VALBELLE, in a low voice, and with sadness.*) It takes a love like mine to be capable of such a sacrifice.
ADELINE. (*To DELCOUR, in a low voice.*) How it exalts you in my eyes!
COUNT. (*To the COUNTESS.*) Let's go celebrate the greatest moment of my life. (*To his wife and his son.*) A person would have to be his father and your husband to really understand the value of life!
FÉLIX. Oh, father! Let's put off my wedding at least for a couple of days. Decorum demands it.
COUNT. (*To DELCOUR.*) My friend, I found sixty thousand francs addressed to you in the villain's wallet. A note said that the sum of money came from your father.
DELCOUR. It was only meant as payment for a crime, if I had wanted to commit it. My father had nothing to leave me. I want nothing to do with that money.
COUNT. Take it, Delcour. This gift can only make up for the villainy of the man who offered it to you.
DELCOUR. It would insult my integrity. I want nothing to do with it. I would rather live poor and honest than accept something from a man whose memory I can only scorn and despise.
VALBELLE. We forgive him for everything.
DELCOUR. (*Vigorously.*) What's the difference? You were only his victims. He made me his accomplice.
VALBELLE. (*Eagerly.*) Ah! my friend, I wish I had another daughter to give you. With feelings like that, you ought to make everyone who comes in contact with you very happy.
DELCOUR. Whoever only pays attention to goodness, and does nothing but good deeds, his reward is in his heart. For him, that's enough. (*To MADAME DE VALBELLE.*) Ah, Madame, I will occasionally need to be reminded of that truth.
VALBELLE. (*Her feelings aroused.*) Let us go inside. Let's prepare to celebrate this happy day. There will be, in all of this, some

things that we will never say, that we will be satisfied to feel. (*Pointing to DELCOUR.*) Madame Verneuil, we never really knew this young man. He deserves both our esteem and our most genuine affection.

COUNT. May he never share in our misfortune. We must make amends for the harshness of his own. Isolated good fortune only makes us happy. Spreading joy to those around us is the real happiness on earth.

END OF THE THIRD AND FINAL ACT

The Haunted Tower

Introduction

Originally part of *The Tricks of Love* but eliminated from the final draft known as *The Marriage of the Arts*, Sade's one-act *opéra-comique, The Haunted Tower*, is first mentioned in the *Descriptive Catalogue of 1788* where Sade notes its significance to the plot of the larger work. He writes:

> The young count who has not been able to succeed in the first four episodes, finally gets rid of his rival at the end. He makes him disappear in a haunted tower, and the wedding of the young count to his beloved occurs in the last of the scenes that follows the opera.

The only other allusion to this opera-comique lies in a letter written by Roulhac de Maupas, the director of the asylum at Charenton to the Abbé Montesquiou in September 1814. In the letter, Roulhac takes issue with Sade's practice of giving the inmates of the asylum his manuscripts to copy. Upon reading the manuscript entitled *The Haunted Tower*, the director found the work, "a terrible opera without wit, without spirit, suggesting a less than mediocre talent. Should the work be performed, it would certainly only provoke yawns and cat-calls."

Despite his poor opinion of the work, Roulhac does admit, however, that the opera does not demonstrate the perversity and degradation that people have come to expect in Sade's writing. On 6 March 1801, Sade had been arrested as the author of *Justine* and *Juliette*, two highly controversial novels and subsequently imprisoned at Sainte-Pélagie until 14 March 1803 when an incident involving the author's "bestial passion" for a young inmate forced his transfer to Bicêtre Prison, generally referred to as "the mob's Bastille." A month later, he was moved to the asylum at Charenton where he was judged to be in a constant state of "incessant licentious insanity." There Sade began producing amateur theatricals using patients as actors (though there is some evidence that professionals from Paris also went to the asylum to perform). The audience for these dramatic presentations was composed of the intelligentsia and nobility of the First Empire. In an undated letter in May 1810, Sade wrote to the lady-in-waiting of the Queen of Holland to ask about the number of tickets she would need for their next performance, and to thank her for the interest she took in their work. Though it is generally agreed that Sade presented many of his own plays at Charenton, there is no evidence that *The Haunted Tower* was ever performed there.

The clearest account of Sade's theatrical ventures is found in a report dated 2 August 1808 from its severest critic, Dr. Royer Collard. After claiming that Sade's one delirium is vice and complaining that he enjoys too much freedom in the asylum (the doctor had just received a report that Sade was living with a woman—Mme. Quesnet—whom he claimed was his daughter), Collard criticizes the asylum for building a theatre without consideration of the possible harmful effects "of such a tumultuous proceeding upon the mind." He explains:

> De Sade is the director of this theatre. He presents the plays, hands out the roles and directs them. He is also the asylum poet. For example, at the dinners of the director, he writes an allegorical piece in his honor or at least some couplets in his praise. I ask your excellency to remedy such a horrible condition. How can such things be in an insane asylum? Such crimes and immorality!

As a result of Collard's repeated complaints, the theatre was eventually removed from the asylum and concerts and balls were installed in its place. According to Dr. L. J. Ramon, a large number of outsiders including theatrical celebrities were invited to the balls:

> The hero of the ball was above all the celebrated Trénitz, choreographic luminary of the period, whom they decked out in the finest attire which it was not always easy to make him give up without some resistance or struggle. De Sade was the organizer of these festivities and shows. So it is not astonishing if among the shortcomings of the administration of Charenton prominence was given to the bond between the Director and de Sade.

Finally on 6 May 1813, as a result of renewed protests, all theatrical events were halted at Charenton. A little more than a year later, the Marquis de Sade was dead.

It is interesting to note that in November 1789, the year after the first mention of this play, a three-act English opera called *The Haunted Tower* premiered at Drury Lane in London and managed to accumulate eighty-four performances in its first two seasons. Composer Stephen Storace's first full-length English opera to a libretto by James Cobb, the English *Haunted Tower* was, according to historian Roger Fiske, "the most successful full-length opera that Drury Lane staged in the entire century."

Set in the days of William the Conqueror, Cobb's *Haunted Tower* opens on the seacoast of Kent where Lady Elinor has recently arrived from Normandy to accept the hand of Edward, son of the newly created Baron Oakland (actually an upstart, named by the king to replace the true Baron who had been banished). Lady Elinor has a secret lover, Sir Palomede, who has followed her from France in the hopes of preventing the marriage—not a difficult assignment since Edward secretly loves a village girl named Adela whom he has passed off to his father as Lady Elinor in the hopes of marrying her before the deception is revealed. Arriving at the castle, Sir Palomede is discovered to be the son of the real Baron Oakland (and thus owner of the premises). When he goes to the tower to collect his father's armor, he frightens the bogus baron's servants who have been secretly stealing wine for some time (perpetuating the myth that the tower was haunted by the ghost of the original Baron Oakland). All is revealed and the two pairs of lovers are united.

Although both Sade and Cobb employ the device of a bogus haunting to enable true love to succeed, the plot of the English work differs greatly from Sade's in its setting and dramatic usage of two pairs of lovers, disguises of identity as well as social status, and an eleventh-hour melodramatic discovery of the long-lost heir to the castle. However, in spite of significant discrepancies in the plotting, both works rely heavily on the Gothic horrors of the climax and the potential for a varied musical score. In fact, a close examination of both librettos shows a striking similarity in the lyrics and situations of several songs that seem to serve parallel functions in both shows. For example, Juliette's opening air in Sade's version, "Love, listen to my sorrow," evokes Adela's "Whither, my love!" in Cobb's libretto. Both pieces depict long-suffering heroines yearning to be reunited to their long-lost lovers in lyrics that suggest images of bondage, lovers' tokens, and an obsession with the lover's image. Lorville's lament, recalling his lover left behind, "Oh! Juliette," is echoed in Cobb's libretto with Charles's "My native land I bade adieu," in which the noble servant character philosophizes about the girl he left back home. In both airs, the characters singing imagine that the intensity of emotion has changed on the part of the women involved. In the English work, Charles accepts the situation with wry humor; in the French, Lorville responds melodramatically, with images of bondage and death.

THE HAUNTED TOWER

Opéra-comique in One Act

CHARACTERS

The Baron, *the owner of the chateau where the actions occurs*
De Grouffignac, *collector of taxes in the Canton and Gascon districts*
Lorville, *young infantry officer, Juliette's lover*
Louise, *young woman attached to Juliette*
Juliette, *the Baron's daughter, Lorville's lover*
A notary
The ghost of the tower, *a non-speaking role*

(*The action occurs in the courtyard of the mansion, decorated with trees and flowers. An old tower can be seen at the rear of the stage, left. When the curtain rises, JULIETTE is seen sitting on a mound of grass.*)

JULIETTE. (*Sings.*)
Love, Love, listen to my sorrow,
And if you are able, charming deity,
Come deliver me from my bondage,
And give me back my lover.
Alas! Since he cannot hear me,
Go, fly, Love, carry to him
The sad tones of my woe.
Tell him that everything I see
Reminds me of his tenderness,
And causes him to live within my heart.
If I see a flower,
His lovely face is in the bloom;
If my hand sketches a picture,
It's either of his features or my chains.
Ah! Good heavens! What slavery!

What fate! What torment is mine!
Love, Love, listen to my sorrow,
And if you are able, charming deity,
Come deliver me from my bondage,
And give me back my lover.

(*Louise enters, inconspicuously.*)

JULIETTE. Ah! There you are, Louise.

LOUISE. Yes, Miss. I was trying to get your attention, but I discovered that I was hardly able to do it.

JULIETTE. Ah! Lorville's absence is the least of my worries. To make matters worse, besides the bitter grief of being separated from all I love in the world, I have to endure the hideous destiny of becoming the wife of the first rustic who disenchants that tower. (*She looks toward the tower.*)

LOUISE. It's true that the Baron, your father, must be terribly provoked or frightened by the noise in his dungeon to sacrifice his only daughter in the hope of getting rid of it. What's more, if you ask me, this business will only exchange one evil for another. And between one devil and the next, I would prefer the invisible kind that only occasionally makes noise, to the she-sprite who'd make a racket every day in the house after she's been married against her will.

JULIETTE. You think I'm evil then?

LOUISE. No, but I know that you don't like what gets in your way, and a lifetime with a husband who doesn't please you is an awful obstacle to have before you. You're in a pretty pickle! Take me, for example, as docile as a sheep. But I tell you, should a similar situation arise, I'd become a hundred times more vicious than the devil in your cellar. (*Sings.*)

Ah! If ever against my will,
A husband seeks to enchain me,
I would make it my supreme desire,
My happiness, to pester him.
During the day, at the house, a great racket,
Threats, moods, whacks and slaps in the face.
At night, perhaps the greater effect,
No more noise, no touching, nothing.
Yes, you believe it, in this day and age,

Women without exception,
Must imitate men in every way
To be their mistresses.
Ah! If ever against my will,
A husband seeks to enchain me,
I would make it my supreme desire,
My happiness, to pester him.
(*Spoken.*) Anyway, has it been decided that you'll only marry the man who succeeds in your father's enterprise?

JULIETTE. Ah! The only thing that consoles me is that there have already been more than thirty who've tried and failed. This will discourage the others. I would rather not marry at all than not have the man I love.

LOUISE. But, tell me, please, Miss, where does the noise come from? I've heard so many stories about it that I don't know what to believe. I've never been bold enough to ask you directly.

JULIETTE. You know that the Baron, my father was in the service. One day, one of his friends made a remark about some woman the Baron was courting at the time. It was only a joke, but little by little the conversation heated up and they started fighting. My father had the misfortune of killing his friend. Dying, the man looked at my father to assure him of his forgiveness, and to ask him to embrace him one last time. This frightening image never leaves my father's head. Every time he turns around, he imagines seeing his friend. At every hour of the day, he thinks he hears him. Peace is declared, he leaves the service and retires here to his country estate. No sooner does he get here when he hears groaning in the tower. He thinks it's his friend. He tries to enter but he cannot go in. His remorse weakens his courage, and he gives up the venture, but he still wants to know the cause of the noise. To satisfy the ghost of his friend, if it is indeed his shade that has come to pester him, he has promised his daughter to whoever would succeed in showing him the cause of the racket, or in rescuing him from the ghost. I know that his motives are pure, but does that make me less the victim in this disastrous situation?

LOUISE. But, Miss, you have to send word to Mr. Lorville about what's going on. The enterprise is worthy of that young military man. Why haven't you already thought to offer this adventure to him since the crown of love awaits the heart of the victor?

JULIETTE. Ah! Can you believe that I haven't done that? My letter went out a long time ago. No response. Ah! Lorville, Lorville, you've abandoned me. (*She sings.*)

The moments of our rapture
Have been forgotten in your heart.
In the arms of another mistress
You imagine you'll find happiness.
Those tender bonds of childhood,
Your hand is pleased to sever.
Must you, in your infidelity
Abandon them today?

In vain do you destroy the bonds.
See the course of those streams:
Their waves fleeing the shore
Leave their traces in the tide.
In such a way, that flame burns inside me,
And fills me with love.
You can extinguish it in my soul
But you cannot erase it.

You are suspicious of my tenderness:
Ah! If I die in this place,
Come and ask if I left behind
Some proof of my passion.
Come ask the mountains,
Their echoes will reaffirm it.
Come run through the countryside,
Its trees will show you.

(*Spoken.*) Tell me, Louise, do you really believe that Lorville doesn't think about me anymore?

LOUISE. Ah! Miss, have a better opinion of yourself. (*Sings.*)

It's in the stars that forever
A young lover will love you.
Cupid was told each lover desired

To create his beloved himself.

As soon as he created your beauty,
Jealous of his model,
The rascal shattered all the features
That would have made you beautiful.

For you, the fire of feeling
Will never consume itself.
Gazing at your eyes for a moment,
In him, will rekindle desire.
(*Spoken.*) Ah! Trust that Lorville will reappear the moment you least expect him, attempt the adventure and emerge triumphant. What's that noise I hear?
(*A sound from the tower is heard, at first rather softly. The women are disturbed. They sing the following duet.*)
JULIETTE. Ah, what a frightening racket!
LOUISE. Do you hear that racket!
JULIETTE. Oh! Yes, I hear that racket!
TOGETHER. And I feel that my courage
Is about to leave me.
LOUISE. I think it sounds like chains.
JULIETTE. Oh! It's much worse than chains!
It's not the time to joke.
Ah, what a frightening racket!
LOUISE. (*Spoken.*) Oh! Heavens! In the six months we've been here, I haven't heard such an awful noise.
JULIETTE. That's because this is the month when my father killed his friend.
LOUISE. That must be it then!
JULIETTE. (*Sings.*)
He's the one ferociously producing it,
He's the one who's causing this disturbance.
It's typical of ghosts
In the time of their misfortunes.
Ah! I'm afraid he's growing angry.
LOUISE. (*Sings.*)
In faith, if I were the Baron,

I'd leave the house
To the devil that inhabits it.
I'd leave the house
To the devil that inhabits it.

JULIETTE. Often they get angry
At the time of their anniversary.
If no one can appease them
They stamp with great thumps.

BOTH. (*Pressed close together.*)
Ah! I'm afraid he's growing angry.
In faith, if I were the Baron,
I'd leave the house
To the devil that inhabits it.
I'd leave the house
To the devil that inhabits it. (*The noise stops.*)

LOUISE. Listen. The noise has stopped. And who is the hero, Miss, who's going into combat today?

JULIETTE. You wouldn't know him. Just another one of my faithful admirers.

LOUISE. Who then? Mr. Grouffignac, the district tax collector?

JULIETTE. You guessed it!

LOUISE. That braggart transplanted from the banks of the Garonne . . . that boring collector with a mind filled with numbers, who only talks about the beauty of arithmetic and the neatness of his calculations?

JULIETTE. He's the one.

LOUISE. Well! I would really like that one to succeed; he's always inspired a certain interest in me.

JULIETTE. Don't make fun of my misfortunes.

LOUISE. Eh! But I'm not laughing. Don't you know that you'd live happily-ever-after with that man? Every week he'd check the household account; he'd teach you the mysteries of new math, and the "company-way." Ah! Please. Become Mrs. Tax Collector!

JULIETTE. If you continue to tease me, I'm going to get really angry.

LOUISE. Ah! Stop getting upset, Miss. How can you dread this misfortune for a moment? Won't he have to go inside the tower?

JULIETTE. Yes.

LOUISE. And you think that the devil will give back a tax collector once he's got him? But here comes the Baron, your father. Come on. Come on. Set your mind at rest. As for me, I've a good feeling about all of this.

(The BARON enters.)

THE BARON. Well! My daughter . . . well, well! My beloved child, did someone tell you he arrived?

JULIETTE. (*Somewhat troubled.*) Who, father?

BARON. Lorville, that fool, that rash creature.

JULIETTE. (*Very troubled.*) He's here, father?

BARON. (*Noticing his daughter's concern.*) Very well! Look, Louise, look, when you say that she's not interested in him . . .

LOUISE. But that's not interest, sir, that's surprise; and there's a great difference between a daughter who's astonished and one who's interested. I assure you that your daughter is not at all concerned with Mr. Lorville. Alright! Alright! I know her heart by heart, and if she'd let me tell you a secret . . .

BARON. Tell me. Tell it to me. I tell you she'll have nothing to get angry about.

JULIETTE. Louise.

LOUISE. Miss, you speak in vain, you shouldn't keep a secret from a father, and above all from a father who's so concerned about the happiness of his daughter like the Baron here. Hold on, sir. Do you want me to tell you everything?

BARON. Eh! Why hide anything from me? Really, that awful subject of Lorville concerns me. I hold the military in the highest regard, but since he's come here, I swear that I feel a kind of aversion to giving my daughter to a man in a uniform. With regard to all others . . .

LOUISE. Very well! Sir, set your mind at rest. Miss Juliette is too smart, she understands your point of view too well to make that kind of choice. She is undoubtedly ready, since you want her to be, to sacrifice herself to the victor of the tower. But I won't hide it from you, sir, that she would like the laurels to rest on the forehead of the tax collector.

BARON. (*Enraptured.*) Grouffignac! My best friend! Is it really true, my daughter? Let me give you a great big hug!

JULIETTE. Really, father, it's nothing. But, Louise, don't you think you're exaggerating in saying such things?
LOUISE. And why, Miss, since they exist?
JULIETTE. (*Blushing and lowering her head.*) It's . . . it's that really . . .
LOUISE. (*Interrupting her; to the BARON.*) Look, look, sir, how modesty fights feeling. Ah! How respectably a well-brought-up young lady behaves at a time like this!
BARON. Don't blush, my child. Grouffignac has everything necessary to captivate the heart of a sensible girl.
LOUISE. Undoubtedly. He's an orderly man.
BARON. Prudent, honest.
LOUISE. A man of importance. A man absolutely withdrawn from the oddities of youth.
BARON. Of those aberrations which are so dangerous . . .
LOUISE. (*Quickly.*) For a young wife . . .
BARON. That's worth more than all the little soldiers . . .
LOUISE. Like that Lorville.
BARON. A rake!
LOUISE. A gambler!
BARON. A little fop!
LOUISE. Because he has a good body . . .
BARON. All women, young or old, like a good body . . .
LOUISE. Oh! It's all the same to them. The young ones for pleasure, the others for their money.
BARON. A dissipated, profligate, fast, loose, idle, unsteady, schoolboy, if there ever was one!
LOUISE. Who'd ruin his wife in two weeks' time.
JULIETTE. (*Softly to LOUISE, peevishly.*) Lighten up, Miss Louise. Why, why, you think you're funny, don't you!!
BARON. Ah! Were I to say everything . . .
LOUISE. (*Who doesn't appear to have heard what JULIETTE has just said to her.*) Speak. Speak, sir. I tell you it's all right with Miss Juliette.
BARON. This summer, at Strasbourg, playing black-jack, he lost twenty-five thousand francs in an evening.
LOUISE. Twenty-five thousand francs!

BARON. And to make amends for his foolish behavior, he kidnapped the daughter of the burgermeister and went to Prussia with her.
LOUISE. The daughter of the burgermeister!
BARON. The burgermeister!
JULIETTE. (*Very concerned.*) He kidnapped a girl, father? (*To herself.*) Ah! The monster! That's why he hasn't written me. (*Aloud.*) Eh! What's he doing here?
BARON. His father, you know, is a friend of mine and he's asked me to keep on an eye on his son while he's waiting for his affairs to be settled. The burgermeister wanted to raise a fuss. There are a lot of men who get upset when their daughters are abducted! And the young man wrote to me eagerly, having heard about what's going on here, and the prize I'm awarding to the winner. He asked me for permission to take advantage of the situation, to present himself in turn. But I hope he'll arrive too late. Grouffignac is due to go into combat tonight. I'm convinced that after him there'll be no more danger, and we'll all live happily-ever-after.
LOUISE. But, sir, if by chance your hopes are shattered, if the tax-collector is frightened, or beaten . . .
BARON. That's not possible.
LOUISE. I understand, but just supposing . . . frightened, or beaten, I say, there'd be a need to go into combat after him. And who do you suppose that'll be, if you please?
BARON. I couldn't oppose Lorville's attempt. Those are the rules. But should he succeed, I couldn't allow it. My daughter could refuse him, and he would have no more claim upon her.
LOUISE. So much the better. I'm glad you explained that. I wanted to put Miss Juliette at ease.
JULIETTE. (*Ready to faint.*) I hope that he will not come here. Excuse me, father. I don't feel well. Please allow me to withdraw for a moment.
BARON. (*Alarmed, first to LOUISE, then to his daughter whom he holds in his arms.*) She's growing pale. She's staggering! What's the matter with her? Is it the evil spirit?

LOUISE. Yes, sir. It just made itself heard in a peculiar way, and it said things that went straight to the heart. That is certainly what's wrong with Miss Juliette.

BARON. Go, go, Juliette. Don't mind me, my child. I will come up and join you in a little while with our beloved Grouffignac.

JULIETTE. Oh! No, father, don't trouble yourself. At the moment I need rest and solitude. (*JULIETTE exits. LOUISE tries to follow her. The BARON stops her and draws her to center.*)

BARON. Why are you making me nervous, Louise? Was the ghost speaking?

LOUISE. Not precisely, sir. Not in real words, but in the noise of chains, and irons, you might say he was dragging all of hell behind him.

BARON. Eh! That's what it does usually. You just said that it talked and that bothered me.

LOUISE. Fear, as well you know, exaggerates things.

BARON. Enough of this. I was very pleased with you just now. Well! What do you think of what I said about Lorville?

LOUISE. What! Sir, would that have been a little white lie on your part?

BARON. Precisely. I can tell you everything. I know you're a woman who's wise and discreet. You have to continue to help me. I need you to back up the story about the twenty-five-thousand-francs loss and above all the one about the burgermeister's daughter.

LOUISE. Oh! Sir, rest assured.

BARON. Listen, my child, you'll excuse this little lie. It was necessary. Never would this Lorville make Juliette happy. He is brave, straightforward, honest, I know it, but light, frivolous, and even something of a ladies' man. I can connect him with three or four women!

LOUISE. Ah! Sir, all that does not displease us as much as you think. You can't imagine that a woman could be so impractical, sometimes, as to prefer such fools to those substantial and stiff men, who might easily not have a single vice, but on the other hand, not have a single virtue. (*Sings.*)

The one very straight, very sheepish, and very ugly
Tells us nothing except for the package.

If he is the rough draft of merit
He is the picture of boredom.
And by an unconceivable art
You always see that Cato,[12]
Never knowing how to be likeable,
Makes us renounce good sense.
The other is the image of the Zephyr,[13]
The butterfly is less nimble.
It's not love at all that inspires him,
It's the sweet pleasure of variety.
He understands the ways of pleasing;
He knows quite well how to treat us.
So in spite of all you can do,
You have to go off with him.
(*Spoken.*) In short you see, sir, how the tax collector, Mister Grouffignac, will make your daughter perfectly happy?

BARON. I am absolutely convinced of it.

LOUISE. Do you want me to tell you why? It's because you like him, and there's a father's injustice: you always believe that your children ought to have either your eyes or your tastes.

BARON. But didn't you tell me just now that my daughter was in love with him?

LOUISE. Yes, sir, that's what I said.

BARON. Very well!

LOUISE. Very well, sir, that union will be very happy, and don't say I didn't warn you. Besides, there's nothing so well-matched than a sixteen-year-old girl and a sixty-year-old man. People call that a marriage of convenience.

BARON. Quiet. Quiet. I think I hear him. Come on! Put on a happy face.

LOUISE. Me, sir? That will not be difficult. I love that man with all my heart. I'm telling you that in case you decide that I'll have to marry him!

(*Mr. Grouffignac appears, out of breath.*)

GROUFFIGNAC. (*Speaking in a Gascon dialect.*) Forgive me, father-in-law (since I hope that you allow me to call you that

---

[12] Marcus Porcius Cato Uticensis (95-46 B.C.), remembered for his moral integrity, tenacity, and absolute distaste for political corruption.

[13] The Greek god of the west wind.

sweet name). I had promised to come to see you: it was impossible for me—an audit of accounts—a diabolical affair! These guys who say they've paid their taxes and always end up owing. Often I'd rather pay out of my own pocket than to see myself having to go to such extremes. Every time you have a heart . . .

LOUISE. And a sensitive heart, isn't that right, sir!

GROUFFIGNAC. Sensitive? Yes, sensitive. That's the word! Father-in-law, I've always liked that there girl; she has a face that's altogether out of this world! Well, the dear girl, how is she?

BARON. She just became indisposed. It's nothing. Female problems. You know, my friend, that those machinations are always perfectly planned. There's always something to mend.

LOUISE. Above all before the wedding.

GROUFFIGNAC. (*To The BARON, motioning to the tower.*) It comes from that, doesn't it? From that. Oh, we're going to finish that affair tonight.

LOUISE. Sweetly, sir, sweetly. Don't imagine going close to it like you're collecting the poll tax. It's a little hard to digest, I'm warning you. And if you had heard the racket it was making a few minutes ago . . .

GROUFFIGNAC. (*Trying to appear indifferent.*) Well, all right! But I've taken all that into account. All the events of this world can be explained by arithmetic. By carefully multiplying the divider by the quotient you always get to the bottom of everything. (*Here a noise is heard in the tower. GROUFFIGNAC trembles and becomes frightened. He stutters his next line.*) Yes, you always get to the bottom of everything. Isn't that what I intend to do?

BARON. (*Equally affected, but in a less comical way.*) Yes, truly, that's it.

LOUISE. (*To GROUFFIGNAC.*) Sir, do you want me to get you pen and ink?

GROUFFIGNAC. (*Still trembling.*) What for?

LOUISE. To multiply the divider by the quotient.

BARON. (*Leaving.*) My friend, you'll have to excuse me. Every time I hear this noise I get such cruel memories. I will, nevertheless, witness your victory since I am sure that heaven reserved it for you alone. I'm going to prepare your armor. I'll send my daughter to you.

(*The noise ceases and GROUFFIGNAC regains his composure.*)
GROUFFIGNAC. At your convenience, Baron. I hope that I'm the one to deliver you from all this distress; and I am perfectly sure than there's nothing supernatural about it. They're just grand effects produced by simple causes.
BARON. Goodbye for now. (*He exits.*)
GROUFFIGNAC. He's a very respectable man, the Baron.
LOUISE. And very attached to you, sir.
GROUFFIGNAC. Yes. I actually think he likes me a little.
LOUISE. A little? Amazing. He thinks the world of you. If you only knew the person he's rejecting to give you his daughter.
GROUFFIGNAC. (*Astonished.*) He's rejecting someone?
LOUISE. (*Mysteriously.*) Someone of importance, sir. At least don't go making me betray myself. I'm in someone's confidence and was strongly advised not to tell you anything. But I can't keep a secret from you, I'm so attracted to you!
GROUFFIGNAC. Ah! Count on my discretion and gratitude. (*He gives her a book.*) I already want to make you feel the effects of that last sentiment.
LOUISE. What sort of present are you giving me here?
GROUFFIGNAC. It's a new, complete edition of Barème's *Books of Accounting* for which I have the greatest admiration.
LOUISE. (*Refusing it.*) Keep it. Keep your Barème. Sir, these masterpieces do not suit everyone's inclinations. Mine are too coarse to appreciate the sublime depth of this work. My sentiments will be the same, and you can rest assured that I will tell you all you want to know. Yes, sir, you have a rival.
GROUFFIGNAC. And what is he?
LOUISE. A young officer: handsome, built, fashionable, and who very certainly will be preferred to you, if you do not succeed in your adventure.
GROUFFIGNAC. The adventure of that tower?
LOUISE. Yes, sir.
GROUFFIGNAC. Ah! Shit! That messes up my calculations.
LOUISE. Why is that?
GROUFFIGNAC. It's because . . .
LOUISE. Yes?
GROUFFIGNAC. I thought . . .

LOUISE. Out with it!
GROUFFIGNAC. Well! I thought that the Baron, happy with my good will, would perhaps let me out of the test. That's the direction I was leading him in.
LOUISE. Ah! Am I to understand that you're not terribly interested in the adventure?
GROUFFIGNAC. That's not it entirely. But after all . . .
LOUISE. But after all you'd like it just as much if someone other than you came forward?
GROUFFIGNAC. It's just that, you see, my child, we collector people rarely allow ourselves to get involved with foolish passions that lead a man into inevitable danger. The great and profound spirit that governs our science is more impressed than others with the intrinsic value of life. It doesn't like to squander it needlessly. And then besides: (*Sings.*)
Victory is uncertain,
Courage is fickle.
Yet, if it were on flat ground,
Or at the edge of a shore;
In vain have I read through Barème.
Never will it tell me
To go and expose myself
To this adventure.
(*Spoken.*) And then besides, they wouldn't be able to replace me.
LOUISE. Of course, sir, that's the coward's way out. Take heed at least. Your rival will be there. He will accomplish what you don't dare to do. And then it's goodbye to Miss Juliette. You'll drive that poor girl to despair because she loves you so deeply.
GROUFFIGNAC. Really?
LOUISE. On my honor.
GROUFFIGNAC. Tell me again. I get the feeling that it will revive my courage. She loves me a lot, then?
LOUISE. Inconceivably.
GROUFFIGNAC. Ah! You fill me with joy!
LOUISE. (*Sings.*)
To love you, to cherish you, and to please you,
This lovely child is resolved.
Just fly recklessly into combat,

And Juliette will do all
To love you, to cherish you, and to please you.
GROUFFIGNAC. (*Sings.*)
To cherish her, to adore her, and to please her,
For my part I promise as much.
LOUISE. At sixty years old, alas! That's a lot to accomplish
When you promise that child
To serve her, adore her, and to please her.

GROUFFIGNAC. (*Snickering, and speaking.*) Ah! Ah! Ah! Yes. Yes, but I'll continue to say, and I'll prove it through mathematical principles, that it would be infinitely better if this adventure ended without me.

LOUISE. And I, sir, who do not understand mathematical principles, can demonstrate, without arithmetic, that if you throw away an opportunity, you are lost, because at that very moment, there's someone else ready to replace you. This somebody else is a child of Mars, accustomed from his youth, to face danger. Cupid will furnish him with his weapons. He will succeed, and you will be inconsolable. Think long and hard about this. Here comes my mistress. Come on. Be steady, and above all, don't shilly-shally.

(JULIETTE enters.)

LOUISE. (*Softly to JULIETTE.*) Remember it's essential that you appear to love him.

JULIETTE. My father told me you were here, sir. I'm eager to see you. Why didn't you come right in?

GROUFFIGNAC. Darling Juliette! I was just shooting the breeze at the moment with your darling Louise. We were talking about you. The only consolation of a lover in his beloved's absence is to talk about the tender object of his affection.

JULIETTE. Oh, good sir, you're always trying to make me believe that you take a special interest in me. Can I hope that it is so?

GROUFFIGNAC. (*Passionately.*) If anything in the world can be proved to you who are lovelier than a goddess, it's certainly that. In the ten rules of mathematics, we don't have a proof more solidly established. Look here, Miss, it is so true that you're always in my thoughts, that again this morning, thinking I was signing a receipt, I unconsciously put my name on a love letter!

LOUISE. (*To her mistress.*) Well, what can I say! But they're proofs nonetheless. And it seems to me that somebody ought to give herself to him.
JULIETTE. It's certainly common to be unconscious of what you desire.
LOUISE. (*Softly, to GROUFFIGNAC.*) Listen to her.
GROUFFIGNAC. (*Softly, to LOUISE.*) I'm at the height of joy.
LOUISE. (*Softly, to GROUFFIGNAC.*) Hold on to that thought. (*Softly, to JULIETTE.*) Keep talking to him in the same way.
JULIETTE. Do you want me to think, sir, that attractions as meager as these can captivate a man who, thousands of times, has seen all of the beauties in the province at his feet?
GROUFFIGNAC. (*In a normal voice.*) It's true that my life has been a modest success.
LOUISE. Somebody's young.
GROUFFIGNAC. Somebody wants to please.
JULIETTE. Somebody's done well for himself.
GROUFFIGNAC. Undoubtedly, but never has a beauty like yours been caught in my net, and those charms that you seem to be unaware of—those captivating delights which you have stolen from the altar of Venus—I find them incomparable, and I'll prove it to you whenever you like. Permit me to sing a short impromptu song on this subject that came to me this morning. You inspired it, Apollo dictated it, and I yielded to the ecstasy. The words and music are my own.
(Sings a Grand Air "Buffa.")[14]
My love is not a problem.
Your sweet attractions have resolved it.
To love you is a system of behavior
Always sustained by my heart.
You have borrowed from the Graces
The addition of so many beautiful traits,
That they have divided
All their beauty into a single you.
(*Spoken.*) Hey! They have divided . . . charming, isn't it?
(*He sings.*) My love is not a problem.
Your sweet attractions have resolved it.
To love you is a system of behavior

[14] A comic, patter aria.

Always sustained by my heart.
JULIETTE. Oh! It's truly delicious. I want you to give it to me.
GROUFFIGNAC. I'll teach it to you on my viola d'amore.
JULIETTE. By the way, aren't you the one who's supposed to fight today? (*She takes a green ribbon from her hair and gives it to him.*) Here, I want your armor to carry this ribbon. It's the color of hope. The same sentiment will burn in our hearts.
GROUFFIGNAC. (*Enthusiastically.*) Heavens, what a present!
LOUISE. Well, sir, where might you be going with that?
GROUFFIGNAC. A new Orpheus, I am ready to descend to hell except, perhaps, that the famous son of Clio only went to looking for his wife and I'll be hurling myself down there to earn one. *(He sings an "Air de bravoure.")*[15]

With such a present from the object of my adoration,
Success is no longer undecided.
Can a person waver still,
When love awards the prize?
Indeed, no danger will shake me
From earning such a reward.
Ah! When beauty crowns us
How pleasing is the victory.
With such a present from the object of my adoration,
Success is no longer undecided.
Can a person waver still,
When love awards the prize?

(*When he begins to sing the first verses again, a noise is heard in the tower. His voice begins to tremble. He sings out of tune and his voice cracks while trembling close to the ladies.*)
LOUISE. What's wrong, Mister Tax Collector? You're acting like you've caught a cold.
GROUFFIGNAC. It's nothing. It's nothing. It's just a coughing fit that comes over me every once in awhile. Excuse me, Miss. (*He starts to exit.*)
JULIETTE. What? Are you leaving me in this situation?
LOUISE. That's not very nice, sir. Don't you see that Miss Juliette is ready to faint?

---

[15] A bravura aria is one with a great many technical difficulties and ornamentation to display the singer's abilities.

GROUFFIGNAC. No, no, not at all. Miss Juliette has a sturdy constitution that's really an honor to her sex. (*Running away.*) Please don't worry about me. (*Gradually the noise stops.*)
LOUISE. Why, Miss, you know you've got a real hero there for a lover. I wouldn't know how to congratulate you for such a conquest.
JULIETTE. What does it all mean? Everything you had me say, making believe that I loved that character, and telling my father all those horrible things about Lorville . . .
LOUISE. Ah! You don't know much about politics. When a father opposes our way of thinking, don't you know that *he's* the one who has to change. There he is now absolutely convinced that Lorville doesn't matter to you at all. And as soon as that young man gets here, and everything happens somewhat contrary to your father's expectations, it seems to me that it was essential to act as I did. On the other hand, Grouffignac would never have decided to go into the tower without your reviving his courage with a few expressions of tenderness. So there, my behavior is explained. Am I so terribly wrong now?
JULIETTE. No, but what good does it all do when Lorville's been unfaithful? And when I have the most convincing proof?
LOUISE. You have the most convincing proof?
JULIETTE. Didn't you hear what my father said?
LOUISE. Of course. (*Aside.*) Let's leave her in the dark. The less she knows the better. Besides all will be made clear to her eventually. (*She turns around to determine the cause of the noise she hears coming out of the castle grating.*) Oh! Heaven help us. Here he is, sooner than I thought. It's him, Miss, it's him.
JULIETTE. Who is it, who?
LOUISE. Him, I tell you, he's getting down from his horse. He's in uniform.
JULIETTE. One more time. Who is it?
LOUISE. Eh! Lorville! Didn't your heart tell you? Ah! Now, at least don't faint.
(*Lorville enters in uniform.*)
LORVILLE. We meet again, oh! My dear Juliette. After such a long absence, may I be allowed at last to fall at your feet?

JULIETTE. (*Coldly.*) Undoubtedly I ought to be grateful to you for your eagerness.
LORVILLE. Oh! Heavens, is this the welcome I should have expected from you? What did I do to deserve this?
JULIETTE. (*Coldly, throughout the scene.*) You've just now arrived in Paris, sir?
LORVILLE. (*Still surprised and uneasy.*) Yes, Miss. Certain affairs having delayed me longer than I had anticipated—longer than I wanted—I've . . .
JULIETTE. Oh! I'm not asking for details, sir. Sometimes they require pretense and certain mental reservations.
LORVILLE. (*Quickly.*) Mental reservations toward you, Juliette? Ah! Read inside my soul, it's open to you. And let my mouth interpret the fire that burns in there for you alone.
JULIETTE. Ah! I believe you in advance without explanations.
LOUISE. (*To LORVILLE.*) Certainly, that's to put you at your ease. Now tell us what you want to say.
LORVILLE. Ah! Louise, my dear Louise, please explain to me this unusual behavior.
LOUISE. Then please tell me where you see the slightest appearance of unusual behavior on our part.
JULIETTE. Your complaints would almost make me believe, sir, that I have neglected certain rules of propriety.
LORVILLE. Ah! Juliette, rules of propriety? Was that what you were talking about before?
JULIETTE. (*Still cold.*) But it seems to me that I've not missed a single one of them where you're concerned.
LORVILLE. (*Quickly.*) You're driving me crazy. I don't know what I'm doing or saying anymore. Here's your letter. Here it is. (*He takes it out from his breast pocket.*) It never left my heart. I wanted to leave the day after I received it, but my father stopped me. Despite my protests, he kept me from leaving for three weeks. Every day I hoped to escape and carry my answer to you in person. That's why I haven't written. Nevertheless, I gave an account of my goings on to your father. Punish me, Juliette. Punish me. But don't destroy me. I've already confessed all of my sins to you. I haven't any more and I won't have any more.

LOUISE. How eloquent lovers are! I've always admired such glibness!

JULIETTE. Where were you stationed this summer, sir?

LORVILLE. You know very well it was Strasbourg, Miss.

JULIETTE. They say it's a beautiful city.

LORVILLE. Oh! I found it sad and horrible. Anywhere you're out of my sight will hardly seem charming to me.

JULIETTE. I was assured, however, that the people there were delightful.

LOUISE. (*Mischievously.*) Yes, someone told us about a burgermeister's daughter whose eyes captivated everybody's hearts.

LORVILLE. A burgermeister's daughter? I assure you that's a mystery to me. In Strasbourg at the moment, there's only one old burgermeister who's widowed and childless. You'll have to be a little clearer about this.

JULIETTE. (*Running in front of GROUFFIGNAC who is entering.*) Ah! Here's our dear Mr. Grouffignac. Excuse me, Mr. Lorville, but Mr. Grouffignac is a man to whom I owe a great deal, and whom I have reason to treat well.

LORVILLE. A man you have reason to treat well, Miss? (*To LOUISE, while JULIETTE goes to the tax collector.*) Oh! Louise! Oh! My dear friend, please explain all of this to me.

LOUISE. Why, it's all self-explanatory.

GROUFFIGNAC. (*To JULIETTE.*) Here I am, here I am, oh, rose plucked from the heart of Flora. Forgive me if I'm a little late. I had to settle an account with some taxpayers in arrears. The haste to come and multiply the active fires of my soul by the rays from your beautiful eyes made me, as you might expect, disregard all that they owed, and I gave them more than twenty-five pistoles out of my own pocket. But is there a sacrifice in the world that can equal the possession of so many delights? And those adorable eyes, that alone govern my soul—with any kind of luck, can they be governed as well?

JULIETTE. You're always so nice.

GROUFFIGNAC. And always so beloved, I hope.

LORVILLE. (*Softly, to LOUISE.*) Who is that character?

LOUISE. (*Softly, to LORVILLE.*) Shh. Shh. He's our fiancé.

LORVILLE. (*To LOUISE.*) Your fiancé. So he likes to throw money out the window.
GROUFFIGNAC. (*Softly, to JULIETTE.*) Who's that young man?
JULIETTE. (*Softly, to GROUFFIGNAC.*) The son of a friend of my father's. Don't let him bother you. (*At this point, LORVILLE approaches JULIETTE and LOUISE closes in on GROUFFIGNAC. They act naturally and are guided by the desire of getting certain information about the people they are approaching. In this way, the two women occupy each one of the corners of the stage. This position does not change until noise is heard coming from the tower.*)
LORVILLE. (*Softly, to JULIETTE.*) I am not surprised by anything. Miss Louise has told me everything.
GROUFFIGNAC. (*Softly, to LOUISE.*) Then he's my rival?
LOUISE. (*To GROUFFIGNAC.*) Yes, so take hold of yourself and try not to tremble if we hear the noise coming from the tower.
JULIETTE. (*To GROUFFIGNAC, aloud.*) I expected to see you fully armed. It won't be long now before my father comes to open the lists of combat for you.
GROUFFIGNAC. Yes, Miss, and I await with the greatest impatience. The Baron is going to let me know a few minutes in advance so that I can put on the armor he's picked out for me and decorate it, as you might expect, with the precious ribbon you gave me. (*He shows his hat with the ribbon tied in a bow around the crown.*)
LORVILLE. Miss, you're the one who distributes the spoils of combat. That makes it easy to understand why a certain person is acting so ecstatically around here. But following the rules of chivalry, it seems to me that he ought to deserve the victory, before wearing the symbol of it. Ordinarily such favors are given only after the competition.
GROUFFIGNAC. (*To LORVILLE.*) It pleased the beautiful hands of my incomparable mistress to decorate her worthy knight beforehand. Is there something in that that disturbs you, sir?

LORVILLE. Oh, no! Sir, nothing disturbs me about you. I'm only amazed by it all. (*Ironically.*) That is to say that you're the one who's fighting today.
GROUFFIGNAC. Who'll win, sir, who'll win.
LORVILLE. Oh! I understand entirely that it's the same thing. Fighting and winning can only be synonymous when it comes to you, sir. It's just like Caesar. (*To JULIETTE.*) And when my turn comes, Miss, will I also receive a token from these lovely hands?
JULIETTE. My father isn't counting on any new exploits after Mr. Grouffignac.
LOUISE. After the ghost is destroyed once and for all, what do we need with more attempts?
GROUFFIGNAC. See how it's proven algebraically!
LORVILLE. (*To GROUFFIGNAC.*) I am not as entirely convinced as you are, sir. (*Softly, to JULIETTE.*) And you want to become the wife of that maggot?
JULIETTE. (*Softly, to LORVILLE.*) As certain as you wanted to be the husband of the burgermeister's daughter.
LORVILLE. (*Softly, to JULIETTE.*) Me! Good God! What a hoax! Ah! May one be as true as the other. That's all I ask of heaven! (*A noise is heard from the tower. JULIETTE and LOUISE tremble. GROUFFIGNAC huddles close to the women. LORVILLE walks fiercely to the foot of the tower and looks up at it.*)
LORVILLE. Ah! Ah! There's the devil that's making so much noise. (*To GROUFFIGNAC.*) Well! Sir, that must be electrifying to you, and your impatience isn't as great as it appears. Good Lord! Do you want to exchange places with me?
GROUFFIGNAC. Without the benefits.
JULIETTE. Don't get so excited, gentlemen. Here comes my father who is going to explain everything. (*The noise stops. The BARON enters.*)
BARON. Ah! Mr. Lorville, Congratulations on your arrival. You know what this is all about, and since I find you here with Mr. Grouffignac, can I assume that you have been properly introduced? When he's returned victorious from combat, my friend is doing me the honor of marrying my daughter. (*To LORVILLE.*) We hope, sir, you'll stay for the wedding.

LOUISE. (*Quickly.*) Oh! Mr. Lorville could ask for nothing better, sir. He loves parties and dancing. (*LORVILLE moves impatiently.*)
BARON. Come on, son-in-law, the armor is ready. Go put it on. (*Looking at his watch.*) You've only got twenty minutes, and you know the reasons I have for being exactly on time. (*He starts to leave.*)
LORVILLE. (*Stopping the BARON.*) Please, sir, a word. I don't infer even the slightest distinction between the combat of this hero and his victory. Nevertheless, as there is now only one man on earth, who can hope to chain victory up to his chariot, it is possible that Mr. Grouffignac might experience the sort of cowardice that threatened nearly all of the other candidates. Could I hope that, in such a case, you would permit me to take the place of my formidable adversary, along with all his rights?
BARON. First of all, the premise is impossible. I know the bravery of my friend too well to be able to doubt his success for a moment. And as far as his rights, you astonish me!
LORVILLE. And why is that, sir?
BARON. Louise, have you completely forgotten what somebody told us?
LOUISE. Why, sir, whatever I know, I got from you. Just a little while ago, you're the one who said to Miss Juliette and me that Mr. Lorville had tried to abduct the burgermeister's daughter in Strasbourg.
LORVILLE. Me! Good heavens! Please, sir, don't believe it. The impossibility of the accusation strikes down the very lie itself. And were this action even possible, I am incapable of committing it. You are aware of your old friendship with my father. I do not blame you for having forgotten it, seduced by a lie. But the reparation that I demand, and which you cannot refuse me, is that you grant me, after the gentleman here, both his place and his rights.
BARON. It is impossible for me to refuse either of your requests. But I tell you that they are unnecessary. If you knew my friend's courage, your demands would seem useless to you.
LORVILLE. Your confidence in the bravery of such a man leaves me with the greatest hope.

GROUFFIGNAC. What pride! Ah! The youth of today!
LORVILLE. (*To GROUFFIGNAC.*) Go, sir, go arm yourself, pad yourself too, if you like. You will go up the first since you've stolen that honor from me. But whether you return or not, I'll follow right behind you, you can count on it.
GROUFFIGNAC. (*To the ladies.*) What insolence in that little head! (*To the BARON.*) Let's go, my friend, let's go because I feel myself getting hot under the collar, and it's for helping a friend, not taking revenge, that I should reserve the strength of this arm. (*They exit.*)
LORVILLE. (*With the greatest passion.*) What! You're marrying that character, Juliette? And you could believe that the lover captivated by you, the lover who adores you, could imagine the existence of another who is your equal? No, I will never forgive you for being so unfair. It's an insult to you. It isn't worthy of you. (*Sings.*)
Oh! Juliette! Oh! Juliette!
Could a heart embraced by you,
Could the object of your affection,
Break faith with you?
I've spent my days in tears
Far away from your sweet attractions,
And you bring me uneasiness
When I return to your arms.
Don't you trust my fidelity,
Don't you trust your lover?
Could it be that absence
Has weakened the feelings inside you?
Ah! To destroy your image,
To overwhelm my passion,
To shatter the memory of your heavenly face,
They'd have to break my heart.

I will idolize you without end:
Aren't you the world to me?
No, no, you're no longer my mistress
With the power to dissolve our bonds.
Even in my swooning soul,

Your eyes will read after my death:
He lived for his love,
In dying, he still loves her.
LOUISE. Good grief, Miss, at the moment, I think the best thing you could do is forgive him. There's nothing wrong with him, except for a little fondness, foolishness, and carelessness! Maybe your father just told a little white lie and believe me, (*Slyly.*) I know a little bit about that. There wasn't even the slightest appearance of wrongdoing.
JULIETTE. You louse! Why didn't you tell me.
LOUISE. I would have robbed you of the pleasure of reconciliation, the greatest joy there is in love. (*Aside.*) Besides, I never say what I know.
JULIETTE. (*Tenderly, to LORVILLE.*) You've always loved me, then?
LORVILLE. (*At JULIETTE's feet.*) Oh, unrivaled delight of my life, can you doubt it for a moment?
JULIETTE. (*Sings.*) Yes, yes, I'll love you unceasingly.
LORVILLE. (*Sings.*) Can you doubt my tenderness?
JULIETTE. I could have doubted your tenderness.
ALL THREE. (*Sing.*) How sweet is the moment of forgiveness.
The god of love stifles judgment.
JULIETTE. He doesn't have to make amends.
LOUISE and LORVILLE. (*Sing.*) It must, it must disappear,
ALL THREE. This dark and provoking suspicion,
JULIETTE. From the moment that tenderness
Makes us lose or stifle our judgment.
LOUISE. (*Sings.*) Love each other, love each other, unceasingly.
LORVILLE and JULIETTE. We love each other, we love each other unceasingly.
LOUISE. And never may your tenderness,
LORVILLE and JULIETTE. And never may our tenderness
ALL THREE. Ever need forgiveness.
JULIETTE. (*Sings.*) Yes, yes, I'll love you unceasingly.
LORVILLE. (*Sings.*) Can you doubt my tenderness?
JULIETTE. I could have doubted your tenderness.
ALL THREE. (*Sing.*) How sweet is the moment of forgiveness.

LOUISE. (*Spoken.*) All this is well and good, but it's not enough to be reconciled. You still have to see to the rest of this business. At the moment, since you two are only thinking about love, I'm the one who'll have to worry about everything else. Always remember that it's important to encourage the tax collector. We have to give him confidence. It's absolutely necessary that he goes into the tower, and I warn you that he won't go in if the two of you continue to get on his nerves. (*To LORVILLE.*) And you, sir, above all, keep your temper and your tongue under control. Here they come. I tell you I'll give up on both of you if you don't listen to what I say.

(*GROUFFIGNAC is dressed from head to toe in antique armor: arm-braces, thigh-pieces, corselet, gauntlets, a helmet on his head, and a spear in his grasp. He carries JULIETTE's ribbon over the shoulder.*)

LORVILLE. (*Breaking into laughter at the sight of GROUFFIGNAC.*) God damn! Mr. Tax Collector, there you are, bomb-proof!

LOUISE. (*Laughing, in spite of herself.*) It'll take a battering ram to break through that.

GROUFFIGNAC. (*Sluggishly.*) In a situation like this, these precautions are the result of wisdom. They ought to be in inverse ratio to the dangers at hand. One of our great authors has said that it was always necessary to put the means in place of the extremes, and the extremes in place of the means. From which I conclude . . .

LORVILLE. (*Interrupting him.*) From which I conclude that you're impenetrable and very attractive like that, really!

(*Here follows a Quintet , a concerted ensemble piece.*)

LORVILLE. (*Sings.*)

It's the god Mars flying toward victory,
Adorned with flowers and gifts from Cyprus.[16]
Who wouldn't envy his conquest and his glory
When Venus herself bestows the prize?

ALL. (*Sing.*)

It's the god Mars flying toward victory,
Adorned with flowers and gifts from Cyprus.

GROUFFIGNAC. (*Sings.*)

[16] In Greek mythology, Cyprus was noted as one of the birthplaces of Aphrodite.

Ah! It's true I'm flying toward victory,
Adorned with flowers and gifts from Cyprus.
LOUISE. (*Sings.*)
While fighting, think of Juliette.
Think of the knots that must be forming in her hands.
Fly to cut the laurel tree which is waiting for you,
Fly, fly, a myrtle branch is covering her heart.
ALL. (*Sing.*) While fighting, think of Juliette.
Think of the knots that must be forming in her hands.
GROUFFIGNAC. While flying there, I'll think of Juliette,
I'll think of the knots that must be forming in her hands.
JULIETTE. I am the reward for your adventures.
The god of love is on your side.
When his torch comes to guide bravery,
Doesn't that insure immortality?
BARON, LORVILLE, LOUISE. She is the reward for your adventures.
The god of love is on your side.
JULIETTE. I am the reward for your adventures.
The god of love is on your side.
GROUFFIGNAC. She is the reward for my adventures.
The god of love fights on my side!
BARON. My friendship is relying on you,
Don't betray its hope most sweet.
After the thorn, a rose is born.
(*Indicating his daughter.*)
If you deserve her, this rose is yours.
GROUFFIGNAC. Your friendship is relying on me.
I will serve its hope most sweet.
ALL. It's friendship that's relying on you,
Don't betray its hope most sweet.
GROUFFIGNAC. No, no, you can always believe
That you've ignited the fire in my heart.
I was a man and inappropriate to glory.
With love, you have made me a god.
ALL. It's the god Mars flying to victory,
Adorned with flowers and gifts from Cyprus.
GROUFFIGNAC. Ah! The die is cast. I run toward victory,

Adorned with flowers and gifts from Cyprus.
ALL. It's the god Mars flying toward victory,
Adorned with flowers and gifts from Cyprus.
Who wouldn't envy his conquest and his glory
When Venus herself bestows the prize?

(*GROUFFIGNAC walks boldly toward the tower. As he does, the noise begins again, louder than before. The music continues and depicts the racket of the ghosts in the tower. Frightened, GROUFFIGNAC returns, trembling in his boots.*)

GROUFFIGNAC. (*To the BARON; the noise stops.*) My dear Baron, I have not put my affairs in order. If I do not return . . . goodbye, Juliette, maybe I'll never see you again. Goodbye, Louise. I beg the Baron to give you fifty louis from the petty cash in my briefcase.

BARON. (*Quickly.*) Oh, my friend, your misgivings could have killed you. Throw them away and think only about the glory that awaits you.

GROUFFIGNAC. Ah! That's too much to think about. I'm going in.

(*When he has entered the tower, the racket starts again. Noises and frightening tremors are heard. The music ceases during the following short scene which should flow, even during the noise, with the greatest speed.*)

BARON. Don't worry, daughter, I have the greatest hope.

JULIETTE. Ah! What noise! Father, do you hear his cries?

BARON. He will return. He will return triumphant.

(*A silence during which the noise gets louder and the cries stop.*)

LORVILLE. He will never reappear. This is becoming serious. Let me go. Let me go, you've got no reason to stop me.

(*A quartet of sung dialogue follows during which the noise that matches the music continues with great force.*)

LORVILLE. (*Sings.*)
He will not return alive,
I must fly to his aid.

JULIETTE, LOUISE, BARON. (*Sing.*)
No, in no way go to his aid.

ALL. (*Sing.*)
Ah! What a racket!

LORVILLE. Honor obliges me;
I must fly to his aid.
JULIETTE. (*Frightened.*) He's dead. Oh! I'm certain of it.
(*To LORVILLE.*) I'll crush you with my hatred
If you run in there against my will.
LORVILLE. (*Grabbing the sword.*) No, no, I'm going in, and I have to.
(*The two women throw themselves at him and hold him back.*)
JULIETTE. I'm crushing you with my hatred.
LOUISE. She's covering you with her hatred.
JULIETTE. If you run in there against my will.
LOUISE. If you disobey our law.
BARON. (*To his daughter.*) Ah! Your feelings betray you.
Your love appears against your will.
LORVILLE. (*Struggling between the women.*)
No, I want to run in there, let me go.
JULIETTE. (*Still holding on to LORVILLE, and answering her father.*)
They had to be discovered,
And you see them against my will.
BARON. You see, Louise, she loves him.
JULIETTE. Oh, father, I implore you
Keep his madness forever in check.
LORVILLE. (*Still struggling.*)
Eh! No! No! I'm being dishonorable.
BARON. You see, Louise, she loves him.
JULIETTE. Very well! Yes, it's truc, I love him.
But stop him from running inside.
LORVILLE. (*Struggling unceasingly.*)
Eh! No! No! Honor is calling me.
When its voice inflames my courage,
I must conquer or die.
LOUISE and JULIETTE. Stop him from running inside.
LORVILLE. (*Getting away from the women, he hurls himself inside the tower, a sword in his hand.*) Eh! No! No! When honor calls me,
I must conquer or die.
(*The noise gets lo*uder.)

JULIETTE. Oh! Father, I'm going to die,
Help me. Everything is leaving me.
BARON. (*Brooding over his daughter.*) My dear child! She's shivering.
LOUISE. (*Holding JULIETTE in her arms.*)
Heavens! Here she is, ready to die!
BARON. (*To his daughter.*)
My dear child! She's shivering,
Look at me.
JULIETTE. (*Weakly.*) I don't see anything.
LOUISE. Don't worry, everything will be all right.
JULIETTE. Don't worry, it's nothing.
BARON. My dear child, I forgive you.
LORVILLE. (*In the tower.*)
Ah! Those rascals! Those scoundrels!
BARON. Do you hear that! Ah! What a commotion!
JULIETTE. (*Opening her eyes.*)
Yes, I hear it! Ah! What a commotion!
LOUISE. You hear it! Ah! What a commotion!
JULIETTE. Oh! God! How he tortures me.
LOUISE. Oh! God! How he tortures us.
(*LORVILLE comes out of the tower. His hair is a mess, his hat is gone, his sword is broken. He is struggling with a horned phantom that shoots fire everywhere. They wrestle one another, one on top of the other in turns. They cover the length of the stage, coming to rest on a trap which opens under the phantom's feet. He falls inside and the flames which surge up from the pit appear to engulf him. Here, shocking music should be used to portray the fight and its aftermath. As soon as the phantom appears, JULIETTE faints into LOUISE's arms and the BARON, very frightened of the ghost he sees, flies to the aid of his daughter. All of this happens very quickly. The Quartet begins again.*)
BARON. (*To the women.*)
Oh! Heavens! Oh! Heavens! Alas, I'm dying!
It's my friend, I'm not mistaken!
LORVILLE. (*To the BARON, then to JULIETTE.*)
Sir, sir, what a vindication!
Ah! Juliette! Ah, my love!
Come round, come round!

There's no longer a ghost in the tower.
Come to your senses.
JULIETTE. (*Revitalized, and falling into LORVILLE's arms.*)
What a stupid thing to do!
Ah! I see it.
ALL. What a vindication!
BARON. What courage!
Were you afraid?
(*Everybody is on stage.*)
LORVILLE. Oh! No! Never! But when I think of it,
Sir! Sir! What a vindication!
What passion and what violence!
BARON. And Grouffignac?!
LORVILLE. On my honor,
I think they ate him in revenge.
ALL (*Except LORVILLE*). They ate him?
LORVILLE. (*Trembling.*) It's horrible.
ALL. Oh, good heavens, what vengeance! What vindication!
LOUISE. It's more like he was scared to death!
LORVILLE. (*To the BARON.*) In their rage, they ate him.
Finally your peace of mind begins,
Remember my goodwill. (*Pointing to JULIETTE.*)
THE WOMEN. (*To the BARON.*) Your peace of mind finally begins.
Think, think of his goodwill.
BARON. (*Coldly.*) That's fair! I must bear it in mind.
THE WOMEN and LORVILLE. Yes, honor obliges it.
LORVILLE. (*To the BARON.*) Give me my reward.
BARON. (*Coldly, as above.*) Yes, it's fair. I must bear it in mind.
LOUISE and JULIETTE. Give him his reward.
LORVILLE. Do not deny me my happiness.
LOUISE and JULIETTE. Do not deny him his happiness.
BARON. (*To LORVILLE.*) But tell me about what happened inside . . .
(*To LOUISE.*) Ah! I can't get it out of my mind.
(*To LORVILLE.*) He was there, you saw him.
LORVILLE. He was there, yes I saw him.
THE WOMEN. He was there, we saw him.

BARON. Oh! It was very easy to recognize him.
LORVILLE. But the fact is he was beaten.
BARON. (*To LORVILLE.*)
Christ, tell me again about what happened.
(*To LOUISE.*) No, I can't get it out of my mind.
(*To LORVILLE.*) Tell me about the ending.
LORVILLE. Eh! No, no, no. Now only a notary
Can put an end to this properly.
JULIETTE. It's time, it's time, father,
Since your ghost has been defeated.
ALL. Let's go find the notary
Since the ghost has disappeared.
BARON. (*To the wings.*) Somebody find a notary
Because my ghost has disappeared.
JULIETTE. (*Throwing herself into her father's arms.*)
May I embrace you, father,
Your ghost has disappeared.
ALL. How happy we are,
It has disappeared.
BARON. (*Sung simultaneously with the following line.*)
I would have never believed what happened.
THE WOMEN. We would have never believed what happened.
ALL. Really! Hail the military!
Both its courage and its virtue.
(*Seeing someone enter unexpectedly, JULIETTE utters a cry of terror.*)
BARON. What's the matter?
JULIETTE. (*Frightened.*) Ah, good Lord! Father,
It's the devil. I've seen it again.
ALL. Eh! No, no, it's the notary
And the devil has disappeared.
It's the notary.
It's the notary.
The notary.
The notary.
Since the devil would have been wearing horns.
(The notary enters.)

BARON. Sir, you are undoubtedly carrying the contract that I had you draw up for the most unfortunate of men.
NOTARY. Yes, sir. In coming here, I heard about the tragic end heaven reserved for him and the happy success of the gentleman here. (*Pointing to LORVILLE.*) But Baron, I'm afraid that there has been a little bit of fraud here. You know as well as I that the dead don't ever come back to life, and perhaps it would be good of you to enlighten me.
BARON. You're right, sir. Actually I smell something fishy in this whole business. Help me, please, unravel this mystery.
LOUISE. (*Eagerly interrupting.*) I alone can explain it to you, sir. All that you've just seen is my doing. I knew your weakness. I took advantage of it. I was afraid of the influence that awful Gascon had over you. He was never the man who was meant for your daughter. I was trying to get you to see that, so I put obstacles in his way I knew he couldn't handle. The victory must belong to Miss Juliette's only love. He, too, was manipulated by my tricks. The men I put in the tower fought off the Gascon and surrendered to Lorville. There was no danger to either of them. I only wanted the retreat of the one and the success of the other. I carried it off. Now, can you blame me for trying to secure the happiness of two lovers who are so well-matched?
BARON. (*Happily, to LOUISE.*) No. But you are a very clever creature, Louise, and I won't trust you in a pinch. (*To the young people.*) My children, you wanted this. (*He signs the marriage contract.*) May heaven grant you happier times!

VAUDEVILLE[17]

BARON. How great a burden is a daughter!
To let her do what she wants is very dangerous,
But if love burns in her eyes,
To restrict her is even more difficult.
Foolishly, then, a person exposes himself
To injustice even when he's right.
You have to forgive certain things

[17] A French satirical song with a simple, folk-like melody, the vaudeville gave rise to the *comédie en vaudeville*, a precursor of the *opéra-comique*.

When the devil is in your house!
NOTARY. Ah! How right is a father to complain
Since his wicked children,
Without consulting him or trusting him,
Are inclined to obey the laws of others.
But that which makes him out of sorts at first,
Soon guides him to the truth.
You have to risk certain things
When the devil is in your house.
LOUISE. Pretty girls are often seen
Laughing and crying at the same time,
To invent a hundred foolish pranks
To get their choice approved,
Which papa strongly opposes.
Afterwards he changes his mind; it's the right thing to do!
He knows you need to hurry the thing
When the devil is in your house.
LORVILLE. Perhaps I would have preferred
A little less mystery in my love affair;
But in this case, I would have sided
More with the father than the daughter.
For rarely does love compromise,
It always wants to be right.
A person starts thinking about these things
When the Devil is in his house.
JULIETTE. (*To the audience.*)
Ah! If the haunted tower
Was successful where you're sitting,
To render it less dangerous,
Gentlemen, please applaud.
The author will think there's something wrong
If you all happen to agree with him!
But, hurry up, do what he suggests
'Cause the devil is in his house.

THE END

The Marriage of The Arts or The Tricks of Love

Introduction

Cited in Sade's *Descriptive Catalogue of 1788* as *The Tricks of Love; or, The Six Spectacles, The Marriage of the Arts* originally consisted of six individual plays or "episodes" which functioned as illustrations of the main dramatic action presented through backstage scenes. Of the six original episodes, *Cléontine; or, the Unfortunate Girl*, a drama in the English style, and *The Haunted Tower*, an opéra-comique, were eliminated to become independent works (*Cléontine* would resurface as *Fanny; or, The Effects of Despair*) leaving a tragedy, *Euphémie de Melun*, a comedy, *The Briber* (subsequently entitled *The Dangerous Man, The False Friend, The Immoral Man*, and *The Friend of the Day*), a fairy comedy, *Azélis; or, The Punished Coquette*, and a ballet-pantomime finale. The manuscript published by Pauvert in 1970 is dated 1810 and was copied by an inmate at Charenton where Sade spent his final years.

A document dated 27 February 1791 indicates that some of the plays in *The Tricks of Love* had been circulated to various theatres and, evidently, accepted:

I, the undersigned General Agent of Dramatic Authors, am contracted to receive from the various producers of provincial spectacles throughout all of France, the royalties which are due to Mr. de Sade according to the rate to which he has agreed and following the conditions set down in the power of attorney which he has given me for the works specified below. To wit:

At the Théâtre de la Nation: *Sophie and Desfrances*, comedy in five acts.
At the Théâtre Italien: *The Immoral Man*, comedy in one act.
The Jealous Man Reformed, comedy in one act.
At the Théâtre du Palais-Royal: *The Virtuous Criminal*, in three acts.[18]
At the Théâtre Lyrique et Comique Rue de Bondy: *Azélis; or, the Punished Coquette*, in one act.

Framery.

After several readings of *The Immoral Man*, Sade was finally invited to rehearsals of the play at the Théâtre Italien on 24 January, 3 and 14 February, and 3 March 1792. On 5 March 1792, *The Briber* (the play's most recent title) was slated to open as the curtain-raiser for Grétry's *opéra-comique*, *Friendship Put to the Test*. Due to the overwhelming clamor caused by a political faction in the theatre, the play was withdrawn and *Suite des Petits Savoyards* (*The Company of Little Chimneysweeps)* was performed in its stead.[19]

Although none of the plays that make up *The Marriage of the Arts* has ever seen a successful production, the work remains Sade's greatest achievement, if only in terms of its dramatic innovations. In his attempt to create a sense of realism, Sade clearly anticipates nineteenth-century developments in stagecraft and dramatic theory while remaining firmly grounded in eighteenth-century French theatre practice. Arguing that these plays are "uniquely Sadean" in the author's attention to "theatrical elements and to the dramaturgical styles of the time," Annetta Foster also suggests that *The Marriage of the Arts* demonstrates a "strain of traditional morality

[18] *The Jealous Man Reformed* was likely an alternate title for *The Bedroom*; *The Virtuous Criminal*, an alternate title for *The Madness of Misfortune*.

[19] For more information regarding the riot, please see the introduction to *The Bedroom* in volume two of this series, and notes to *The Dangerous Man* below. See also Pauvert II 606 ff., Foster 294 ff., and Lever 381.

that has not hitherto been acknowledged or, indeed, even recognized" in Sade's work. While the play-within-a-play technique might demonstrate the author's fondness for English Renaissance stagecraft, the Marquis exploits its potential in a kind of anticipation of Genet; and by creating a medley of plays all based on the same action, but from different perspectives, Sade foreshadows the work of Joanna Baillie, the English nineteenth-century dramatist who opted to design plays in which the entire action centered around a single emotion. Arguably the finest episode of the series, *Azélis; or, The Punished Coquette*, also heralds nineteenth-century spectacle melodrama as well as the absurdist theatre of Ionesco, and the grotesqueries of Michel de Ghelderode.

Of Sade's major critics, Annie Le Brun is the only one to discuss *The Marriage of the Arts* at length and calls attention to the "essentially 'optical' composition of the piece" in which "the true dramatic interest resides less in the entangling of the plots than in the general perspective of the entire plot, presented from these different points of view. . . . The multiplicity of points of view leads to a multiplication of the planes on which the action will unfold, as if theatre's only function is to split reality into fragments of unreality, which then reorganize according to the whims of theatrical illusion."

It is also significant to note that the ballet-pantomime that completes the work is an occasional piece written to celebrate the marriage of Napoleon (recently divorced from Josephine) to Marie Louise, daughter of Emperor Francis I of Austria in April 1810. It seems clear that, through this work, Sade was hoping to convince the Emperor to pardon him and release him from Charenton.[20] Previously, on 17 June 1809, Sade had written to Napoleon begging for his release:

> Sire,
> Mister de Sade, the father of a family in which he sees, for his consolation, one son who distinguishes himself in the army, has for nine years, in three consecutive prisons, been leading the most miserable life in the world. He is in his seventies, almost blind, and overwhelmed with gout and with rheumatisms of the chest and stomach that cause him horrible pain. Certificates from the

[20] See Foster 282 ff..

> doctors at Charenton, where he is now, attest to the truth of these statements and authorize him at last to ask for his freedom, declaring that he who grants it will never have grounds to regret it. He ventures to call himself, with the greatest respect, the most humble and obedient servant and subject of Your Majesty, Sire.

Again Sade's efforts were in vain for on 18 October 1810, Napoleon's Minister of the Interior, Montlivet, recommended that Sade be put in solitary confinement, forbidden outside communication, and denied the use of writing materials. Although Coulmier, the director of the asylum, resisted Montlivet's recommendations, clearly the Emperor agreed with them, for on 9 and 10 July 1811, sitting in Privy Council, Napoleon decided that Sade should remain at Charenton.

Maurice Lever argues that Napoleon was not merely "carrying out a routine official duty" when he signed the warrant maintaining Sade's incarceration:

> The author of *Justine* was not entirely unknown to him: he was familiar with the book and with Sade's reputation and detested both. On Saint Helena the former emperor of the French vented his wrath once more: he said that as emperor he had heard a summary and thumbed through the most abominable book ever engendered by the most depraved imagination: this was a novel which, even at the time of the Convention, he said had revolted public morality so that its author had been locked up and remained so ever since, and he believed he was still alive.

Sade's final attempt at freedom had failed but, undaunted, the Marquis proceeded to draft another novel, *Adelaide of Brunswick*, and continued to stage plays at the asylum theatre. In January 1812, patients began to complain to the minister of the interior that they were living in miserable squalor while the asylum was wasting money on expensive parties and theatrical spectacles. Lever cites a vehement complaint from an unknown patient, dated 19 January 1812:

> Excellency,

> What would you say about a hospital where balls and concerts are given two or three times a week, and splendid dinners on occasion, while the wretched patients are treated like criminals, most of them sleeping on straw like dogs with a small piece of tattered cloth for a blanket? Yet that is all they have to protect themselves against the rigors of the climate. How many, Excellency, musbe claimed by the cold? Alas, if the dead could speak, how many people would sign my little petition!

Though theatrical performances continued through the year, and were attended by celebrities such as Cardinal Maury, the archbishop of Paris, the halcyon days of the theatre at Charenton were over.[21] On 6 May 1813, the theatre was finally closed. To make up for the loss, Sade began the fair copy of his *Secret History of Isabel of Bavaria*, attempted once again to convince the Comédiens Français to produce his tragedy, *Jeanne Laisné*, and developed an intimate, sexual relationship with Madeleine Leclerc, a 16 year old girl, to help him pass the time.

Nowhere in the dramatic works is the unquenchable energy of Sade's personality better expressed than in *The Marriage of the Arts*. Originally written before 1788 and revised four years before his death, the work shares the violent spirit of *The One Hundred and Twenty Days of Sodom*, which Le Brun argues Sade was writing at the same time, as well as the mystical, sentimental, almost religious fervor of the later occasional works. However the plays are viewed—historically, theatrically, psychologically—the work provides a penetrating insight into Sade's intellect and imagination, and remains, according to Annetta Foster, the "most ambitious dramatic work of Sade and the most fascinating as an historical document of drama and theatre during the artistic drought of the First Empire."

[21] For occasional verse written by Sade for Maury and Coulmier during this period, see the verse translations at the end of this volume, the introduction to *The Festival of Friendship* in this volume, Pauvert III, 435 ff., and Lély 620.

THE MARRIAGE OF THE ARTS
or
THE TRICKS OF LOVE

In Alexandrines, Iambic Pentameter, Free Verse, Prose, Music and Songs

The glory of your endeavors is marked by the obstacles they present for you to overcome.
Villaret[22]

Thoughts

On the creation of this work, and some advice to those who will perform it.

In 1726, Daiguespierre had produced something similar to the outline of what you are about to read, but he was far from fulfilling the goal of this work, which consists in putting the exposition of the "Great Whole" in a kind of prologue, making this prologue run in between the acts in such a way that it would become the main play to which all of the others are only incidental; in short, to arrange things in such a way that each episode, set up in the exposition of the plot, contributes to the main action, and becomes the complication and the resolution of this standard, basic play.

That is what gives this, I think, an absolutely new look, another example of which will not be seen in any other dramatic work.

Count Verceuil is in love with Émilie. He learns that he has a rival and, in order to take possession of his mistress, he disguises himself as an actor because he knows that Mr. Desclapon, his lover's

[22] French actor, theatre manager, and playwright who died in 1766. He is known for *The Winter Quarter*, a play written in collaboration with Bret, Godart, and d'Aucourt

father, has a passion for the theatre, and that by offering him his talents in this field, and those of the artists he assembles for that purpose, he will be able to reach his goal. That is the background for this piece. Now, to succeed, Verceuil employs all of the means suggested by his imagination. The first is to make use of Émilie in the performance of his plays because he knows quite well that in this way he will find the opportunity of speaking to her about his love. Another of his methods lies in his choice of plays for public performance: in each one, he wants Mr. Desclapon to see the misfortunes threatening a father who sacrifices his daughter to his own ambition. When he discards this first approach, he uses another: to show Émilie the dangers of infidelity, and to what misfortunes the women who yield to it will be subjected.

As a result, in the tragedy called *The Siege of Algiers*, you see a father abandoning his family because of ambition, and causing, through this mistaken ambition, his own misfortune and that of his two daughters. The marriage of the oldest hurls him into misery, and that of the youngest, which is nevertheless more satisfactory, exposes her and her lover to dangers which they would never have known if this wisest of fathers hadn't stopped keeping an eye on his daughters' behavior.

In *The Dangerous Man*, a father openly sacrifices his daughter to his ambition to make up for the loss of a fortune that was taken from him by the treacherous scoundrel to whom he is ready to give his daughter. What a lesson for Émilie's father! The rogue is ready to carry her off, the lover wards off the blow, unmasks the villain through the intervention of a friend, punishes him cruelly, and wins the object of his desires.

There is another kind of lesson in the fairy comedy. Here Verceuil actually speaks to his mistress; it is sweeter, but when Cupid gives him the rod for punishment, should he not put it back into the hands of the Graces?

Finally, the Count reveals himself and shows, at the same time, the powerful reasons he had for ousting his rival. Émilie confesses that she loves Verceuil and the marriage is concluded.

Let us move on to some fundamental advice for those who will perform this play.

It is essential to remember that what are called backstage scenes are all the ones that make up the plot of this work and upon which all the rest is an elaboration, that is to say, to make myself even clearer, those which are occupied by Mr. Desclapon and his entourage; everything else is of secondary importance, even though the daughter of the estate might be performing the primary roles in the various plays.

Despite the fact that the explanations of the episodes might either be stated or simply indicated in the backstage scenes, the necessary information has been adequately repeated in the episodes so that each of the little plays might create complete entities, to give those who would like to perform them individually the ability of removing them from the body of the work. It can be done. Each part of the whole is complete by itself. You want to connect them? Everything hangs together; everything is made to go hand in hand, to contribute to the same goal. But an objection presents itself here.

If these plays about to be produced are extemporized by the Count, how does Mr. Desclapon's daughter Émilie have time to learn the roles?

First of all, not to exaggerate this objection, it is only she alone who is employed in the Count's plays; all of the other roles you find are filled by the actors of the company. But could we do without her and him? We ought to suppose then that the author's memory is good enough to learn quickly what he's written, and that his mistress has an interest powerful enough for her to enter her lover's plans to overcome every kind of difficulty. Besides, a bit of illusion needs to be created, and what asks for that more than theatre? We have to believe that everything that can be possible is possible in the given situation, and especially when you can't do otherwise.

Nevertheless, as we have just said, everything can be separated. Perform the whole thing or leave out the backstage scenes and perform separately whichever of the plays you like, it's up to you. The backstage scenes connect the episodes, but each episode can be performed on its own, without the backstage scenes, and it is because of this novelty that the work seems worthy of some leniency. Let it be remembered, above all, that the actress given the role of Émilie must absolutely fill the primary roles of the episodes.

It is also necessary to see to it that the curtain is never lowered except where indicated.

When an episode is finished, the stagehand brings back Mr. Desclapon's study, the principal location of the play. The actors who are undressing at that time reappear in negligees, and the backstage scenes continue. Things get underway for a new episode. That is when the scene changes and allows the scenery necessary for the next episode to be visible. But there is no need for the curtain to be lowered; it should be lowered only when it is indicated.

Perhaps people will say that in *Azélis* and in the ballet, the stage is full when the episode begins, and that the curtain should be lowered so that the characters who ought to be in motion have the possibility of getting into position. I say that you have to be really careful, however necessary it might appear, in dropping the curtain so often in a play that has no stopping point to speak of, and where the action is virtually continuous. This lowering of the curtain—completely breaking the action—would be horribly out of place here. This is how I solve the problem.

Mr. Desclapon's study should have very little depth; it should hardly extend to the second set of wings. Thus, the stagehand is no longer short of space in which to set up his flats. He works behind the study and when the study disappears, there are no more than two pieces in front to move, all of the ones in the back are ready. Regarding the characters who are supposed to be in motion when the episode begins, what prevents them from placing themselves at the edge of the backdrop for Mr. Desclapon's study? That puts them almost onstage when the study disappears and lets them approach the footlights when the scene-change is carried out. That is what has to happen then, and that is the reason you see at the beginning of each episode: "the scene changes and represents" and not, "the curtain rises and reveals."

As for the orchestra, it must not be heard between the end of each episode and the backstage scenes immediately following them because these backstage scenes depend on the episode that has just been performed. They are the continuation of it. The break indicated by the orchestra would be thus out of place. It should only occur when, after the performance of the backstage scene that follows the episode, we set out to show something new; and we have been careful to put precisely at each of these locations the word, "orchestra," that corresponds to the end of act one, end of act two, etc., in traditional comedies and indicates that break brought about by the music.

Mr. Desclapon's study is, in a word, the principal location of the action; it must always be regarded as such. It is the one that changes into the different settings required for the different episodes, and it is the one that reappears when each episode is finished. I have clearly indicated every time the stagehand has to bring it back into sight, and I suggest that directors pay very close attention to see that all of this is done with precision.

It is hardly necessary to inform the actors who would want to perform this play that there must be an essential difference between the delivery of the backstage scenes and that of the episodes. This difference is well established by what governs the various styles. When you are in Mr. Desclapon's room during the backstage scenes, you must speak as if you are in someone's home; in the rest, you play the comedy and, however simple the tone of the comedy must be, you know, nevertheless, that it must have more color and more force than the tone of ordinary conversation. But this repartee, however natural it may be, must never exist in the backstage scenes with the exception of the places where Verceuil demonstrates that he's an actor. The difference that is called for and established here ought to be the same as that of the flowers of a tapestry in relation to the background on which they roam. Shouldn't these flowers stand out from the background, and isn't that the reason they're placed on a very simple canvas?

The ballets should be performed with all possible spectacle.

I beseech the artists not to deviate from anything that is stipulated above. They could not do so without upsetting the illusion, the maintenance of which, you see, already requires a large dose of tolerance in a work like this.

The set designer will be aware of how much we have tried to help him by not only working out for him the greatest possible means of displaying his ability, but also by allowing the backstage scenes to begin only with the sight of a huge garret in a space where he must, in so little time, create such magnificent effects.

THE MARRIAGE OF THE ARTS

(An Episodic Comedy)

CHARACTERS

In the Background Scenes

Mr. Desclapon, *owner of the house in which the action takes place*
Émilie, *his daughter*
Count Verceuil, *Émilie's lover, disguised under the name of Belval, an actor*
Mr. Vieuxblanc, *engaged to Émilie*
Marton, *Émilie's companion*

The setting is in Mr. Desclapon's mansion, a few miles from Paris. The scene is set in a very small study in the mansion.

DESCLAPON. Ah! I'm delighted to chat with you for a moment, my dear Marton. This room is empty, and while my friend, Mr. Vieuxblanc is finishing his game of cards with my daughter, we could easily talk here without anyone interrupting us.
MARTON. Well, sir, what's going on? You know how fond I am of your interests.
DESCLAPON. Here's what's happening: you know that tomorrow my daughter is marrying Mr. Vieuxblanc, that rich financier she's with right now. And based on the fondness you know I have for festivals and plays, I would like you to think of something that could celebrate this great event. Talk to me a little about what we could come up with.
MARTON. Really, sir, to tell you the truth, in this situation, my imagination isn't coming up with anything.
DESCLAPON. And why?

MARTON. It's just that in the marriage you're talking about, I don't see very definite happiness for Miss Émilie, and when my mistress is distressed, it's impossible for me to be in a holiday mood.
DESCLAPON. What do you mean, distressed?
MARTON. But in all honesty, can you believe that she's marrying whole-heartedly your Mr. Vieuxblanc, a man who's three times her age? At the age of sixteen, with Hebe's face,[23] Flora's luster,[24] the Graces' figure,[25] it's hard to love a man like the one you're giving her. I certainly want to believe along with you that Miss Émilie has never been so inclined, but when you're created like her to inspire love, you're very close to experiencing it—loving or being loved—Ah! Sir, if you only knew how close they are!
DESCLAPON. Has she said something to you about this?
MARTON. Not exactly, sir. But if her mouth is silent, her heart speaks, her eyes are expressive. And between us girls, we take all of that as a hint.
DESCLAPON. I swear I'd be very angry if Vieuxblanc didn't suit her. He's been a friend of mine for fifteen years.
MARTON. Do you think that gives him the right to become your daughter's lover?
DESCLAPON. He's a reasonable man.
MARTON. That quality isn't found in Cythera's code.[26]
DESCLAPON. Terribly rich!
MARTON. There's still nothing there for love.
DESCLAPON. But this man is happy-go-lucky. He has all the talents that please my daughter.
MARTON. (*Aside*.) Except the talent to please.
DESCLAPON. He's wild about the theatre, and he's wonderfully well versed in it.
MARTON. (*Aside*.) Hang on! We'll have her perform for him.
DESCLAPON. He's already given my daughter a lot of lessons, and under the instruction of so good a teacher . . .
MARTON. Her talent is decided upon, right?

[23] In Greek mythology, Hebe is the goddess of youth.

[24] In Roman myth, Flora was the goddess of flowers and the spring season.

[25] In Greek mythology, the three Graces were goddesses of charm, beauty, nature, human creativity and fertility

[26] In Greek mythology, Cythera was an island sacred to Aphrodite.

DESCLAPON. Ah! Why, she's not too bad already. I think that if fate had intended her for the stage, she would have been very successful. Then think—create—dream up something and let me in on your plan tonight so we can act accordingly. Something trivial: a town festival, a pastoral play, all sound good. We're out here in the country and our neighbors will appreciate anything. I'm going to see if their card game is finished. You'll come and tell me when you've come up with something. (*He exits.*)

MARTON. (*Alone.*) I didn't want to say anything. I was wrong, nevertheless. How unhappy she'd be with the husband who's intended for her, especially if what they tell me is true! But her lover, Count Verceuil will soon put an end to this. I hope it won't be long coming: he'll expose everything. (*Looking toward the rear of the set.*) Why, what's that fellow looking for? Oh, heavens! It's the Count. How dare he come here?

(COUNT VERCEUIL enters shabbily dressed.)

VERCEUIL. Well, my dear Marton! Is this the way you reply to what I told you yesterday?

MARTON. Really, sir, when I saw that your affairs were taking a turn, I preferred not to reply, convinced that would hasten your arrival here. Tomorrow, Émilie must be Vieuxblanc's wife. Was it really a waste of time writing to inform you of this?

VERCEUIL. That news crushes me. I knew it all the same: I placed some reliable people around the neighborhood, and I've been informed by them about absolutely everything that was going on. But I'm here to disrupt the arrangements, and I hope that the scheme I've come up with is forever going to guarantee me the hand of your beautiful mistress.

MARTON. Oh! I rely on you for tricks. Few people create them better and even fewer make them succeed so well. Is that then what brings you here?

VERCEUIL. Shhh! Be quiet. I'm a country actor and, what's more, a director! My name is Mr. Belval and in order to combine all these perfections, I'm an author. That last characteristic explains the splendor of my attire.

MARTON. What's your plan?

BELVAL. Having heard about the passion Mr. Desclapon has for the theatre, and passing by his estate with my company, I've come to offer him my services.
MARTON. Very nice!
BELVAL. He won't fail to ask us for something. I'll suggest that we allow Émilie to participate in our performances; he'll agree. Maybe he'll even suggest it himself. It will be the first opportunity to speak freely to that dear object of my heart. In the rehearsals, I'll paint her a picture of my love. I'll express it to her in the performances, and since I have a great deal of the world at my command, (*Mysteriously*.) if she wants me to carry her away, I'll create some special effects and make her disappear like Persephone in a trap, or like Venus in a cloud.
MARTON. That's really what they call the "Tricks of Love." In a word, lo and behold! You've become an actor. What you told me yesterday made me a little suspicious about this plan. Are there many people in your company?
BELVAL. It couldn't be fuller. I've got three people for every specialty; twelve supernumeraries, sixty musicians, two composers, ten featured dancers, fifty ballet-dancers, three chorus-masters, twelve children, four special effects men, six painters, two designers, three prompters and sixty female singers.
MARTON. Sixty female singers?
BELVAL. Yes, really, whom I hired in Paris and who are harder for me to direct than fifteen regiments of dragoons!
MARTON. Ah! Sir, that's really what they call a company on the rise! Well, you couldn't have come at a better time. I've been put in charge of coming up with something to enhance the occasion of your lover's wedding. You'd certainly like to be in charge of the celebrations, wouldn't you?
BELVAL. That's not entirely what I had in mind. I'll go along with the effect; it serves my plans the best, but as for the reason, it won't be exactly as you said. And if Desclapon sees his daughter married tomorrow, I swear to you that it won't be to Mr. Vieuxblanc. Right now, I know too much about him to be afraid of him.
MARTON. But she's decided on him all the same, sir, and I think you'll have a lot of trouble making her change her decision.

BELVAL. (*Spiritedly.*) Her decision? Her decision is to love me. She told me so. She's incapable of lying to me.
MARTON. Well, yes. But a father's wishes?
BELVAL. Oh! We'll change those. I could ruin his friend with a single word, but I'd rather force that scoundrel to relinquish his place to me through examples or hard lessons. (*After a moment's thought.*) I agree that it might be more reliable to carry Émilie away first and explain to her father later, but that method is dangerous. Leave it to me. I'm going to turn all of that over in my mind. I'll talk to Émilie, about the circumstances, about my love. We'll be successful, you can be sure of it! Of course! We're conquering a fortified city! You don't want to be overcome by an old fool like your master. Go, announce me. Desclapon has never seen me, neither has his friend, Vieuxblanc. That's already something vital. You'll find out the rest.
(*MR. DESCLAPON, ÉMILIE, and MR. VIEUXBLANC enter.*)
DESCLAPON. (*Never casting his eyes on BELVAL.*) Well! Marton?
MARTON. Well! Sir, luck favors us much better than my mind. It sent you this gentleman expressly to serve your plans.
ÉMILIE. (*Softly and spiritedly to MARTON after recognizing the Count.*) Oh! Heaven! Who did I see, Marton?
MARTON. (*Softly, to ÉMILIE.*) Pretend not to notice and don't let your heart betray you.
DESCLAPON. (*Eyeing the Count up and down, scornfully.*) Who have we here?
BELVAL. (*Very quickly.*) Sir, I'm a doctor, alchemist, historian, laureate, spiritualist, symphonist, engineer, algebraist, academician, physiologist, logician, botanist, musician, genealogist, pyrotechnist, hypnotist, painter, organist, poet, astrologer, pilot, ventriloquist, and actor to serve you.
DESCLAPON. (*Softly, to MARTON.*) Marton, do you think that man's got all his marbles?
MARTON. Oh, yes, sir! It's just that he's a great scholar and sometimes science rattles the fibers of the brain.
DESCLAPON. Those certainly are trades for dying of hunger, sir.
BELVAL. Well, I'm still not wealthy, but I'm young and haven't lost hope of making my way. *Audaces fortuna juvat*![27]

[27] Fortune favors the brave.

VIEUXBLANC. And what's worse, he's a Latinist, sir!
BELVAL. Oh, yes, sir! I know Greek, Hebrew, Syrian, Celtic, Slavic, Teutonic, Malayan, Arabic, Calabrian, Chaldean, and Chinese.
ÉMILIE. Then you've traveled a lot, sir?
BELVAL. Not tremendously, Miss. I've still only been to Persia, Lapland, Spitsbergen,[28] Greenland, Kamchatka,[29] twice to Japan, the Maldives, Golconda, Siam, the Congo, Monomotapa,[30] Visapour,[31] three times among the Caffres,[32] five times with the Hottentots, and eight times in America.
DESCLAPON. Why, he knows everything, Marton! What good wind is blowing him our way?
BELVAL. A very simple event, sir. In Paris, I received orders from the Emperor of China to assemble a full company of actors that he intends to set up in Peking. My task is done. We're on our way. Our route goes through your town. Having heard about your inclination for these kinds of pleasures, I didn't want to leave without paying you my respects and giving you a few samples of our abilities.
VIEUXBLANC. What! The Emperor of China wants a French company? I was unaware of that. It seems to me the newspapers still haven't said anything about it.
BELVAL. They won't talk about it, sir. (*Mysteriously*.) It's a secret operation to which his Highness is treating his Mandarins.
VIEUXBLANC. A French theatre at the Chinese Emperor's palace! Most certainly this is a project that's a credit to the art and which really justifies the inclination that I've had for it all my life.
DESCLAPON. Why, my dear Vieuxblanc, today there isn't a court in the world that doesn't have a French theatre. (*To BELVAL*.) Sir, I accept your offer with thanks, and since all of us here like that diversion, we'll join you. You'll use us and perhaps you'll find us not unworthy of you.

[28] The largest island in Norway.
[29] A peninsula in northeastern Russia.
[30] A kingdom in southern Africa.
[31] Capital of the Kingdom of Decan, India.
[32] A race of people in southeastern Africa.

BELVAL. Unworthy, never. You're the one, sir, who honors us. And as for your request, it's the simplest and easiest thing in the world to carry out.
DESCLAPON. Well, daughter, here's the one who's going to make a decision about your abilities. The gentleman will be able to judge them, and after hearing his opinion, it'll be easier for you to select a genre.
BELVAL. (*To ÉMILIE.*) Has the lady ever acted before?
VIEUXBLANC. No, sir, she's a beginner.
BELVAL. With a face like that, talent is almost unnecessary. She only has to appear!
DESCLAPON. You have too good an opinion of her, sir. Take it from me, don't respond until after the test.
BELVAL. The lady will blossom when she pleases. And what is the genre for which you feel you have a special gift?
ÉMILIE. (*Deliberately.*) Why I think lovers suit me, perhaps, better than anything.
BELVAL. (*Alternately controlling his emotions and expressing them.*) Oh, yes, I agree with you. The roles inspired by love. (*Half softly to her, half stuttering.*) And I'd even bet that when that little god wants to win somebody's heart, you're always the one who inspires him. (*Returning to normal.*) It's very certain that with such a pleasing voice, with such flashing eyes, it's not a question of when you want to express life's sweetest emotion, I tell you, it's only a question of giving yourself up to nature.
VIEUXBLANC. Absolutely! Nature. It's that damn nature I can't seem to convince her about!
BELVAL. (*Spiritedly.*) Well, I'll take it upon myself, sir, to teach the lady everything I know on that subject. The first point, Miss, is to feel. You have to have soul. You'd almost need to have an object for your feelings . . . yes, really, an object.
DESCLAPON. (*Indicating VIEUXBLANC.*) Well, here he is!
BELVAL. (*Surprise mixed with contempt, but greatly disguised.*) Who, the gentleman? Ah! The gentleman! Of course. Yes, the gentleman for example. (*With the utmost skill and the most focused passion.*) Well, Miss, in the emotional bits, always have in front of you the person you love most in the world . . . like now. Address everything you say to him, just as you would do it yourself, even

if it wasn't in the part. You'll see his eyes responding to you. His heart will fly to his lips to tell you what's troubling him. He'll rebel against the obstacles that prevent him from marrying you. He'd want there to be only you and he in the entire universe—your soul nourished by him alone. (*Entirely with abandon.*) He'll tell you a hundred times that he adores you; he'll swear it to you. You'll assure him in return, and to convince him further, you'll let something of the fire which he's ignited in your heart show in those delightful eyes. (*To DESCLAPON with absolute composure.*) And that's what they call "Nature," isn't it, sir?

DESCLAPON. (*Completely amazed.*) Yes, definitely! Sir, there you're developing some great talents in us.

BELVAL. (*With the utmost composure, and taking a pinch of snuff.*) Nature, sir.

VIEUXBLANC. It has served you wonderfully. A person can see that you feel your art, and that you know its entire domain.

MARTON. Well, sir, what will you give me for making such a discovery?

DESCLAPON. Let's see. Let's get things settled: what have you got ready?

BELVAL. (*Quickly.*) Everything, sir: Molière, Boursaut, Scarron, Destouches, Racine, Crébillon, Corneille, Voltaire, Regnard, Haute Roche, Palaprat, La Chaussée, Sainte-Foix, Gresset, and Marivaux.

VIEUXBLANC. Sir, that's a lot to choose from. But I have an idea. Listen to it, Desclapon, I'm sure you will approve. Everything the gentleman just told us we know by heart. To celebrate tomorrow's event which will make me the happiest of men, it seems to me that it would be more gratifying to present something entirely new at your reception, especially since the gentleman told us he was a poet.

BELVAL. Something that would fit the occasion, right, sir?

VIEUXBLANC. Absolutely.

BELVAL. (*Spiritedly.*) I'll see to it. You only have to pick the genre.

DESCLAPON. What do you mean, pick the genre? Are you in a position to succeed in all of them?

BELVAL. Succeed, no. My pride doesn't extend that far! But I skim the surface of all of them. And to convince you, rather than have a full-length play followed by a short one, if you like, I'll entertain your audience with three dramatic works, all working towards the same objective, and in completely different genres.
VIEUXBLANC. Oh! Of course, that'll be something new.
DESCLAPON. What! Will you unite tragedy with comedy?
BELVAL. We'll begin with a tragedy, followed by a character play . . . it's actually somewhat serious but we'll lighten things up with a fairy comedy, and finish with an extravaganza! What do you think about this plan?
MARTON. (*To DESCLAPON.*) Oh! Really, sir, you've never seen anything like it.
DESCLAPON. Most certain! And I can't thank fate enough for the delightful acquaintance I've just made.
BELVAL. Wait to praise me, sir, until you've heard me. Perhaps you won't be tempted to do so in a couple of hours. Besides, what I'm suggesting to you here is for the purpose of trying out . . . of discovering your daughter's talent. For once she has performed in three different genres, it'll be easy for us to determine what's right for her.
DESCLAPON. Let's get everything ready. It's been a long time coming for me to enjoy what you've promised.
BELVAL. Marvelous! But I need some floor space. I have stage sets, machines, chariots, temples, palaces, explosives, canon, thunder, mountains, deserts. I need a lot of space for all of that.
MARTON. (*To DESCLAPON.*) Well, sir, behind there you have a huge garret. It seems to me that the gentleman could make do with it well enough.
DESCLAPON. Most certainly. (*Into the wings.*) Open up, open up, all of you. Let the gentleman see if these premises can suit him.
(*A curtain rises and permits us see a great empty space, having absolutely nothing in it that would be appropriate for a theatre. It is dimly lit.*)
BELVAL. (*Looking over the space.*) That's exactly what I need, sir. My technicians will become immortal here, and today you know that scenery contributes greatly to the success of a production!

What do the colors of the poetry matter when the painter's are so brilliant? (*The backdrop is lowered.*) We're going to start, sir, with the tragedy about the siege of Algeria, a historical event from the reign of Louis XIV into which I've merged the story of the Marquise de Frêne, sold by her husband to Algerian privateers, the period of which is a little removed from the one that creates the boundaries of my play. I'm going to play your daughter's lover; I'm giving her the lead role. Let's get to work. The improvisatory nature of everything we're doing should increase its value.
DESCLAPON. My goodness! This young man electrifies me. I believe we'll be a success.
MARTON. If you'd like to be even more certain, sir, let the public know how badly you want it! (*Everyone exits and the curtain falls.*)

ORCHESTRA

It is essential to warn, once and for all, that the orchestra must never be heard at the end of the episodes; only after the end of the backstage scenes is the entr'acte played.

FIRST EPISODE OF THE MARRIAGE OF THE ARTS

EUPHÉMIE DE MELUN or THE SIEGE OF ALGIERS

Verse Tragedy in One Act

And all passion, since it is extreme,
By trying to hide, betrays itself.
Jean of Naples, Act 2.[33]

CHARACTERS

Selim Hamet, *the Dey of Algiers*
Euphémie de Melun (Émilie), *niece of the Count de Melun who is in command, a prisoner of war, loved by the Dey*
Azémar de Melun (Belval), *the Count de Melun's son, in love with Euphémie and a prisoner of war like her*
Constance, *a French woman, the Dey's slave, older than Euphémie*
Ibrahim, *a Christian refugee having converted to Mohammedanism*
Black African Slaves
Melun and his Officers of the French Squadron
Algerian Soldiers
French Detachments
All the Women in the Dey's harem.

[33] A tragedy by Jean-François de La Harpe (November 20, 1739 – February 11, 1803).

COSTUMES

Euphémie and Constance wear Eastern costumes.
Ibrahim wears a Turkish costume.
Azémar is dressed as a slave.

The stage reveals the Dey's garden, planted with lemon trees, orange trees, and other African trees. To the actor's right are the towers of the Seraglio; to the left, the ocean, and the French navy in the harbor; and in the distance, the ruined walls of the city. The day is barely dawning.

CONSTANCE. What! While facing a hostile enemy,
Thinking only of you, too fair Euphémie,
The Dey of Algiers causes a myrtle tree,
Which his hand reserved for your beauty,
To spring up amidst the cyprus trees.
Far from pleasing you, this highest privilege
Seems to plunge your soul into the deepest
Turmoil. Ah! Maintain your woman's rights
And capture the love of the brazen despot
Whose court we make up; and gratifying
If you can, the fervor of his esteem,
Shatter . . . shatter the fetters of vile servitude
By giving us a beauty for a queen
Who soon will deliver us all to freedom.
EUPHÉMIE. Ah! What a happy moment, my kind friend,
What an enchanting moment for your dear
Euphémie, if by tightening the bonds
Which are so pleasing to us, I succeeded
At last to put an end to our distress.
CONSTANCE. But you would have to yield.
EUPHÉMIE. No. I will have
The courage which, in these sad surroundings,
In the midst of slavery, would be able
To preserve you for the object of your
Passions, despite all the attempts of an
Audacious monster.
(*Passionately, and taking her hand.*) Let's unite against

His barbarity. Soon we'll see again
Our blessed country; my heart promises
It to me, and those vile champions who
Disturb the quiet sweetness of the harem,
Beaten, dismayed with the efforts of France,
They will not resist its manly power.
See those burning remains, those ruined battlements,
See those walls knocked over, those strongholds
Destroyed; in short, everywhere the effect
Of those flying sledgehammers that, carrying
In their bowels a thousand dreadful deaths,
Proceed to show the likeness of the lightning
From the heavens or the fires from hell
To this wicked people. I glory
Completely in seeing them defeated.
It is my dearest hope, and soon victory,
Which will fasten Mars securely to the
French flag, will come to soothe our misfortunes
And determine our plans.
CONSTANCE. Since a ray of hope
Can dispel your cares, for a moment,
At least with me, deign to forget your chains.
EUPHÉMIE. Ah! Can I, Constance? Does the power exist
Within us to forget such obvious wounds?
Picture for yourself all my misfortunes:
I was born in France. There, underneath
The old roof where I had come into being,
Were two warriors, since war was over,
Relaxing their courage in the shadow
Of the laurel tree. Both of them conveyed
To me the blood of which I'm proud. They were
My father and his brother. Close to them,
Just like me, the good-natured and dear child
Of that beloved brother grew up quietly.
The sweet routine, alas, gave birth to that need
To fall in love, of which the heart is not
The master. Nothing could yet change that pleasant
Emotion whose fervor was electrified

By the hand of love, when ambition,
Separating the two brothers, disturbed
Those passions so dear with its designs.
My father sought to add yet another
Illustration of his fame in the army.
He leaves. Eternal God whom I implore,
One day, may you repay my fervent vows
To the father I adore! We never
Saw him again: that was the beginning
Of our calamities. My mother died
Because of it, but to complete our hardships,
A sister whom I loved, and who had raised me,
Was soon taken away by a cruel husband
And, succumbing underneath the weight
Of the most horrible misfortunes, alone
With destiny my heart was left to struggle.
About this time, I heard the martial trumpet
Call Frenchmen to the boundaries of the earth.
The African pirate, inflated
By empty success, dared to make other
Attempts against Louis. Our men are taking
Arms; and these heroes united by revenge,
Have Melun at their head.
Oh, heavens! I've told you everything . . .
CONSTANCE. *(Interrupting, passionately.)*
Is it Melun who's leading us to victory
On these premises?
(*Pointing to the Dey's palace*.) In vain I asked
That ferocious tyrant for the name
Of his conqueror without his ever
Consenting to deliver it to me.
EUPHÉMIE. What can interest you about that soldier?
CONSTANCE. (*Still disturbed*.)
Through the bonds, which perhaps . . . finish telling
Me your story. Don't conceal anything.
You should be able to read in my heart
All the interest I have in asking
It of you.

EUPHÉMIE. Melun said goodbye to me.
His ties with me arose, as I told you,
Through the blood of my father to whom he was
A friend even more than a brother.
He suspected my passion; I hid nothing
From him. "Brave soldier," I said to him,
"Azémar is my blessing, Euphémie
Is his only hope. Do not separate them.
I am going to serve France, to earn
My lover through deeds of valor, to fight
At his side, to energize his fervor,
To crown his head with laurels with my hands,
To earn my conquest through the greatest exploits.
I idolize a hero, and it is in
His eyes, next to you, uncle, in the midst
Of danger, that you will grant me the triumph
To which I aspire. You'll guide my steps,
You'll consent to teach me; and from both
Of you, in the end, I'll learn in turn
How someone serves his king, country, and love!"
Melun agrees. His son becomes my brother-
In-arms. Armor soon covers my feeble
Charms. I don't know whether I was obliged
At my age to my features for the gift
Of gathering together his noblest
Qualities, or if my heart, struck with his
Heavenly likeness, stamped, in spite of myself,
His features on my face, but I resembled
Him. We fly into combat; everything
Staggers, everything succumbs to the efforts
Of his arm. The dead men who exerted
Their strength beneath his blows, succumbing
To that hero, respected his bravery.
One assault ruined us; we ran to the
Battlements. My heart, driven by love,
Was defending Azémar when fate
Betrayed us. You know all the rest. They take me
To the Dey. Though not easily, I've still

Been able to protect myself from his
Lethal love.
You know to what methods my mind resorted
To convince him that Azémar is my
Brother. He believes it and allows him
To devote himself to working in the
Garden deliberately to please me.
Through these clever and roundabout means,
I've finally been able to speak to him
Twice since our confinement. That's my fate,
My friend. Keep your promise. I've hid
Nothing from you. Now tell me the cause
Of this uneasiness and agitation
Which, at the faithful recitation of my
Sad adventure, seemed to tear the life
Right out of you, against your will.
CONSTANCE. (*In tears.*)
You, whom I pressed against my heart so long,
You, for whom my friendship framed my youth,
Have you forgotten the dawn of your life?
Don't you recognize your sister? Don't you
Recognize Sophie?
EUPHÉMIE. (*Thrusting herself onto CONSTANCE's breast.*)
What do I hear? Ah, good heavens! Forgive
My mistake. Immediately, all your
Features spring up again in my heart.
I was so young then, that's my only excuse.
Nature has spoken, its voice is no longer
Indistinct. And since my tears can flow
While I'm in your arms, this fate has no more
Troubles that can overpower me.
(*After a long pause given to tender emotion.*)
And your husband, God almighty?
CONSTANCE. Let's forget the culprit. I shut my eyes
To him a long time ago; he is no
Longer excusable. For a long time,
Pride sustained the love inside of me,
But what a deadly change of heart for the

Illusion! (*Mysteriously.*) My enslavement is his work.
Into the heart of Italy, the villain
Carried me away, feigning the desire
To travel through places whose ancient splendor
Still might interest an observing eye.
One day he disappears. A vile privateer
Comes suddenly to announce my wretched
Misfortune to me. I had been sold.
Alas! Such were the means by which that worthless
Spouse destroyed our bonds.
EUPHÉMIE. God, what treachery!
CONSTANCE. I had to set out for these dreadful places.
Detestable monsters got a hold of me;
The rest you know. Let's cut short this already
Too lengthy narrative
Because Selim is coming into view.
EUPHÉMIE. (*Terrified, detaining CONSTANCE.*)
Oh, my most tender friend, do not part from your
Dear Euphémie.
(Enter SELIM, and a group of Eunuchs and Black Slaves.)
SELIM. (*To CONSTANCE.*) Withdraw, Madam. As soon as I appear
With her, let everyone immediately
Leave me in peace.
(CONSTANCE exits.)
EUPHÉMIE. What! You're taking away from me the harmless
Pleasure of speaking to a relative
About my misfortunes. You prove yourself
To be more of a tyrant than a husband.
If we were married, good heavens! How would
You behave?
SELIM. In such a case, like now,
Your master, Madam.
Here, we despise the weaknesses of the soul
Which, demeaning us beneath the yoke
Of your Western rules, enables you to
Encroach upon the holiest of our rights.
EUPHÉMIE. Ah! Don't utter that horrible blasphemy!

You don't know then, my lord, how one loves?
No, no! You're ignoring the sweetest
Of pleasures if you neglect the art
Of creating desire. Believe me, Selim,
Follow our example; Cupid has temples
Only in our hemisphere. There, only
The most ardent vows are offered up
To him, and there, it is our own hands
That enchain us. By lending us arms,
This sweet influence has its purest fires
Without losing any of its charms.
SELIM. These sentiments, Madam, have few attractions
For us. The hand of the Eternal God
In varying our features, also knew how
To vary the core of our personalities.
One doesn't look at things in the same way
In the two hemispheres. Each people has its
Laws, its culture, its virtues, which the
Neighboring peoples dare to abuse.
We condemn your morals, we criticize
Your customs. To you, ours are absurd
And savage. But when sense guides us and leads us,
We comply with the customs of the country
In which we live. Let so wise a lesson
Enlighten you today. I'm raising you
To my level; if this tie might please you,
Accept it, madam, and consider it certain
That an unending refusal, eventually
Enlightening me about your shameful contempt
Of which I know too well the cause, perhaps
Might expose you to the greatest misfortunes.
EUPHÉMIE. What, my lord! In the midst of the dangers
This day brings, can you, without terror,
Concern yourself with love?
(*Turning toward the city.*) Your city set
Ablaze by French fire, its precincts exposed
To the swords of French soldiers, the fear, the cries,
Don't they chill your passions and your spirits?

SELIM. No, no, all those setbacks don't trouble my soul;
Those destructive calamities don't snuff out
My flame. According to our holy teachings,
Their sinister effects are God's impartial
Judgment. They were written in advance
In the book of fate, and for God who watches
Them with indifference, the innumerable
Human victims of these hardships are like
A grain of sand carried off by the tide.
So these disasters are nothing, Euphémie,
Compared to the amorous ecstasy
Of my steady soul. And soon, to shorten
The delay, I should certainly conclude
My marriage before any success
On either side puts obstacles in the way
Of the happiness that I expect
From one of my slaves.
EUPHÉMIE. Great God! What a speech! Ah! Forgive me, my lord,
I can only accept laws from my heart.
As long as you embitter it by this
Horrible way of doing things, how can
You hope that it will ever love you? In a
Fit of rage you will acquire a wife
Who could only see you through the eyes
Of horror!
(*Trying to pacify SELIM who is becoming irritated.*)
For a few days, suppress
So much impatience. On my behalf, open
Your heart to leniency. Its price will be
A nice reply.
SELIM. (*In an icy rage.*) I give you one hour.
And if, after this interval some traces
Of your scorn remain, no longer hope,
Madam, of obtaining any favors.
But it is not against you that my hate
Will act; it's not your heart my hand will strike.
No. To make my revenge more closely fit

The insult, someone else will feel the effects
Of my rage; and my furious arm,
Directing its blows, will be able, you'll see,
To lead them back to you.
EUPHÉMIE. What can be the object of such a threat?
Who could deserve it? Please explain yourself.
SELIM. Oh, don't presume, cruel woman, to abuse
Even longer a heart so jealous
With such piercing eyes. That unworthy
Christian whom my goodness tolerates
And allows you to see here as your brother:
I know that he isn't. That's the impostor
Whose spilled blood will pacify my rage.
EUPHÉMIE. (*Very passionately*.) No, Selim, you're mistaken.
SELIM. (*Very quickly*.) Well, come now, madam,
If he is not your lover, then become
My wife. Follow me. Everything's ready.
EUPHÉMIE. Try to deserve me.
SELIM. (*With cold and deliberate anger*.) I intend to fulfill
So great a duty, but by showing you
The object of your delight under
The terrifying machinery
Of the cruelest tortures. Seeing your eyes
Fastened on his sufferings, your tears
Overflowing in front of my eyes,
That's how I will earn the honor of this
Bond. I'll make you pine away to provoke
Your animosity,
And happy to acquire some feeling from you,
I will, at least, enjoy your horror for me. (*SELIM exits.*)
EUPHÉMIE. (*Alone*.) Heavens! Heavens, where am I? In what distress
He leaves me. Sad and baneful object of all
My affection, by loving you, I lose you.
By saving you, I die. There never was
A more appalling fate! Why, here he comes.
Good heavens! My heart, trembling with too much
Emotion, dares neither to long for, nor

To endure his presence.
(Azémar enters. This scene ought to move quickly.)
AZÉMAR. Oh, you whom
I idolize! Oh, dear and sacred object,
Let us take advantage of this day,
So long desired. Let's flee. Let's distance
Ourselves from that terrible tyrant.
Let's escape our bonds.
EUPHÉMIE. That is no longer
Possible. (*She is about to run away.*)
AZÉMAR. (*Stopping her.*) You're making me shiver.
Explain those tears to me.
EUPHÉMIE. If I love you,
You die; and if you live, I die.
AZÉMAR . Good heavens!
I understand!
EUPHÉMIE. Do you have any weapons
Left?
AZÉMAR. Absolutely!
EUPHÉMIE. Go and get them.
AZÉMAR. And why
These sudden fears when we can . . .
EUPHÉMIE. That villain!
I think that this hand, sooner or later,
Will destroy his vile scheme.
AZÉMAR. No. Don't
Expose yourself to that grievous danger.
I understand our troubles, but there is
Another way. We can escape from here,
You can be certain of it! An old man . . .
Honesty is painted in his eyes.
He has in his gaze, that fire, that nobility,
That spirit that interests me in you.
Nature has chosen, I think, to adorn
This Frenchman with your features in order
To win hearts on its behalf.
EUPHÉMIE. Where was
He born?

AZÉMAR. On the banks of the Seine. Ibrahim
Is his name, and it's easy to see that
He was born from blood made to be worthwhile.
Yet, he managed to renounce our laws;
He betrayed his God. His misery
Was the cause of it. Misfortune embitters
A man, and very often makes him liable
To take arms against whoever disturbs
His happiness. Renouncing his belief,
In such a case, is a mistake, but whatever
Incense the Almighty prefers, when virtue
Burns it, it has the right to please Him.
And if that mighty God wants a real worship,
His hand built its altar in the heart
Of the just man.
That wretched old man, bemoaning his life,
Was asking to return to the bosom
Of his native country. One never
Leaves it without eternal regret.
He managed to get some kind of access
Through a soldier, and as early as
Today he should be leaving for France.
He took me into his confidence
About his daring plan, offering both
Of us the chance to participate,
Without risking, he says, the slightest danger.
EUPHÉMIE. We cannot. Too many people are watching
Us. Let the old man's care reserve itself
For you alone. Go alone and leave me.
While you're in flight, I'll prevent anyone
Here from following your tracks. Go. Run.
Fly as soon as possible. Let nothing
Get in your way. At the very same moment,
Revitalize our soldiers at the breach.
Fight for your love, and to be worthy of her,
Dear friend, let your courage teach you to risk
Everything. Then I will become the price
Of your conquest. This plan fascinates me;

It fires my brain. Azémar, it adds to the
Cause—to the law—the law to serve France
That is so powerful in you. Consider,
My dear beloved, that by risking your life,
You're serving love and country at the same time.
Far from you, unable to take part
In your endeavors, to join in your success
As I did before, I'll have, at least . . .
I'll have, in my wretched bondage, the honor
Of being the prize offered your courage,
And of having achieved, through the gift
Of my faith, the laurels your commander
Promised to his king.
AZÉMAR. Beloved heroine!
Ah! Your thoughtfulness ever increases
The value of your tenderness. But I
Tremble too much about your fate here,
And I'd rather fight a hundred times
Before your very eyes. Let's flee. Let's flee
These walls. I beg you, in the name of love.
You'll serve your prince and country so much better
By returning with an arm still ready
To conquer.
EUPHÉMIE. Ah! You haven't guessed my glorious plan,
And you're only jealous.
AZÉMAR. Oh, God! Can I
Refrain from it when on you alone,
Alas, my happiness depends?
EUPHÉMIE. You win.
All right. I surrender to your wishes.
My sister is in these apartments and I'll
Run to tell her.
AZEEMAR. Your sister's in this harem?
EUPHÉMIE. Heaven brought her back to me.
AZÉMAR. You see
My soul is touched by this gift so dear. Ah!
Fly to find her and return immediately.
Above all, think, Euphémie, about the fate

That awaits us.
EUPHÉMIE. (*Trembling, indecisive.*) Azémar, I'm trembling.
AZÉMAR. Ah! What's bothering you?
EUPHÉMIE. Alas, my heart is broken when I leave you.
(*Trembling.*) What if the tyrant's hand clapped me in irons?
AZÉMAR. Ah, if he tried . . . no, nothing in the world
Could prevent me from crossing these walls.
His heart would answer to me for such an
Extreme offense, and led by love and hatred
Simultaneously, I would either
Carry you off, or lose my life.
EUPHÉMIE. No. Fear nothing, friend, when I adore you.
Heaven's watching out for what your lover craves.
Goodbye. (*She goes back into the harem.*)
AZÉMAR. (*Alone.*) What terror, then, has just dismayed her?
Ibrahim is coming. I have to put my
Mind at ease.
(IBRAHIM enters.)
IBRAHIM. (*Spiritedly.*) Everything is ready.
Let's hurry. That Asian poison, delectable
Ambrosia of the sons of Mohammed
Whose different effects on their rough minds
Either drives them mad or makes them drowsy,
Has overcome those soldiers without morals,
Without discipline. Let's take advantage
Of the opportunity.
AZÉMAR. What God
Causes you, oh, generous mortal,
To bring about my good fortune? Alas,
Forever, you bind my heart in chains.
At this very moment, Euphémie
Is on her way to meet us. How I fear
The delay she's causing us. Her sister
Is the excuse: she wants to take her
Away from the imperious yoke which could have
Dishonored her. Because of this delay,
I fear I'm giving up the hope of going
To the shores of France today. While she's

Carrying out such benevolent
Responsibilities, tell me, what fate
Brought you here? Our sorrows are appeased
By pitying those of others, and I'll
Forget my own to sympathize with yours.
IBRAHIM. Young man, you asked for it; then, listen to my
Misfortunes. But by learning about them,
Also discover my regrets. At age
Sixteen, I was serving in the army,
And already victory had seen me,
Under Harcourt in the fields of glory,
Share from time to time the harvests
Of laurels, with which that great man always
Surrounded his soldiers. When a preference,
Hardly deserved, for which my soul grieved
Secretly, for a long time, barring
My courage from taking a dangerous course,
Caused me to bring the qualities of Mars
To marriage. I thought I would find peace
In the bosom of my family.
A futile hope! Oh, my daughter! Oh, my daughter!
Was it by breaking the sweet bonds of your heart
That peace and happiness should have arisen
Within me?
AZÉMAR. (*Disturbed.*) You broke the bonds?
IBRAHIM. Ah, forgive
These tears. Foolish ambition aroused
My uneasiness. Its treacherous voice
Always knew full well how to mislead me.
Thinking I was becoming famous,
I brought shame upon myself. Unhappy
At court, out of revenge or resentment,
I wanted to serve against France.
Algiers was, at that time, at war with Louis,
And to make my extraordinary crimes
Even worse, defiling the sacred
Character of France, I took up arms
Against a king for whom my father died.

That is when I felt mortal despair
Spring up every day in the guilty heart
Of the deluded citizen who, in a
Blind rage, selfishly dared to give up
His country. As if the Almighty
Hadn't placed within his heart, the love
Of country as the most important virtue.
It took its revenge through my regrets.
All the most disgusting things possible
Were offered me by these horrible people.
I thought I could serve them, but they rejected
Me. I thought I could move them, but they
Detested me. Ah! Always, some vile stigma
Of contempt must become, alas! the only
Prize for betrayal. That Selim, that tyrant
Who causes your sorrows, has made me
Lament my fate more than any of them.
Often I wanted to flee; and my wife's tears,
Like sparks of fire permeating my soul,
Seemed, by burning it, to attract it
Every day toward those beloved tokens
Of our sad loves . . . toward those cherished fruits
Of our former rapture, whom my sinful
Weakness had caused me to abandon. Ever
Since that time, no pleasure soothed my sadness.
Everything proceeded to crush or tear
My heart to pieces. And the incredible
Power of those emotions, every day
Directing my eyes toward France, proved to me
That there's nothing but misery for a man
When he's betrayed his God, his king, and country!
AZÉMAR. Ah! I am deeply grateful to you for this
Sincere confession; but your repentance
Is too ardent, father, not to have
Already appeased the wrath of a God
So merciful and tender a long time ago.
What's your name?
IBRAHIM. I still must keep it a secret.

You may believe, however, that this name
Both honors me and is a credit to me.
But let's leave some details incomplete
For the moment. I will reveal them
When the time comes.
(*A loud noise is made in the direction of the port.*)
God! What did I just hear? Ah! The watch
Is waking up. I judge from the sounds striking
My ear that we have delayed too long.
Make them hurry, my son, and as for me,
I'm going to discover the cause
Of this commotion. *(IBRAHIM leaves.)*
AZÉMAR. Why has that story caused confusing
Emotions which I can't control to rise up
In my soul? The persecuted man
Always deludes himself with so much skill!
But I haven't a clue about this awful
Delay! What could Euphémie be doing
In this time of danger? Ah! I think
I can still see her fear and her tears.
Who's approaching? Surely it's her sister.
(Enter CONSTANCE.)
Ah, God! What kind of trouble am I in?
Madame, at this moment, are you coming
To reduce or increase our afflictions?
Have the chains of the one I adore
Been severed?
CONSTANCE. Noble blood of the Melun
Where I have drawn life, you must appeal
To your most steadfast courage. We cannot
Follow you. Alas! We're being watched.
Alone, avail yourself of the relief
Fate intends for you, and return, my lord,
Weapons in hand, to carry your Euphémie
Away from that inhuman monster.
AZÉMAR. (*In the utmost distress.*) I was
Born unlucky. I knew it, Madame.
Born for all the sorrows which tear a heart

To pieces,
But I'll swear to you, I didn't think
That heaven would torment me to this degree.
(*In despair.*) If the tie that binds us and my dreadful
Grief can make you generous on my behalf,
Go, right now, and let your sister know
That nothing can pacify my torment
And my sorrow; that I cannot leave
Without you and without her. And that
In order to end your cruel punishment
(Alas! I want to), I must shed all my blood
Here, to take you away from that villain,
Or run him through.
CONSTANCE. You add to our misfortunes
By your opposition. Go. Someone
Is waiting for you. And the vile vengeance
Of the tyrant whose anger your eyes inflame
Will come down again upon each one of us
Any moment now. Go, my lord, go,
And return to convince us that there is
No danger you cannot overcome
When your prize is Euphémie and her sister.
AZÉMAR. (*Confusion and passion.*)
Ah! Far from tempering my resentment
You're aggravating it. And I think I
Understand you. Yes, that hurriedness,
That fervent prayer, that uneasiness,
That insulting desire to drive me away
From here, I understand it all, Madame,
It's all very clear to me. Selim
Is less frightening than Euphémie says;
He knew how to triumph over his proud
Enemy, and while I'm here venting
My sorrow unsuccessfully, he's earning
The heart of my deceitful lover. Well!
Let her adore him! I consent, Madame.
Yes. Yes.
Let her have both his passion and his hand.

Never will my incensed heart regret it!
I don't imagine I'd have any regret;
One day, if it burst forth, or I retraced
The detestable tale of this event
In my memory, it would force
Its arrogance even more successfully
To smash the altars of a hated cult,
A cult that I renounce, and that her cruel
Hand itself worships through the bond it is
Preparing. Believe me,
I could imagine creating these bonds
So sweet, without complaint, without sorrow,
And particularly without anger.
I adore her and hate her, I condemn her
And forgive her. One after the other,
I pity her, defend her, and blame her.
Forgive my condition . . . but if it can
Appeal to you, go on my behalf
And drag her out of the arms of my rival.
(In tears, he throws himself at CONSTANCE's feet.)
If you refuse to grant this supreme favor,
I'll kill myself before your very eyes.
(*Seeing EUPHÉMIE enter.*) Oh, heavens! It's her.
AZÉMAR. (*Rushing toward EUPHÉMIE.*)
Ah! What kept you in that deadly abode?
EUPHÉMIE. (*Spiritedly.*) Your interest, mine, and that of our love.
You wish it, I'm going with you, but your
Death is certain; nothing can save you
From the inhuman rage of that jealous
Tyrant if we don't escape.
AZÉMAR. We must
Hurry, without losing a single moment.
(*Anxiously looking all around.*)
But Ibrahim! Oh! Heavens! He's supposed
To come back here. Without him, without
His help, what could I attempt to do?
He alone arranged for the small boat

That's waiting for us, and if he does not
Appear, we'll flee in vain.
EUPHÉMIE. (*Very disturbed.*) He's not important.
Let's hurry. Follow us, oh, my Constance!
(*AZÉMAR clasps one of his arms around EUPHÉMIE's waist and they go off left, that is, in the direction of the port. CONSTANCE follows them. Enter SELIM, and groups of Eunuchs and Slaves. These two scenes should proceed with the utmost speed.*)
SELIM. (*Furious with his slaves.*) Punish her guilty impertinence
Immediately and stop the effects
Of their betrayal!
(*Forcefully, the slaves pull EUPHÉMIE from the arms of AZÉMAR, and they restrain him in such a way as to prevent him from using his hands. He is returned in this condition.*)
EUPHÉMIE. (*Fainting into CONSTANCE's arms.*) I'm dying!
SELIM. Wretched
Creature! What were your plans?
AZÉMAR. (*Surrounded by slaves, but less restrained by them.*)
To carry Euphémie away from your
Unholy passion: to avenge, all at once,
Love and nature, God, my religion,
My country and my honor.
(*After a short pause.*) I abhor life.
Strike me. Strike without fear!
EUPHÉMIE. (*To AZÉMAR.*) Ah! Don't provoke
Him. He holds all the power over your life!
AZÉMAR. Could I want to preserve it for myself
When these loathsome days would be no more
For you?
SELIM. (*Grabbing his sword. To AZÉMAR.*)
I'm going to satisfy you.
(*To EUPHÉMIE.*) Give me your pledge, Madame, and swear
That, at that very moment, you'll consent
To my excessive love.
EUPHÉMIE. (*Throwing herself at the Dey's feet.*) You win, Selim.
I'm on my knees before you. Spare Azémar,
And my hand is yours.

AZÉMAR. (*Boldly. To EUPHÉMIE.*) Oh, heavens! What are you
Doing? (*To SELIM.*) Tyrant, I am freeing her.
Dare to run me through. Dare to gratify
Your rage, but surrender all claims to her hand.
You'll never possess it!
(*With one hand held by EUPHÉMIE at his feet, SELIM makes a movement with the other in an attempt to stab AZÉMAR. The movement is interrupted by the catastrophe which happens unexpectedly.*)
IBRAHIM. (*Running at the head of the French troops in order to hurl himself at SELIM, he stops. Seeing the tyrant's sword on AZÉMAR 's breast, he says spiritedly to SELIM.*)
Monster, don't complete your horrid crimes!
Melun's going to punish them; he's just
Been informed of them. Tremble for your
Subjects and see your city in ashes!
(*A shower of bombs, launched from the French ships that are in the harbor, flies through the air, swoops down upon the city and destroys the buildings. Meanwhile, SELIM, who is in a fit of rage, seizes the two women, brings them close to AZÉMAR, causing them to be restrained by the eunuchs who previously seized the young man.*)
SELIM. (*Passionately, to IBRAHIM.*)
You have betrayed me, treacherous one,
And your vile race must answer to me here
For the fate that threatens me. Before
Your eyes, this steel is going to tear their sides
To shreds.
IBRAHIM. (*In despair.*) Stop your blows, barbarian!
They're killing my children.
AZÉMAR. (*Surprised.*) Oh, heavens!
(*A second shower of bombs succeeds in annihilating the city. The two women have fainted in the arms of the slaves.*)
SELIM. (*Rapidly to IBRAHIM.*) Calm the horrible effect of those
Volcanoes whose fire desolates us
Or my hand slays them. (*He is about to strike them.*)

IBRAHIM. (*Retreating with his troops toward the edge of the gardens, and raising his hands and his voice toward the fleet.*) Stop, my friends, stop! Good heavens! You're thrusting
A sword into my paternal breast.
(*At that moment, a company of African soldiers with an officer at its head enters hurriedly from the interior of the city.*)
OFFICER. (*Spiritedly to the Dey.*) Come fight, Selim.
(*Rushing to the head of this company, SELIM rids himself of the three captives who remain, nevertheless, in the hands of the slaves.*)
SELIM. Oh, rescued in the nick
Of time!
(*To IBRAHIM who is rallying the French troops and who is opposite the Algerians.*)
Approach now, you fearsome enemy;
Come, I'm no longer afraid of you.
(*The two companies charge one another vehemently. But as soon as the fighting begins, luck deserts the Dey and IBRAHIM seizes the day; and running hurriedly toward the captives with a few soldiers, he releases them. Then everyone runs off at the same time: the slaves who were restraining the prisoners as well as the company of African soldiers which the French detachment is driving into the city. The firing from the ships has ceased.*)
AZÉMAR. (*As soon as he is free, to IBRAHIM.*) Venerable old man, what mighty God
Guides you?
IBRAHIM. Oh, my dear Azémar, soon you
Will know everything. Look at that uproar.
(*Then the French crowd into the city and repel the Algerians who throw themselves haphazardly into the ruins where the king's troops are following them.*)
The *fleur de lis* at last is an insult
To the Turkish standard battered down!
Friends, the city is taken!
(*To the two women.*) And you,
Touching objects, Melun's nieces, you're my
Children. Embrace your father.
EUPHÉMIE. (*Throwing herself into IBRAHIM's arms.*) Oh, moment
Full of charms!

CONSTANCE. (*At the same time as her sister, and falling at IBRAHIM's feet.*)
How many times for you
Have our tears flowed!
AZÉMAR. (*Very quickly.*) You their father? Oh, good
Fortune! What a happy day for us!
The Eternal Being finally brings you
Into harmony with our desires!
IBRAHIM. (*Very emotionally.*) Ah! Receive from my hands, the object
Of your affection.
(*He joins EUPHÉMIE with her lover; then, to his two children and to AZÉMAR.*)
Thus I can make amends
For the sins of my youth.
AZÉMAR. Your children's love
Will comfort you.
IBRAHIM. Let's go find Melun. And let's
Gather for him the objects that he
Impatiently desires and mix some flowers
With the laurels of France.
(*At that moment, MELUN, leading the officers of the squadron, lands on the shore. He walks in front of his family, and there is a moment of recognition. While this group exits toward the city, a large group of women, lightly restrained by the French soldiers come out and perform a ballet that ends the play.*)

(*MR. DESCLAPON's study immediately comes into view again; the following background scenes are played there. It is absolutely necessary to remember that the entr'acte occurs only after the background scenes. At that time, the curtain is lowered to prepare for the setting of the play that follows, and it is only there that the orchestra is heard.*)

CONTINUATION OF THE MARRIAGE OF THE ARTS

DESCLAPON. Sir, you must be pleased with my daughter.
BELVAL. Certainly, sir. No one could show greater talent. And did the play suit you?
DESCLAPON. I like your Ibrahim a lot, he's a gentleman, a good Frenchman. If he's made a mistake, he's corrected it and that's how I like people to be.
BELVAL. There's no doubt about it, sir, that's how everybody should behave. Ibrahim had taken false measures to attain his own happiness and his children's bliss; he had been led astray by the false principles of ambition. He repents; he gives his daughter to the lover she adores. Oh! you're right, sir. That's how all fathers should act.
VIEUXBLANC. Right, right. That's the moral of the play. When you arrange the events, it's very simple for them to come out the way you want them to. (*To BELVAL.*) What are you going to do for us now?
BELVAL. (*Staring boldly at VIEUXBLANC.*) *The Dangerous Man*, sir, a character comedy in one act, and in verse. I take the liberty of asking you to be somewhat attentive to this piece.
VIEUXBLANC. (*Awkwardly.*) Certainly that character offers something.
BELVAL. Some truths, sir. Some truths.
VIEUXBLANC. Well, yes, but all of that doesn't seem to me to be entirely appropriate for a celebration.
BELVAL. Full of people who'll perhaps think in a completely different way.
DESCLAPON. The gentleman makes a lot of sense! I think we should hear his play.
BELVAL. (*Referring to VIEUXBLANC.*) I'm disappointed that the gentleman won't be able to play the leading role.
VIEUXBLANC. Oh! I don't have a good enough memory; that would be too long to learn.

DESCLAPON. Yes, yes, we'll be glad to give you the utmost attention, and my daughter will play . . .
BELVAL. The victim. I mean to say the sweetheart and I'm the lover, as timid as he is star-crossed in his claims.
(MARTON enters.)
MARTON. Come on, gentlemen, they're getting impatient. Can't you hear the stomping and the canes? And they haven't even started dressing.
ÉMILIE. Oh, God! I'm on my way. Marton, you'll rehearse with me while I'm getting dressed.
MARTON. Yes, yes. Let's hurry. I'm right behind you.
(*ÉMILIE gets away; VIEUXBLANC gives her his hand.*)
MARTON. (*To BELVAL.*) Well, how far did you get?
BELVAL. To the best of all the lessons. Listen to my play, and you be the judge of the effect it should produce. (*They exit.*)

ORCHESTRA

(*Only at this point does the entr'acte occur. The curtain is lowered and the stage is set up for the following episode.*)

SECOND EPISODE OF THE MARRIAGE OF THE ARTS

THE DANGEROUS MAN[34]

Verse Comedy in One Act

CHARACTERS

Count Saint-Fal, *the dangerous man*[35]
Mr. Pontac
Florival (Belval), *Adelaide's lover*
Adélaide (Émilie), *Mr. Pontac's daughter*
Darneuil, *Florival's friend*
Dubois, *Count Saint-Fal's servant*
A Messenger, *dressed in a chestnut brown cloak*
Servants

(*The action takes place in Paris, in a townhouse shared by Count Saint-Fal and Mr. Pontac. The stage reveals a drawing room, at the back of which the audience should see the door to Mr. Pontac's apartment. It is eight o'clock at night.)*

DUBOIS. Really, I don't understand you anymore!
For two months, like a hermit, like a recluse,
You've confined your conquests to this town house.
My lord Count! It is, I fear, some new trap
That you're setting, even though this respite
Seems to put my doubts to rest.
SAINT-FAL. No, it's done, Dubois; I'm infatuated.
And the beauty so titillating and so lively

[34] The title, *The False Friend*, was erased by Sade.

[35] "The false friend" was erased by Sade.

That happened to lead me into these surroundings
Enchains me, in short, to her feminine charms.
(*Acting benevolently.*) But if my soul is delighted with this project,
It's because I'm able to reward the pains
And trouble you take on behalf of my desire.
DUBOIS. Sir, sir, let's put my needs aside;
My only need is to be useful to you.
SAINT-FAL. Oh, no, honestly, there isn't anywhere
In this city, a servant more punctual,
More thrifty and more indispensable.
Don't blush, I'm saying what I think.
It's time, then, for me to reward you.
Here's how it's done: I want to give you
A pretty little future, at least until your death,
By marrying you off. Yes, really, married life
Seems to me to be suited to your inclinations,
To your age. I can see you already in your house,
Managed peacefully by your serious and sensible mind,
Making everyone who surrounds you happy,
Because of the cheerfulness prosperity gives us,
Playing host to me four times every year,
And bringing me your children in your arms.
(*Phlegmatically.*) What's bothering you?
DUBOIS. Yes, truly, sir, I swear to you,
These details so lovely in nature,
And so movingly portrayed by you
Have really touched me, very much.
Be that as it may, sir, what can I do
To serve you in the new affair
That manages, at last, to plant you here?
For, if you have the generous desire
To make me happy, it's really necessary
For me to spend my life in your service as well.
What is the subject of this new plan?
SAINT-FAL. Listen to me: here it is in three words.
The old man, Pontac, whose daughter I adore,
Just inherited a large family estate
Which, luckily, caused a legacy to go to him,

For he is poor and in despair.
That wretched man whom misery draws near
Falls for sure, if, through some difficulty,
This inheritance gets away from him.
(*Mysteriously, and with a malicious attitude.*)
Now, I have more than two hundred affidavits,
And an enormous trunk of documents
That are going to prove that this property
Which was left to him,
Should more properly belong to someone else.
(*Softly, and laughing malevolently.*)
And meanwhile, the whole business is a sham!
Everything absolutely, justifiably belongs to him,
And this is only a clever trick I use,
Along with the help of some handwriting experts,
To reach my goals quickly.
DUBOIS. Very well, sir. And your soul's not completely
Healed then from deceit!
SAINT-FAL. Ah! Is a person cured of his oddities that way?
You have to cling to nature, my friend;
When it stamps a particular character on us,
We have to yield, divert our thoughts, and keep quiet.
DUBOIS. But where will this lead us?
Seeing you thrash about like that,
Will the old fogey you hold in your fist
Release his beloved Adélaide ?
SAINT-FAL. Poor Dubois, I see with regret
That you're making little progress in my art.
It's by striking the most sensible blow
That a person draws nearer his goal,
And it's by striking the most sensible blow
That it's possible to achieve your objective
In the most skillful way.
Dear Pontac is absolutely unaware
That I have anything to do with his estates;
And the resources that I have in my power,
The secret route, in a word, that I'm taking,
Is unknown to Pontac and his people.

In order to blind him to the fact,
I pity him, I comfort him,
I promise him the use of my credit.
He respects me, and my perverse mind
Forces him to worship me
While I'm putting him in irons!
I have coerced him into talking about a marriage:
I have his word on it,
And without a lot of prompting on my part.
DUBOIS. In that case, sir, why defraud him,
Rob him of his estate, and drive him to despair?
I still can't see what you're up to in all of this.
Would you please inform me more fully?
SAINT-FAL. It's that the girl adores someone named Florival—
A very fine young man, truthful, a real clown!—
To whom Pontac had already promised her.
If they have the estate, the operation's finished,
Considering that, in this case,
They strongly agree with one another.
If they don't have the estate,
The young man will be wrong for her.
They'll go looking for a richer suitor,
And at that very moment,
Florival will be out of the picture.
Now, that being the case,
You know, of course, the husband who is perfect
For them is me. I fit them to a T!
DUBOIS. But if you're going to all the trouble
To get married, why, sir, steal their fortune?
That's what I always come back to;
That, sir, doesn't make any sense to me.
SAINT-FAL. Now I'm beginning to understand
That your mind could never follow me.
You know very well I like your opinion,
Although it's shrewd, scrupulous, and sharp,
And I've seldom seen another servant like you.
DUBOIS. When you praise me, you make me feel guilty.
I'm beginning to see that that's your goal.

SAINT-FAL. You know me!
(*Mysteriously*.) Listen, tonight, skillfully,
Intelligently, at my request,
Get six horses ready to take wing
Swiftly toward the German borders.
DUBOIS. (*Dumbfounded*.) You're running off with her?
SAINT-FAL. (*With the utmost composure*.) You third-rate rogue!
The slightest thing amazes you, and when
Someone behaves differently than the rest
Of the fools, all is lost!
DUBOIS. Good heavens! What atrocities!
SAINT-FAL. I deceive the entire
Family, all at the same time. Secretly,
I'm given the daughter, and I get
Into Pontac's family quietly.
On the one hand, manipulating the plans
Of both the lover and his intended,
I make the pretty ingénue believe
That they're going to make her enter a convent,
Ruthlessly, against her will,
To suffocate the love that occupies her.
And Florival, of whom I love to make
A fool, to him I said that it was good
To use a little deception to get
Together with the sweet object of his
Tender desire. He feels certain that the
Methods I'm using are only intended
To give him back that lovely child, whom I
Am kidnapping today. Besides, he thinks,
Because I've been talking him into it,
That I'm going to arrange a marriage
Between myself and his sister, Alciméade.
I'm deliberately spreading it
Around here. Following that, nobody
Stands in my way. I act in the open,
Without any trouble; and through my skill,
Submissive to my plans, my watchdogs
Become my friends. Our two lovers are

Intoxicated with their good fortune,
And fearlessly, entrust themselves into
My arms. And that, my dear fellow, is how
With some intelligence, serious skill
Combines, to some advantage, the lucky
Talent for inventing things with slander!
A skillful man will always know how to
Charm and take control of all the fools
You find down here, without a lot of trouble!
DUBOIS. I hardly understand this pretty talk,
For, in a word, seeing that her father
Has promised you what you desire, what's the
Purpose of the flight you are preparing?
SAINT-FAL. Poor Dubois! Oh, well, I give up!
The objection doesn't merit a reply.
I'm keeping my mouth shut.
DUBOIS. (*After a moment of thought; looking pitiful.*)
Sir, I hear you.
The state of matrimony doesn't suit you.
Marriage is a legitimate bond.
SAINT-FAL. (*Interrupting.*) Which in itself is nothing that I value.
DUBOIS. (*Interrupting.*) Yes, your mind would have nothing to feed on;
It needs agony to satisfy it.
But with you away, the old man'll blab.
SAINT-FAL. No, no, I shut him up, since by leaving
I put back into proportion the means
That I was holding tight to bias his mind!
No more lawsuit, and the estate stays free.
Pontac wins, and you'll agree with me,
That twelve thousand ducats[36] every year
Do more good at the center of a family
Than the wisest and prettiest daughter.
DUBOIS. Everyone, sir, doesn't think that way.
Honor still has some temples here. Myself,
I say that, in a similar venture,

[36] The ducat was the standard European monetary unit until 1857. A single ducat was worth around $45.00 in 2012 US currency.

Nature would triumph over selfishness.
SAINT-FAL. Oh! It's well known that honor always had
Unassailable rights among the Dubois!
And that's as it should be. Myself, I think
The same way.
DUBOIS. It shows in your nice behavior.
SAINT-FAL. Most certainly. All right! Be very discreet
And have everything ready here tonight.
DUBOIS. If you wanted . . .
SAINT-FAL. (*Interrupting*.) A little reprimand . . .
Isn't that right? Don't you know in advance
That you'll get nowhere preaching at me.
Leave me, then, to my holy design.
It gives me joy, and your sweet wisdom,
Smothering the warmth of my enthusiasm,
Would doubtlessly be a disadvantage
To the project, dear Dubois, which, under
The circumstances, makes you rich forever.
DUBOIS. Ah! You have such a splendid talent.
So shrewdly do you disguise the abyss,
That a person would go all the way
To hell with you!
SAINT-FAL. Here comes Pontac. That's all.
Leave us.
SAINT-FAL. (*Taking a step toward PONTAC who is entering*.)
Ah! Dear Pontac, I was just on my way
To your door. How's everybody doing?
PONTAC. (*Sadly*.) My daughter's better; that lawsuit I'm losing
Has become a terrible setback
For her. The certainty of belonging to
The object of her sweet expectations
Vanishes with that property.
Her heart is tender. She loved Florival.
He worshipped her. It's a fatal blow.
SAINT-FAL. I feel it, indeed, and it is not
Without any difficulty that I see
That bond breaking today. In fact, if you
Don't have anything against me, I'm pleased

To bind myself to you without objection.
But, in this situation, Adélaide
Should agree reluctantly to give
Me her hand. My heart is sincere. It is
Sensitive, kind. And the sweet words that duty
Allows are a small price to pay for her
Tenderness. Think about it.
PONTAC. (*Eagerly.*) Oh! No, no,
Dear Saint-Fal. When you alone relieve
Our sorrow . . . when you express the emotion
And the love for Adélaide that guides you
All the way to wanting to make up
For her misfortunes, will I be opposed
To such great favors? In time, her tears will dry.
You're cut out to calm her apprehensions,
Whoever the husband was to whom
She might have promised herself, within your arms,
She must forget him.
SAINT-FAL. (*Pretending to be gullible.*) Certainly, my only
Concentration will always be to
Anticipate precisely her slightest
Wishes. Between us, our most sacred pleasures
Will be to please the venerable mortal
Who overwhelms us with prosperity
And property.
PONTAC. (*Sadly.*) Property! Oh! No, for I am ruined.
SAINT-FAL. Giving her to me, ah! You've given me
The most invaluable of all properties.
Doesn't she have your pleasant innocence,
Your virtue, your sincerity? To my heart,
She's a goddess! But are you thinking, sir,
About the injustice, alas! The pinnacle
Of fraud and deception that is causing
You to lose, in this matter, a lawsuit
That's indisputable, and so well explained.
At least, I said, out of the entire
World, either the court or ministry
Will remember so much integrity,

A likeable man, full of courtesy,
An old servant who, from his tender youth,
Demonstrated bravery in battle,
And who devoted his rest, ever since,
To discovering and relieving sorrows;
Friend of the arts and filled with eloquence,
A man, in a word, so original
That France, a country teeming with people,
Perhaps, couldn't come up with another
Like him today. I said it, I repeated
It continuously; and everywhere,
I confess, I found your friends, or made you friends.
But, good heavens! What an awful country!
They don't value wit or merit there.
By means of false appearances, a rascal
Gets ahead, and supported by his lies,
Proceeds to drive out men of brilliant merit.
PONTAC. Nothing is more certain, and I am
The victim of it. Almost always now,
If it is skillful and steady, crime
Shamelessly devours virtue. Really,
I'm becoming a misanthrope because
Of it!
SAINT-FAL. (*In the most open and honest manner.*)
Skillfully, the evil-doer
Veils himself, and knowing the need for virtue,
Carefully adorns himself with it
More than anything else. Frank and loyal,
The honest man thinks he can be believed
Simply by the look on his face. The scoundrel
Cheats, he bribes, he charms, he impresses
People, and in that way, he's successful,
While the other, sparing of his pains,
Languishes and dies amidst his chains.
Ah! As I was saying. Certainly
You remember that it's very important
For Adélaide not to know about
The arrangement with which you've honored me

For some time.
Indeed, you know the sensitivity
Of that troubled heart has to be eased.
(*Mysteriously.*) That's the reason I'm convincing people
Here about my marriage to Alciméade.
My friend, if Florival were to speak to you
About it, tell him that, indeed, I am
Considering the idea; that most certainly
It delights and fascinates me; that the
Only thing in all of this that troubles
Me, is the delay. And about your daughter:
Cleverly you have to sound her out
About your fear of not having more than
The choice of pensions to leave her, because
Of the unfortunate situation
You're put in by all the trouble of the
Lawsuit. In this horrible crisis,
My only desire, as you know,
Is to make her happy, and together
With her sweet personality, to look
After you forever.
PONTAC. Ah! My dear Count,
I approve of all of this. You know
That already. I'm planning on it.
SAINT-FAL. (*Cunningly.*) Then why so much hesitation to get
It done? Under these circumstances,
Do you think you can make her accept
The appropriate plan without the convent?
Ah! Trust me. Decide to cloister her.
Too confidant of your rare benevolence,
Too certain, in a word, of so many
Of your qualities, she proclaims to
Whomever wants to listen that you have a
Heart much too tender to force her to give up
Florival. That remark cannot be
Insignificant to me.
You understand that as soon as it exists,
I quite simply must insist that you

Put her in safe keeping for a little
While.
PONTAC. Would my daughter be so bold?
SAINT-FAL. (*As if he is letting what follows escape against his will.*)
She's said
Some other things I wouldn't dare repeat.
PONTAC. (*Provoked.*) What else then? Why, you have to tell me.
SAINT-FAL. (*As if uneasy, and mysteriously.*) There were
Some plans made about leaving you, about
Escaping, about shutting herself up
At her relatives' who soon, she claims,
Will force you to end the quarrel by marrying
Her, without delay, to the young man
Who delights her every inclination.
"My father's good," she says, "he's flexible."
(*Maliciously.*) "You understand me, he's not capable
Of making a firm decision or having
A steady opinion."
PONTAC. (*Very angry.*) What the devil? The brazen hussy claims . . .
SAINT-FAL. (*Interrupting him.*) Great! Anger and resentment!
I should have
Tried harder to keep my mouth shut.
Don't go and dishearten the dear child.
PONTAC. I still must be respected.
SAINT-FAL. Amen. But be especially careful
Not to tell her who the person is
Who just informed you; for you must bear in mind,
My friend, that I have love and honor to deal with
At the same time.
PONTAC. Have no fear. I'll keep
The secret. I'm going to complain exquisitely.
I don't like to be considered so good.
SAINT-FAL. Ah! Why, truly, you're absolutely right.
Almost always, sir, no matter what they
Say, these feelings . . .

PONTAC. Are nonsense. I know it well.
Ah! Ah! The dear child. Tomorrow, tomorrow,
You'll go into the convent and we'll see
If that solitude will give rise in you
To a little uneasiness about
Those acts of kindness of which you have no doubt.
(*Very hot tempered.*) Goodbye, my friend, I'm going off at once
To reprimand Adélaide properly,
To speak to her firmly, and when everything
Is settled, don't worry, I will have served
My heart by swiftly making you happy.
SAINT-FAL. My dear Pontac, above all, don't be angry.
PONTAC. No, my friend, no. Leave it to me.
(*Still very excited.*) Without
Getting angry and with no fit of passion,
I'll tell her to follow me to the convent! (*He exits.*)
SAINT-FAL. (*Alone.*) There's my man, right where I wanted him!
A fool can hardly defend himself
From the clever trap of the hand that moves him.
A little flattery gets you everywhere!
Florival's a little more persistent.
Ah! If I were in his place, maybe,
Like him, I'd want to be enlightened too.
But I see him; he seems horror-stricken.
(FLORIVAL enters.)
FLORIVAL. (*A little forced.*)
My dear Saint-Fal, I'm coming to thank you.
Your heart delights in being kind to me;
You revel in the service of your friends.
SAINT-FAL. (*Fondly.*) All my happiness is in succeeding.
But I deserve very little from you;
Your friendship rewards me quite sufficiently.
Who wouldn't take the keenest interest in such
Pure marriage bonds, which Pontac forbids you!
Right here, for an hour, with all my might,
I fought against his silly resistance;
I tried everything but to no avail.
He says he thinks you're forward,

And since he cannot grant you his daughter,
From this moment on, you finally have to
Withdraw from the bosom of her family,
And that today, you have to leave us.
FLORIVAL. Stopping is hard, and so much the more acute
Since Adélaide is still inflexible
About the option you've suggested to her.
SAINT-FAL. (*Pretending the utmost indifference.*)
I pity you a lot if you refuse it;
Because of the grief that beats him down
And overwhelms him, Pontac seems to me
Quite capable of demanding more
Than a stop-off in a convent.
FLORIVAL. (*Disturbed.*)
What does he intend? What new torture?
SAINT-FAL. If, by chance, he's afraid of violence,
To shatter the plans for your marriage most
Successfully, who says he wouldn't force
Adélaide to take the vows?
FLORIVAL. Adélaide, to be so frail!
I'm responsible for her and know her tenderness.
Wouldn't she consider the rack less deadly
Than taking vows?
SAINT-FAL. (*Phrased very cleverly.*)
Ah! Believe me, her soul
Is weak and gentle; it fears the jolt
Of misfortune. To avoid scenes of
Brutality, it will bow beneath the yoke
Of misery. Away from her, and reduced,
In a word, only to writing her
Occasionally, you would nourish
Your passion by this means, three months, six months,
A year perhaps, or two. Corrupt people
Will intervene: they'll cause trouble, they'll
Prevent you from contacting one another.
They'll tell her that you finally accept
The situation; that you think it's good,
And that you promise to let her obey

Her father. And then, to you, they'll say
She's happy in the monastery, that she
Wants to cloister herself there, that all
Is said and done, and you have to forget her . . .
That she's even the first to insist on it!
Oh! You know everything people can do,
Everything they do, whether they like it
Or not, when time passes and they're separated.
Powerful superiors will maybe
Intercede, and the remorse for having
Killed the master, for eluding all those
Enemies, and for having been able
Without so many worries, to become
Happy through the intervention of a
Reliable friend who favors you,
Will succeed in making you drink the cup
Of misfortune, madly, in large gulps.
Forgive what I say. Blame it on my
Sincere devotion; I would be cold if I
Were less faithful to the feelings I have
Sworn to you.
FLORIVAL. (*Nearly exhausted.*)
Ah! Dear Saint-Fal, my heart
Is convinced. It's troubled by those horrors
And it's frightened. I'm going to see her.
Should I not try, once more, to conquer her dark
Premonitions?
SAINT-FAL. (*With some surprise.*)
What are they based on?
And what feelings between us, dear Florival,
Does she question? Yet, everything proves
My devotion to her.
FLORIVAL. (*Still a little forced.*)
But she doesn't know where you're taking her.
SAINT-FAL. (*With the simplest, most natural expression.*)
To her relatives as you well know.
It's actually my sister's house, but wisely,
She shouldn't seem to be in collusion

With us until the moment we arrive.
Undoubtedly, we will disguise ourselves,
And before the outcome you would go
To ask her about our plan of action
And she would tell you quite correctly not to
Be suspicious of any of this.
If you could be successful on your own,
Without any deception, I'd tell you
To take her yourself! But then do you
Want this to be treated as a planned
Attack? If you fear for your life in any
Way, be more careful. Forgive my complaint,
But condescend to place at least a little
Value on those who are your true and sincere
Friends.
FLORIVAL. (*As before.*) What do you want? I'm describing
The figments of her imagination
For you. Terrified of secrecy,
Her young mind doesn't understand that you
Cannot succeed if the secret happens
To be discovered.
SAINT-FAL. (*Annoyed, but still composed.*)
Really! My dear, I think
I understand you perfectly, and we're
Wrong when we want to become useful
To people who are suspicious of our hearts.
FLORIVAL. (*With contained passion.*)
Saint-Fal, oh, heavens! How mistaken you are!
Aren't there other ways for you to profit
Here? And soon, my dear Count, aren't you marrying
My sister?
SAINT-FAL. (*Coldly.*) Those bonds undoubtedly have a thousand
Charms for us.
FLORIVAL. (*Continuing with spirit.*)
Then those suspicions wrong us
All. Ah! My friend, I know that deception
Is a long way from entering your heart.

SAINT-FAL. (*Completely disinterested.*)
I want to believe that. And to show you
Better that the only objective
That guides me in all of this is to be
Of use to your Adélaide, to serve you
And do you some good, I'm breaking it off,
And listening to no more of this.
Supporting you in such an endeavor
Was undoubtedly a very stupid
Thing to do. I don't want to make mistakes
Like that; they terrify me, and I'm afraid
Of regretting them. Let's never speak
Of it again, I pray you. You've cleared
Things up for me. I thank you for it.
FLORIVAL. (*With more warmth, he is beginning to be won over.*)
Ah! My friend, don't drive me to despair.
SAINT-FAL. (*As before.*) No, Florival, one day you will learn
Whether I was meant for your distrust;
Your repentance will suffice for my
Revenge. All friends are not alike, that's true.
But in my situation, I deserved
A somewhat special treatment. Let there be
An end to it! It's just foolishness!
I knew very well what I was getting
Myself into. At my age, should someone
Involve himself indiscriminately
In activities such as this? No. People
Get in trouble over things like this.
I knew that. So, let's stop it right here!
FLORIVAL. You distress me saying all of that.
(*All the fire of passion.*)
What? Close to port, you would have the courage
To toss us cruelly onto a sinking ship?
That way you'd lose Adélaide and me.
For, at the moment I give you my trust
To steal her away, even from her father,
To carry her to the ends of the earth,
Must I, alas, to atone for my mistake

Die the most dismal death? I idolize her.
She is my existence, my good fortune,
My dearest hope. And to have her, I'm ready
To suffer all the misery that will
Come my way.
SAINT-FAL. Then I surrender to this effervescence.
My heart is weak and always undefended
When someone attacks it with sentiment.
You know that, my tender and charming friend.
Go see her. Go persuade her quickly
To get over everything so we
Can be successful; and tell her to come
Immediately to have a word with me
In this apartment. I want to destroy
The useless worries that her soul is storing
In her gullible mind. Especially
Be careful that Pontac, who's anxious,
Doesn't hear about our daring plan.
FLORIVAL. Adélaide will be here right away.
You can become her master, now, and like
We said, get everything ready for
Tonight, without fuss and without ado.
Ah! Allow me to embrace you now.
(*With ecstasy*.) May my heart thank you a thousand times!
Goodbye, dear Count, goodbye. Look at my tears,
And forgive my reprehensible fears.
SAINT-FAL. (*Alone, with a malevolent joy*.)
He couldn't hide his distress from me.
I'm flattered by it. I like it when people
Recognize me.
They value me when they're convinced that I
Don't have the unnecessary virtue
Of self-sacrifice at the expense
Of my passion. Ah! How he loves her!
And how his young soul passionately
Revealed itself here! Well! Sir, I too
Worship her, and before too long we'll see,
I think, which of the two of us should have

The ability, through greater skill,
Or from more tender vows, to subject her
To the power of his passions.
DUBOIS. *(Entering, looking like a messenger, mysteriously.)*
In haste, here, I come to let you know
That everything is done. When you see three
Or four torches shining over there,
Across from us, both servants and horses
Will be ready.
(*Uneasy.*) But what kind of depressing
Individual was that, who just
Offended me, a little while ago?
He is wearing a chestnut brown coat,
A big hat, and quite the look of a scoundrel.
If he runs into me, he watches my
Expression; when he loses me, he runs,
He investigates. I don't value
That insulting intrigue very highly,
And just this minute, I considered telling
Him so.
Come take a look at the situation
To unravel this dangerous mystery.
It would be hard to see us delayed
By a mishap at the very moment
Of our departure.
SAINT-FAL. What kind of connection could this rustic
Character have with our plan? Besides,
To overcome the effects of fear,
Approach that frightening object, woo it,
Offer it your services. No longer
Be so inexperienced in the trade,
And certainly remember that by coaxing
And caressing, and especially by praising,
We reduce a man and his savage pride
To humbling himself to the most menial
Homage. What we give him, he returns
Immediately. The more we elevate him,
The sooner he falls. With these methods,

I dazzle him and lead him on, without
Straining my mind too terribly, for
What people give always has some price;
What I give back has only the appearance
Of contempt. Do you want some money?
(*He gives him a purse.*)
DUBOIS. (*Taking it.*) Yes, I have more faith in its effects
Than in those of the science you've just
Outlined for me here. I fly to my post,
And without hesitating, simply come
In a moment, to prevent the quarrel
If it's possible. (*He exits.*)
SAINT-FAL. (*Alone.*) The child's afraid.
As for me, I'm afraid of nothing,
And all of this can only turn out well;
Take heart! But wait, I hear Adélaide,
My happy fate is leading her to me.
How beautiful she is! What divine features!
To be bound to her only through shameful
Schemes! There was a time when that gloomy
Idea would have intimidated my soul.
For the time being,
I will be responsible for finding
Some more lively fascinations there.
ADÉLAIDE. *(Entering, proper and simple.*)
A tender friend sends me to you, Saint-Fal,
And you see that I come joyfully
To assure you that I'm not at all
Suspicious of the plans we're making with you.
SAINT-FAL. The word is hard, forgive me, Miss. But to
Affirm with so much enthusiasm
That you have no suspicions at all
Concerning a man, to my way of thinking,
That gives him reasons for assuming
There's a little bit of mistrust. And you
Must admit, under the circumstances,
The powerful knots with which I'm going
To bind myself should certainly have caused

Me to be appreciated differently
In the sweet and reliable mind
Of the wise and prudent Adélaide.
ADÉLAIDE. No, no, sir, I'll say it again. On this
Subject we're not wrong in any way.
Myself less than another, ah! I trust
Your heart too much for mine to suspect it
Of deception; and friendship, the most
Touching bond, broken if you were guilty,
Would be a crime, too horrible and too cruel,
Yes, for my mind to believe or comprehend.
The beloved object of my utmost
Affection just this second did what he thought
Would persuade me the most. You know him:
He's tender, he's vivacious, and yet,
He's never broken a promise to me.
I'm here to see you; I yield to his desire.
I come without concern, even with pleasure,
Convinced, and very happy to be sure
That you yourself will create feelings here
That would lead me to virtues I want to
Respect.
SAINT-FAL. I'm very far from wanting to fight
Them; I idolize virtue far too much.
I find it too indispensable
To happiness, as a way to chill
The inclinations of the heart.
(*Carelessly*.) Ah! Who
Would want it to fade in your features?
Seduced by so much charm, at most, a person
Can languish because of love, seeing it
In your face; but then misled by your
Beauty, what the affected senses
Offer to its image, is soon transformed
By love into respect.
(*Recovering himself*.) After all,
When a woman makes a man her husband,
Just between us, I don't see how virtue

Can suffer by accepting what love
Proposes. Are you in any way
Suspicious about Florival? In that
Case I would applaud your reasons. If
That's the way it is, please tell me. And in
That case don't worry about my taking
The slightest step to promote a plan
That wouldn't have virtue as its objective.
ADÉLAIDE. Me, suspicious of my fondest lover!
Ah! Far from it. Try to understand me
Better. I would place my destiny
In his hands, without any risk, and without
The slightest effort. But you know my father
Absolutely refuses to allow
This affair to be concluded. Our lost
Estates have caused him to change his plans;
His lawsuits overwhelm me with sorrows
And because of my duty, I can do
Nothing about it. I am his daughter.
Indeed, I must submit to any plans
That he might make concerning me.
SAINT-FAL. (*Disinterestedly, and skillfully.*)
You explain the sacred spirit of the
Laws of nature somewhat poorly, I think.
The greatest good that nature can obtain
For us, is unquestionably our father;
Until death, ceaselessly, we owe him
Both respect and gratitude. But if
He delights in tyrannizing us,
By way of that very thing, we can dare
To protect ourselves from his oppressive choice.
And by what barbarous and Homeric right
Does this hard-hearted father intend to
Unfasten the beloved ties which you saw him
Admit and accept?
It seems to me a just man would have said:
"From this moment on, I must unite
This husband and wife who are madly in love.

My daughter's wasting away. I have to
Console her. Florival's in love with her,
And if he's been endowed with a solid
Inheritance of feelings, never will they
Be lacking in possessions." But dismissing
This sweet logic, the one a despotic
Father follows tends to corrupt you
Instead of saving you. Ah! Forgive me.
But could I approve his behavior
And his thoughtlessness . . .
And the match which your obedience
Forces you to pursue in this horrible
Calamity, even at the expense
Of the laws of your heart?
(*Very slyly.*)
That earnest heart whose voice purifies us
Is also fashioned by nature. It has
Its rights, which are also perhaps as great
As those which wrongly we give to our parents.
If you are sensible, listen to it;
It will tell you that you can alternately
Cherish a father and yield to love.
It will tell you that when that unjust
Father tries to abuse his awesome power,
In order to control our sweetest feelings,
We withdraw from him, at least for a few
Moments, as much to escape his wretched
Bondage, as to enter without fear
Into a marriage, which, with time, he can
Only approve of. That's my opinion.
Nothing can save you from the horrible
Hardships to which I see you reduced
If you don't take to flight immediately.
ADÉLAIDE. Ah! How harsh then is my destiny?
I see only misery on all sides!
(*With tears.*) Either I'm going to lose a lover
Whom I adore, or I'm going to flee
From a father whom I respect! I see

It clearly: a convent is my fate!
Ah, well! I'll go. I'll go because I have to.
At least in my excessive misery,
Keeping myself occupied with the only
Object I love, expecting one day
To see him again, I will have the sweet
Pleasure of having done my duty.
SAINT-FAL. (*With a surprised attitude, where the negative shows.*)
Seeing him again, no, no. Be well
Assured that there's a plan to bind you soon
By eternal vows. I swear to it!
ADÉLAIDE. (*Startled.*) Do you think so? Ah! What cruel plans!
SAINT-FAL. (*Firmly.*) They're definite, and that magnificent
Arbitrator, or that tyrant—a title
Which rather suits him better—right there,
This minute, just told me in confidence
That tomorrow he intends to bind you.
(*Mysteriously, and taking her hand.*)
Tomorrow, I tell you, he's going
Far from Paris, to the coast of Brittany;
He's taking you with him, counseling you
Harshly, and enslaving you for life.
(*With the utmost passion, the most intense pathos; gradually, with the utmost skill.*)
For one lonely moment, let your heart
Study the terrifying blow that Pontac
Has in store for it. Will you take that
Terrible vow, which forever steals
A lover from you? Will you bear the cries
Of that lover, and the burden of your
Grievous fears that, tired of his cruel fate,
He might cut it short by stabbing himself?
He'll do it, you can be sure of that.
And to reinforce your chains, to aggravate
Your horrifying destiny, you'll have
The regret of having caused his death.
The sacrificial victim will disturb

Your troubled mind, all the way to the altar.
His sad hand will come to tear you away
From the arms of God, which you have faith
In reaching. Unexpectedly, he will
Arrive in the horror of silence;
Everything will represent for you
His deadly presence. The doleful bell,
Carrying prayers for the wretched mortal
To heaven, will be an appalling instrument
For you, which, murmuring in your guilty heart,
Every day reminding you of him,
Will show him to you underneath the bloody
Dagger! Overcome, a prey to terror,
You will see that quivering phantom hurl
Upon you the sinister inhibitions
Of despair, of heart-rending remorse;
And in the midst of the torment and tears,
Your heart rent by your violent sorrows,
Soon, at the height of terror, you yourself
Will perish, in the prime of your life.
ADÉLAIDE. My soul has no defense against these sights.
Having terrified me with their dismal
Implications, finish destroying
The cry of virtue in my beaten heart.
SAINT-FAL. (*Rapidly, and passionately.*)
Adélaide, listen to nature. It's speaking
To you, and its truly more confident voice
Makes resisting a crime in your eyes.
When it ignited your passion with its
Fire, you were indispensable
To its intentions; nature is also
Tender Cupid's mother. She's the one,
My friend, at the bottom of your heart,
Who's calling you to happiness through that god.
Yield, without fear, to their heavenly commands.
Young and sensitive, old enough to be
Seductive, gather the flowers they sow
At your feet. Their immaculate hands

Are gilding the days with tastes and charms
Which the Fates are spinning for you. Let them
Shine; and far from being obstinate,
Under the influence of their pleasing tones,
Become intoxicated with their mellow
Fragrances, and don't experience
The unnecessary madness of
Resisting the attractions of life.
Life offers only one chance to enjoy them:
Take advantage of them instead of
Allowing them to wither away.
Courageously follow a friend who loves you,
Who bears everything, himself, to please you,
Who would die to overcome your fears.
(*ADÉLAIDE staggers. Her tears are flowing. SAINT-FAL takes her in his arms.*)
Ah! I am victorious. I see your tears!
(*Noticing FLORIVAL.*) Hurry, dear Florival. Her affection
Finally agrees to the plan that leaves her
In the care of a trustworthy friend
Whose sole desire is to reunite you
No matter what may happen.
Now strengthen her courage; I am going
To make arrangements for our happy voyage
And in a little while you'll be able
To judge my feelings and my honesty.
(*SAINT-FAL exits quickly.*)
FLORIVAL. Why those tears when a devoted friend
Intends to do everything to help us?
You certainly see how honest he is!
ADÉLAIDE. Ah! Good heavens! What recklessness! To me,
This venture is both troublesome and painful.
Give it up, Florival, I demand it.
My heart is frightened thinking about it.
FLORIVAL. We are lost, alas, if we refuse.
If you love me, my dear Adélaide,
Follow close behind the friend who's leading you.
Seeing that he's bringing us together,

Is there anything to be afraid of?
ADÉLAIDE. Ah! I see excessively in everything
He tells me, how inevitable
The severe treatment is that my father,
Without qualms, is planning for me.
They agree too well in their accounts.
That deadly bond is true! I would die
Before taking it.
FLORIVAL. Let's find consolation in the fact
That this will take us to the only one
Who's bound to guarantee our destiny.
ADÉLAIDE. But what perils must be overcome
To arrive at port! What if this friend
Betrays our hopes!
FLORIVAL. How could we not have confidence in him?
How could we begin to worry again
When your esteem is the price of success!
That honest fellow understands its worth
Too much to behave toward you in a way
That would make him contemptible in your eyes.
With my heart and soul, I have faith in everyone
Who's felt the influence of your attractions.
Perhaps, alas, they'd like to seduce you,
Adore you, but deceive you? Never.
Come on. Cheer up! No more regrets!
ADÉLAIDE. Against
My will, a dark sorrow devours me.
(*During this line, the MESSENGER happens to creep behind FLORIVAL. ADÉLAIDE becomes frightened when she sees him.*)
What kind of man is this? What does he want?
MESSENGER. (*Giving his message to FLORIVAL.*)
The letter requires secrecy of some
Significance. Read it quickly, and come
Immediately.
FLORIVAL. (*Looking it over very quickly.*)
It's from Darneuil, my best friend.
He says that he'd appreciate it if
I would meet him somewhere nearby without

Any delay.
ADÉLAIDE. I see. It's some new danger.
What does he want, anyway?
FLORIVAL. I don't know
What he's up to, but for Darneuil,
I'm ready to do anything.
(*To the MESSENGER.*) Lead on.
ADÉLAIDE. Oh, God! A duel!
FLORIVAL. No, no. Darneuil
Is sensible. I can see why he might
Require my presence. In a moment,
I'll fly back to your feet.
ADÉLAIDE. I'm not leaving,
In case you don't return.
FLORIVAL. You're making a
Mistake. Ah! Leave without anything to fear!
What reason would you give to a friend,
Whom we have to handle carefully,
To pretend that you can't go along?
Ah! Remember, then, that love, prudence,
Pure friendship, and gratitude—finally,
The despair of terrible bondage—
Make our plans a duty for you.
(*Squeezing her in his arms.*) Touching
Object of my idolatry! You, whom
I adore, alas, more than my life!
ADÉLAIDE. Only hope of my miserable life,
If I lose you, I'll end its flow. (*Alone.*)
(*The sun goes down.*)[37]
Ah! What goodbyes! How anxious I am!
What does that man want, and what's he planning?
Luckily, Darneuil is his friend.
If, however . . . My God, I'm completely
In the dark in all of this. Today,
People are so deceitful in the world,
So few friends are worthy of that name!
Oh, no, never! Never was treachery
Served with so much depravity. Never

[37] Sade's original stage directions read: *Here the footlights are lowered. It is night.*

So much skill, never so much versatility
Has blackened hearts to mask it.
But why be afraid of such a climax
Of horrors!
(Night has fallen completely.)
How we tremble when we're going
To commit evil!
(*She looks at the door to PONTAC's apartment.*)
What are you thinking,
Now, oh, my father? Are you concerned
With the fate to which so much harshness
Reduces me? But is it up to me
To verify your fairness? Forgive me,
Forgive the artifice your cruel heartlessness
Forces me to use!
(*She goes near the apartment.*)
Undoubtedly,
I'm wrong. It was just my happiness
That your fair-minded wisdom desired.
(*She throws herself on her knees in front of the door to the apartment.*)
See anew the guilty daughter at your feet,
Fervently imploring your forgiveness!
Let her live in your good and tender heart.
See her always in the midst of your family
And condescend once more to ask the Almighty
For help to preserve your daughter, in the
Stillness of our days, as in former times.
Ah! Don't think my happiness is completely
Genuine. Can it be by offending
A father?
(*She hears a noise and trembles. She gets up.*)
God! It's the Count. Hurry, there's no more time.
SAINT-FAL. *(Entering, in traveling clothes: his hat over his eyes, his sword under his arm. In a low voice, but curtly.)* Are you ready?
ADÉLAIDE. (*Trembling.*) Yes.
SAINT-FAL. Everything's waiting
For us. Let's go. Let's fly. Let your mind
Be confident. Don't worry. It's the end

Of our troubles.
(*Anxiously.*) What's happened to Florival?
ADÉLAIDE. He went quickly to take care of something
At a friend's house.
SAINT-FAL. (*The greatest dismay.*) Who came to get him?
ADÉLAIDE. A stranger who could give no information,
Who could explain nothing about this
Intrusive concern.
SAINT-FAL. (*Trying to hide his uneasiness.*) What did he look like?
ADÉLAIDE. He wore a brown coat.
(*SAINT-FAL trembles all over his body; a deadly chill seizes him. His words fall from his chest with difficulty. We should hear the clacking of his teeth.*)
SAINT-FAL. Let's go. Let's leave. Let's be off at once!
Everything is holding up the night
In this situation. Take my arm.
What! Are you troubled?
(*They go upstage, right.*)
Are you disheartened
So close to happiness?
(*ADÉLAIDE follows him without taking his arm. Going in front of her father's door, she speaks.*)
ADÉLAIDE. Oh, cruel night!
Oh, my father! Oh, my father!
SAINT-FAL. (*Harshly.*) Speak softer.
ADÉLAIDE. (*Continuing, and without waiting for the reply.*)
Author of my misery, you whom
I adore, and whom I offend, alas!
In my misfortunes, do not abandon me![38]
(*SAINT-FAL and ADÉLAIDE begin to fade into the darkness upstage, when FLORIVAL, preceded by four servants and the MESSENGER, enters abruptly and speaks to the MESSENGER and servants.*)
FLORIVAL. Oh, my friends, save Adélaide.

---

[38] In the Pauvert edition of this play, it is noted that six pages of the manuscript are missing at this point, neatly cut out of the text. Evidently this represents an alteration of the play in an earlier form and is clearly Sade's work as the indication of the final scene is in Sade's handwriting while the rest of the play is in a copyist's hand.

(*Immediately, three servants line the backdrop. The fourth, and the MESSENGER seize the young lady and bring her back downstage; she faints in their arms. Pursuing SAINT-FAL, FLORIVAL says to him as he flees.*)
And you, get out, treacherous and deceitful
Man, or this hand which fury guides, in a
Moment will tear your heart out!
ADÉLAIDE. (*Returning to her senses, and trying to escape from those who are holding her.*)
Ah, Florival, I beg of you, do not
Concern yourself with his baneful life!
(*A loud noise is heard in the street. With everyone holding his position, we can hear the sound effects for a moment. After a little while, DARNEUIL and PONTAC enter hurriedly.*)
PONTAC. (*Spiritedly to his child.*) Oh, my child! It's done. His reign is over.
There's Darneuil.
DARNEUIL. (*Cutting him short.*) Yes, the crime is punished.
ADÉLAIDE. (*Eagerly, to both of them.*)
God, I'm dying! What did he dare to do?
DARNEUIL. (*Continuing, with animation; to ADÉLAIDE.*)
I'm here to shield you from his offenses.
You must recognize that dangerous man:
Through horrors and shady maneuvers
He changed the titles to all of your possessions.
He bribed the witnesses and the judges.
I used to groan, seeing him betray you,
But sooner or later, I was bound
To succeed. The timely foresight of the
Magistrate had managed to shatter
The insolence of that treacherous rogue,
And through diligence, and because people
Were on the lookout for him, he was
Arrested at your door. Straightaway,
I'm called to court. I managed to catch our man
Red-handed, at the very hour the judge
Was ruling in your favor.
FLORIVAL. Ah! Dear Darneuil,

What a useful lesson!
(*To PONTAC.*) Alas, sir,
Forgive the indiscretion to which we
Were driven by the deadly arrogance
Of the wretch who led us all astray.
PONTAC. (*Taking his daughter's hand, and to FLORIVAL.*)
Here's her hand.
FLORIVAL. Ah! At your knees . . .
PONTAC. (*Quickly interrupting.*) Let's forget
Everything. Be eternally happy.
Through the bonds created by her affection,
I want to read repentance in your heavy
Heart for having offended me.
ADÉLAIDE. (*Very touched.*) Father!
(*With a resentful tone.*) Oh, heaven, to what degree do ingenuity,
Treachery, and dark deceit proceed
To draw us into the midst of misfortunes
When eloquence assists in ornamenting
Them!
PONTAC. (*Passionately.*) Let's stay far away from that gibberish
Which custom justifies. Let's have less wit,
And a little more honesty. Let's love
Each other more, and like the good old days,
Let's have less art, and let's be pleasant people.
(*MR. DESCLAPON's study is put in place again and the backstage scenes continue.*)

CONTINUATION OF THE MARRIAGE OF THE ARTS

BELVAL. Well, Marton, are you pleased? Does the lesson seem valid to you?
MARTON. It's only too obvious, sir. Oh! Really, if he doesn't recognize it, I don't know anymore what we'll have to do for him to get it. But are you all in order, and are all your papers ready?
BELVAL. Everything is coming out of the same office. You can be sure that your master won't be able to question a thing.
MARTON. Why not act immediately?
BELVAL. I told you, Marton, I want to speak to Émilie. I know that she was ever so slightly unsettled, and I want to punish her for being fickle. Listen carefully to what's coming: you're going to see a character that may appear minor to you, but this Almanzor will serve as a reflection of dear Mr. Vieuxblanc, and I hope that you'll understand all the allusions to him. (*Seeing MR. DESCLAPON enter, MARTON goes out.*)
DESCLAPON. Well, sir, it seems to me that my Émilie didn't do badly in her role, and it's thanks to your efforts.
BELVAL. Me? Not at all! Really, sir, I don't know how, or why I'm so lucky to cause the gentleman, your son-in-law, to be jealous, but as soon as I try to give a lesson to Miss Émilie, he's always there. I can't manage to get a single word in. Am I meant to trouble him about his happiness?
DESCLAPON. Oh! That's the way he is, easily offended by the least little thing.
BELVAL. If that's the way it is, he'll make your daughter very unhappy. So, that's the husband you intend for her?
DESCLAPON. Absolutely. Don't you think he has what it takes to make my daughter happy?
BELVAL. A slight difference in their ages, and in their personalities, but as for everything else, I'm convinced that . . . even so, be careful of making a mistake, sir. You've just seen an awfully

fatal example of a girl ready to be given to a man who suited her so poorly.

DESCLAPON. The circumstances are quite different.

BELVAL. They're more alike than you think, sir.

DESCLAPON. My daughter has no other inclination. She's only in love with the one I've chosen for her.

BELVAL. That's different. However, if she weren't in the situation you think she's in, the step you're about to take, sir, is one of those in life where you least ought to go astray.

DESCLAPON. I've never seen any feelings in Émilie contrary to what I'm telling you.

BELVAL. Ah! Sir, you know that well-bred young ladies always keep their inclinations secret. When they're born, two very unusual things happen among them: nature makes them pay attention to a heart that their education forbids them to listen to. From that point of view, it seems to me that a wise father should consult his tastes less than his daughter's when he's planning an arrangement for her.

DESCLAPON. Sir, could Émilie have told you something that might be the occasion for what you mean here?

BELVAL. Not at all. But I'm an extremely good judge of faces. I am, sir. I told you. Carefully examining the young lady, your daughter, one easily perceives in the muscles of her face, there, yes, sir, between her two eyebrows, one readily perceives that she's not all that inclined toward the future like you think she is. According to that, it would be very possible that you'd have some grief in store for her by consummating this affair.

DESCLAPON. Ah! Sir, you're depressing me, right in the middle of a celebration. I've definitely thought about what I'm doing. It's set for tomorrow, and I won't disrupt anything at your convenience. Let's get back to the business at hand, and tell me, if you please, the plot of the play that's next in store for us.

BELVAL. Here it is, sir: the island of the Good Fairy is inhabited only by women. Nevertheless, they know that somewhere in the world there are beings of a different sex. They ask the fairy to show them what the other sex looks like. There are some complications, they are smoothed away, and what happens after that to one of the young inhabitants of the island (the obstacles to her happiness caused by a naïve flirtatiousness which she acquired from nature), comprises the very flimsy plot of this trifle whose title is *Azélis; or, the Punished Coquette*. I've written it in free verse to vary the style of the episodes I've had the honor of presenting to you.

(MARTON enters.)

MARTON. Gentlemen, the young lady awaits you. She's ready. Mr. Vieuxblanc is already in place.

BELVAL. (*Breaking away.*) Oh, heavens! I'm the only one who isn't dressed!

DESCLAPON. Tell me, then, have you been indiscreet in any way?

MARTON. About what, sir?

DESCLAPON. Regarding my daughter.

MARTON. Why? Has that young man said something to you?

DESCLAPON. Certainly not. But he's saying that the marriage I intend for my Émilie won't suit her.

MARTON. There's no need to be secretive about that, sir. That's a truth that leaps out in front of everybody's eyes!

DESCLAPON. Ah! It's settled. I want to make her explain herself before completing the arrangements. This all seems suspicious to me.

MARTON. For me, sir, everything's perfectly clear. You're sacrificing your daughter. People have told you that. They're proving it to you, they're making you see it, and you don't want to hear it! Come on, sir, let's go take our seats. They're starting.

DESCLAPON. (*Leaving, and aside.*) Oh! Yes, yes, I'm right. There's something quite extraordinary going on around here!

ORCHESTRA

AZÉLIS
or
THE PUNISHED COQUETTE

Fairy Comedy

In the future, I want the world to know
That often the heart restores the mind.
Voisenon.[39]

CHARACTERS

Toute Bonne, the (Very) Good Fairy, *ruler of the Blissful Island*
Prince Attalide, *ruler of a neighboring island*
Azélis, Euphrosie, Roséide, Zéphirine, *four young inhabitants of the Fairy's island, raised in her palace*
Three young princes, *from Attalide's court*
A group of young ladies, *from the Blissful Island*
Dancers

The Setting alternates between the two islands.

The most fashionable, up-to-date, and elegant attire should be characteristic of these young ladies, especially the Fairy's four favorites. The costumes should be identical, but to distinguish between the four favorites and the women of the seraglio whom they should not resemble, Azélis, Euphrosie, Roséide, and Zéphirine will not wear veils. The

[39] The epigraph is from Abbé Voisenon's three-act comedy in verse, *La Coquette fixée* (*The Reformed Coquette*), published in 1746.

Fairy is dressed like the fairy in the Oracle.[40] *Attalide and the young princes wear masks.*

(The stage reveals a luscious island, shaded by palm trees and coconut palms, orange trees, lemon trees, and a vast amount of shrubbery covered with flowers. The ocean billows on the shore and seems to join the horizon in the distance. Upstage, a little to the right, is a palace designed in the Corinthian style and whose columns are made of diamonds. It is sunset; the last rays of the sun darting perpendicularly on the building make it dazzling to see. We catch sight of a crowd of young women employed in different ways in various parts of the island: some picking flowers; others, fruit. Some are eating fruit on the very tree they're climbing; others are seated at the base of other trees. In short, they all create groups that are as varied as they are pleasantly designed. EUPHROSIE, ROSÉIDE and ZÉPHIRINE, each at a different bush farther downstage, are weaving garlands of flowers. AZÉLIS, seated at the foot of a palm tree a short distance in front of them, is busy reading attentively. The stage picture stays like this for a moment while the end of the overture suggests the sunset and the song of the birds at this time of nature's momentary repose.)

EUPHROSIE. (*Leaving her work aside; approaching AZÉLIS with her garland in hand.*)
What's that book, Azélis?
Give it to me. I want to better myself.
They never let us read.
They want our minds
Enslaved in ignorance,
Even to give up understanding,
To give up suspecting
That we can look forward
To pleasures more perfect for us
Than those attractions
This dwelling offers us.
(*During this line, AZÉLIS's two other companions have likewise approached her, with their garlands in their hands.*)

[40] A popular three-character prose comedy in one act by Germain-François Poullain de Saint-Foix, produced in 1740.

AZÉLIS. (*Getting up, irritably.*)
Ah! What a place to live, and how it bores me!
They're deceiving us. They're deceiving us,
Oh, my dear Euphrosie,
I no longer doubt it now.
(*She throws the book, spitefully.*)
The being who should be making our lives more attractive,
Whose name, you know, we're searching for
All the time . . .
EUPHROSIE. (*Eagerly.*) What is it? Speak, I tell you!
ZÉPHIRINE. (*Vivaciously.*) Ah! Yes, my dear friend,
Give us its name quickly.
AZÉLIS. It's . . .
ROSÉIDE. (*Spiritedly.*) Speak I tell you, quickly.
AZÉLIS. (*A little begrudgingly.*) Well! It's a lover.
EUPHROSIE. (*Full of childishness and naïveté.*)
A lover! What in the world is that?
Is it a tree? Ah, I bet
It's a charming shrub
Which, from its foliage, fresh and sweet,
Causes flowers to bloom constantly,
All around it . . .
Whose fruit is so delicious,
That when you eat it,
You become intoxicated,
As if you were enchanted!
ROSÉIDE. (*As before.*) Oh, yes, yes. Indeed, I suspect
That's the reason Toute Bonne,
The fairy everything on this island obeys,
Strictly warned us
To avoid its holy shade.
AZÉLIS. (*Smiling.*) Poor children, with what kind of cloud
Do they wrap up our minds and our hearts here?
One lover, Roséide, has much more sweetness
Than all the attractions this island shows us.
Ah! We still only know the fears,
The deprivations, the agonies;
And these interesting beings,

Nature gave us to soften them
Are forbidden to our senses
By a cruel deception.
ZÉPHIRINE. Explain yourself, I implore you.
My heart appreciates what you're saying,
But my mind, I assure you,
Cannot imagine it, or understand it.
EUPHROSIE. Yes, more clearly describe for us what a lover is.
AZÉLIS. (*Mysteriously, and gathering them around her.*)
Listen to me carefully. It's a being
Who causes all the passions to blossom inside us,
He promises happiness—he gives it to us;
He gives birth to it.
And when he has made us experience it,
So strongly are we united with him
That he alone, alas, becomes the master
Of all our feelings.
So he alone changes them,
Inflames them, gives life to them.
He becomes our only support.
He is our life's soul,
And in him is our existence.
Always submissive when he wants to please,
Always loyal when he's pleased;
He charms us when he's hopeful,
And flatters us when he's won;
With so much skill, a lover finally enslaves us.
To his victory he adds an enticement so titillating
That, under the weight of the irons
With which he enchains us,
We triumph even in yielding.
ZÉPHIRINE. Oh, how nice!
EUPHROSIE. Let's ask for a lover.
AZÉLIS. One? That isn't enough. We'd all be jealous.
ROSÉIDE. What? We'll each have him one after the other.
AZÉLIS. You poor innocent girl.
Alas! You know little about love.
We would fight over the honor

Of being his wives all the time;
We'd long for the good fortune
Of always being the one he prefers,
And soon, the one most beloved
Would become an object of horror
To her rivals in passion.
Why should we quarrel when our sovereign
Can save us from animosity
By giving each one of us a choice?
It's certainly better, you understand,
For each of us to have her own,
Than to be robbing one another continually
Of our pleasures, our desires, and our rights.
Let's talk to our Fairy. She's sweet and kind.
Let's ask her to give us
The thing our hearts are missing.
ROSÉIDE. Let's ask for it fervently.
ZÉPHIRINE. Ah! We won't get anything.
Because she's invincibly bound by her destiny,
She never has special powers.
ROSÉIDE. Ah! What does it matter, we have to see her.
Since we've never asked questions
About something like that,
We don't know what she'll say to us;
We have to explore her inclinations.
ZÉPHIRINE. Perhaps it's very much in her interest to hide
The happiness of being loved from us?
If we were inflamed by love,
Undoubtedly she'd be afraid
Of certain misfortunes to which
Fate would soon subject her!
EUPHROSIE. What? Are we therefore meant for her pleasures?
AZÉLIS. (*Vigorously*.) Ah! Please, don't believe any of it.
Try as we might to love her, at the bottom of our hearts,
We feel the germ of a more tender flame
Carrying us away to desires
That cannot give rise

To the vain and useless pleasures
We enjoy in these rustic surroundings.
The best way to assure ourselves
Is to cast our eyes on the countrysides;
All creatures have their countrysides.
(*To the one who is nearest to her.*)
See my dove and her pigeon,
When I want to cheer them up,
I put the two of them together;
Love immediately unites them;
Then both of them caress one another,
But with passion . . . ecstasy . . .
Which we'd experience as well,
Because one feels them when one loves.
Ah! We'd feel them too.
ROSÉIDE. Then how are we supposed to behave here?
AZÉLIS. (*Firmly.*) We'll grieve, sulk and complain.
We'll have to make her a little afraid;
People are fooled by too much sweetness.
Let us join together zealously
To shake off the yoke that's making us miserable;
Let's revolt, and grumble,
Let's show our grief and annoyance,
Let's especially object to the tyrannical selection
That ferocious Almanzor,
Whose look alone makes our blood run cold,
Audaciously happens to make here every year.
What? Would benign nature maintain
With splendor so many sweet objects
In these cheerful gardens
For that sole object of horror?
No, no, really! That cannot be!
No, no, I'm absolutely certain of it!
ROSÉIDE. There's some awful secret in all of this.
AZÉLIS. They mask it and they hide it very carefully.
But, at some point when they try to do it,
I will unravel the mystery.
While we're waiting, let's tell the Fairy

That we would prefer death
To the choice of that wretched Almanzor
With whom she's foolishly infatuated.
And that we still want her
To inhabit her island,
Her blissful and fertile empire,
With beings that Cupid created for pleasure.
Do you swear to support me?
ROSÉIDE. Yes, we promise!
EUPHROSIE. (*Spiritedly.*) And instantly we'll curse
The one among us
Who, through weakness,
Or because of some other feeling,
Will dare to betray the oath!
AZÉLIS. We'll let all the garlands
She wanted us to make
Dry up and die.
(*She grabs the garlands from the two girls who are beside her and throws them away. The fourth girl likewise throws her garland down, spitefully.*)
Let's trample underfoot the vile offerings
We were preparing for the god we're fleeing;
When the heart renounces a worship,
By which it was saddened for a long time,
The contempt it adds to the outrage
Is always a sensual pleasure.
They were for Almanzor.
He arrives on this island
And in our idiotic worship,
We were still going to scatter flowers under his feet,
To be the next one
To be pitilessly delivered
To his favors!
But, why is one wife a year
Necessary for his abhorred passion?
I don't understand it, myself.
ZÉPHIRINE. He's a monster. A tyrant!
AZÉLIS. Ah, yes, yes. That so-called necessity

Is only a pretense.
He buys us because of his arrogance;
Love has nothing to do with it.
Let him give us more of a token
Of that delicate feeling . . .
I can easily understand it;
It is our privilege to be fickle:
Receiving much less from a lover
Than we offer him.
It's certainly appropriate
That we should want more.
But him? You can clearly see
That it would be wrong for him to be fickle
Since, in us, he has absolutely
The sweet and holy advantages
Of completely possessing
That which the gods have created
In their own image!
(*Seeing the FAIRY.*)
Good, good. Here she is. Take heart,
And let's pout in earnest.
(*They all separate and run off, each to her side of the stage. There, they lean nonchalantly against some trees. During this first scene, the young women who were filling out the island have gone off gradually so that none of them remains at the beginning of scene two.*)
FAIRY. (*Looking at them, with surprise.*)
Why this aloofness?
What's wrong, my children?
Almanzor is coming with great strides;
Thanks to the pressing north winds
His azure vessel darts forward;
Under the efforts of the diligent oarsmen,
The waves give way without resistance;
And the elements, vanquished by his powerful desires
Seem to yield to so much impatience
As if love itself opened its flanks!
In times past, this blessed day satisfied your expectations:
Your cares and our desires were content

With becoming his lover in turns;
And with a sparkling enthusiasm,
Wanting to appear beautiful in his eyes,
Early in the morning, you placed a budding flower,
Gathered carefully from our fields,
Artistically in your hair
To embellish your youth
With its tender luster.
Today, everyone is silent,
Everyone is deaf to my voice.
You're bored, I see it.
Try as I may, from one extreme to another,
To summon simultaneously everything
That I can imagine or think of
To entertain your minds for a moment,
It's no use. I understand that.
(*During this speech, the four women return onstage and draw closer to the FAIRY, but still with the attitude of carelessness and discontent.*)
AZÉLIS. (*Taking her hand, and firmly.*)
You're forcing us to be ungrateful
Every time the amusement
Is directed only at our minds.
In this instructive book you lent me yesterday,
I have discovered, Madame, another amusement,
And it is . . . oh, yes! It is quite different
Than the pleasures you say can be enjoyed.
It is another sex, as you well know,
That on its own, it says, can set for us
The boundaries of the highest good.
We're no longer children.
Unite us with that sex. It's about time, after all.
What right do you have to hide from us
What they'd show us fearlessly
In the rest of the world?
Does that sex, designed for happiness,
Deserve your anger?
You boast to us about the games
On your charming island,

And then what do you offer that's tempting to us?
Women from every country.
You give them to us
Under a thousand different features,
But they're always women, my lady!
Oh! That's why we're dying of boredom!
ROSÉIDE. Yes, that's the way it is, Madame.
And we want to know about
The object that has given rise
To feelings inside of us
That are so heavenly and so sweet.
AZÉLIS. (*Charming her.*)
Listen, my lady, believe us.
We've been troubled since this morning;
We sigh and we cry,
We ask one another
What's bothering us
And, without being able
To unravel the reasons
Behind what's causing us distress,
We see clearly that what's missing in our hearts
Is the blessed object, the pleasant object
We're anxious about.
Nature, in short, more powerful than your laws,
Can simultaneously show us
Both the mistake that happens to surprise us,
(*Maliciously, lowering her eyes.*)
And the sweet means we have to use
To make its voice triumphant.
ZÉPHIRINE. (*Innocently coaxing the FAIRY.*)
Don't refuse us. Oh, our lovable mother,
By granting our prayer
You'll enjoy our happy fate.
We know that you only seek to please us,
But, if we anticipate your wishes in every case,
Why do you shirk them?
And why put off our marrying?[41]

[41] Here Sade makes use of an indecent pun with the French word *noeud*. The literal slang translation of the line is: *Why put off giving us pricks?*

EUPHROSIE. (*Continuing eagerly.*)
You can't do it without being inhuman.
What do the dangers matter if we scorn them;
We know very well that no matter how careful we are
There are never pleasures without deceptions,
And as for these, we think
That their charms outshines their sorrows.
You don't love us!
FAIRY. Ah! It's your happiness,
Your happiness alone that concerns me,
And if I encouraged your mistake
Soon, you'd be fooled because of it.
People never realize
The dangerous and sweet attractions
Of this seductive phantom
Which now preoccupies you,
Without being bombarded immediately
With dark melancholy,
The fruit of the most sinister regret.
AZÉLIS. And why is that, I ask you?
FAIRY. Ah! Why is that? Because your hearts
Too sensitive and defenseless,
Aren't made to be faithful,
A trait that could spread honey
Over those bonds.
AZÉLIS. And the man? Is he worth more?
FAIRY. (*To AZÉLIS.*) No. And that's why
This union is so full of danger.
One of them too often tries to break loose
Without thinking that he's exposing
The other's heart to grief.
AZÉLIS. (*Somewhat moved.*)
Ah! But why break loose
If nothing's standing
In the way of happiness?
FAIRY. Is it for you to question me
About your taste for infidelity?
You whose foolish inconsistency,

Whose fiery and fickle mind
Knows no other enjoyment
Than the empty pleasure of changing!
AZÉLIS. (*Poorly defending herself.*)
But I haven't loved anything
That was worth the trouble
Of so strong an attachment.
I'd have to decide whether or not
The chain would cause me anguish
In another commitment.
And, besides, it really seems to me
That it matters very little if you're unfaithful.
The object is to keep your lover from being so!
ZÉPHIRINE. That's the way our minds see it.
That soothes our dismay.
AZÉLIS. (*Quite put off.*) The great sorrow I foresee
Is for whichever of the two is faithful.
And by a curious wisdom,
You only have to leave the other,
And you're no longer in despair.
EUPHROSIE. Oh, yes, my lady. Oh, yes.
Our hearts are urging you,
Oh, yes, give us some husbands.
And you'll see that we'll be able
To keep them constantly at our feet.
ROSÉIDE. (*Eagerly.*) Or to leave them, if their affection
Was aroused for someone other than us.
AZÉLIS. (*To the FAIRY, laughing.*)
You see the disciples I'm making in all of this,
And how they're taking advantage of it?
FAIRY. Yes. I see how they imitate
Your indiscreet paradoxes.
All right. I have to make you wise.
Alas! May you be wise at your expense,
And since you want your share of husbands,
Listen to me, my children.
(*She gathers them all around her.*)
Undoubtedly you know that my power is limited

And I cannot deviate from the course
Which has been prescribed to me by fate.
You don't want Almanzor.
Very well! Another is going to appear,
But I cannot prevent him from being free
To choose between the four of you.
But at the moment his desire
Is satisfied, the other three
Will fall into a deep sleep
From which neither his power
Nor your own will manage
To awaken you. That's not all.
That sovereign, although charming,
Is subjected to a destiny that overwhelms him,
And he will take you
To his horrifying island right away.
Never again will you see this touching sanctuary,
So dear to your childhood games;
And in spite of all my power,
Undeniably, you'll have to leave us.
AZÉLIS. Oh! What an unpleasant arrangement!
What! Couldn't you come up with another
That would at least give us the enjoyment
Of each one of us having our own?
ZÉPHIRINE. That would be better, certainly!
AZÉLIS. (*Continuing, quickly.*)
Or, better still, to appease our passions,
Instead of those herds of women
We see here at every step,
Let some men in droves wander about these regions.
Then, instead of being chosen,
It's our turn to choose.
Consult my friends about this important point:
They'll all approve these plans,
Take my word for it.
FAIRY. I cannot serve your fantasies in such a way.
AZÉLIS. (*Peevishly.*) Oh! It's unpleasant to die!
So we have to give up these charming islands!

But what if we were dissatisfied with our husband?
FAIRY. In that case, to get help
You'll have to turn toward the dawn
And call me in a loud voice.
(*She shows them the gestures they will have to make in such a case.*)
Perhaps, I will yet succeed
In being useful to you once.
But the method will be treacherous;
It's the one you want to avoid at the moment.
For you will have left the handsome prince Attalide
(That's the name of the husband who's going to enchant you.)
As I was saying, you will have abandoned his charms
Only to find yourself in tears,
In the arms of that dreadful Almanzor.
The effort that will free you from your bondage
Will be due to him alone.
And through a new marriage,
You'll go with him to begin a new destiny.
Such is the law. I can do no more.
Again, think it over carefully.
AZÉLIS. Ah! My God, how cruel she is!
Can't happiness exist with you?
FAIRY. No. When a husband calls you,
You must leave everything behind to follow him.
Stay unmarried. Then we'll undoubtedly be able
To live together forever.
AZÉLIS. That way is madness.
I don't doubt that it's worse than the misfortune
Of getting married.
Let's discuss this among ourselves for a moment
To decide on what we want to do.
(*The FAIRY goes off toward her palace without leaving the stage.*)
AZÉLIS. (*To her companions.*)
What do you say about this awful fate?
Does it make you afraid?
ZÉPHIRINE. Oh, my God, no!
That incredible sleep alone
Disturbs me for a moment.

But if the prince is fair
I have neither fears nor suspicions.
EUPHROSIE. (*Arrogantly.*) It's more inevitable that I should expect
To attract the desires of a lover.
ROSÉIDE. (*Likewise.*) Oh! No, no. I'm the one he's going to take.
Don't doubt it for a moment.
AZÉLIS. Wasn't I saying that, here, just recently?
When you have to please the same lover,
Each of you values yourself at the expense of the other.
Tenderness and friendship are all forgotten,
And immediately the serpent of jealousy
Is born out of pride.
Ah! Calm yourselves. If he's in his right mind,
I'd be the chosen one instead.
Enough! Let's end this indiscreet discussion.
(*She goes looking for the FAIRY.*)
All right. Strike your wand. Work your magic, my lady!
For, in no time at all, I expect
War to flare up here.
Certainly we love you a great deal,
But, whatever it costs, we want
To make some attempt at the good fortune
We anticipate.
Strike the wand.
Don't let us think about regrets.
FAIRY. (*Tenderly.*) Goodbye, then, my children. Goodbye. Be happy.
And if ever you become aware of your mistakes,
In misfortune, at least, become courageous
And don't blame me for your woes.
(*She strikes her wand upon the stage floor. ATTALIDE, a young prince appears out of the floor and the FAIRY disappears. At that moment, the four young girls hastily get into a diagonal line on the right.*)
ATTALIDE. (*Looking all of them over.*)
Ah! How to decide!

Without any discrepancy,
My tribute is directed to all of them.
Before my very eyes, today,
I see that nature has attempted
To adorn them magnificently!
(*To EUPHROSIE.*) What a slim waist, and what an outstanding figure!
(*To ROSÉIDE.*) Here I find honesty and innocence.
(*To ZÉPHIRINE.*) In that one over there, the luster and youth of Hebe.
(*To AZÉLIS.*) And here are the fruits of love!
(*To himself.*) Why haven't I the power
To take all four to my court?
Never, never has so much elegance
Adorned the place where I dwell!
But I must commit myself,
Since fate seeks to prevent my heart
From increasing its tribute.
(*To AZÉLIS.*) Ah! Azélis makes up for it,
And in Azélis I find happiness!
(*He extends his arms to her. She runs into them. A magical drowsiness seizes the others. They succeed in staggering over the beds of greenery on which they sleep, in a variety of postures. A crash of thunder is heard. The scene changes. The stage now reveals an abysmal desert. It is bristling with dry rocks; a few cypress trees and some pines are still in existence, and here and there a herd of horrible wild animals is grazing on the dry rush that grows at the base of the rocks. The sea breaks upon the reefs with a roar. AZÉLIS's three companions are asleep upstage.*)

ATTALIDE. (*Still holding a terrified AZÉLIS in his arms.*)
You're trembling, Azélis,
And your heart is beating quickly.
The feeling of fear excites it
More than love!

AZÉLIS. (*Frightened, stuttering, and a little cold.*)
Oh, no. My passion is quite sincere!
And every day you'll see me busy,
Happily trying to please you.

(*Anxiously looking all around her.*)
But where do you hold your court
In this dreadful lair?
ATTALIDE. In this somber and solitary place,
In this miserable and wretched country.
AZÉLIS. But if you're a prince, where are your favorites?
ATTALIDE. That breed is hardly necessary.
A monarch is everyone's father equally
And everyone has an equal right to him.
But to the title of friend, which he bestows,
And to which he aspires,
Never can his heart be a party
Through pretended respect
Which self-interest bestows upon him;
Flattery is the mark of the usurper!
In that case, what an easy-going prince
Grants to those he sees groveling
Is a crime, which he is being forced to commit,
Against the strict and severe virtue
Which should teach him without deceiving him.
AZÉLIS. But where are the subjects who pay you homage?
In short, where are the inhabitants of your kingdom?
ATTALIDE. (*Indicating the animals.*)
You see them on this cold pasture;
They come with slow steps to welcome you.
Their reception is simple and wild;
It's like their feelings.
At least, with these courtiers,
Never do artifice and deceit,
Arrogance or bad faith
Hinder, like elsewhere,
The truth from reaching me
Because of too much disrespect.
(*The animals go away gradually.*)
AZÉLIS. Oh, what pleasant affairs of state!
It's not the way of our courts.
And so you're only ruling over bears anyway;
You certainly ought to be bored

With that philosophical taste!
(*To herself.*) This singular individual
Certainly looks a little caustic to me!
(*Aloud.*) Well, my lord, I say it without scorn,
But really, you rule a lousy country!
ATTALIDE. There's no place that love cannot beautify.
These caverns, these deserts
Will become cheerful and dear to you,
If you know how to love.
Sometimes, you have to make a sacrifice to that god,
And hardships strengthen its chains.
As for me, wherever the hand of love unites us,
I'll find the entire universe.
AZÉLIS. I like this courtesy,
And everything you say is charming.
I'm flattered by it, and I feel it.
But it seems to me a person
Should be able to be in love in public;
To be isolated is madness,
And very often dangerous.
You can be sure, if the bond that binds us
Had some witnesses nowadays,
It would be much less dull.
Publicizing your happiness
Gives it a more lively and sweeter appeal;
Then you arouse envy
And all the charms of life
Consist in making people jealous.
ATTALIDE. Don't think that way. A person gets worried,
And irritated showing the seductive sights of happiness.
The public pride that vanity arouses
More easily forgives love's faults.
Oh! Believe me, wherever a person lives,
Wealth, wit, fashion, and awards
Will always be the despair of fools.
AZÉLIS. So may it please you,
But according to my way of thinking,
The great crime is to be bored.

ATTALIDE. And can you be bored when you're in love?
AZÉLIS. I admit that, with you, love is happiness supreme,
But, to vary it,
To keep it from being the same,
You sometimes have to forget it.
For, after all, try as you will to say
That you adore me every day,
Though you might be charming to some degree,
A person cannot always be in love.
In that case, how does he fill up
The gaps in his heart?
ATTALIDE. I burn for you with a passion
That doesn't fear those distressing concerns.
Each day, something new and charming,
Offered to my affection by the hands of love,
Will make my every moment different
By deifying my ecstasy.
AZÉLIS. There's always something tender in your words;
That pleases me and charms me,
But, forgive my vulnerability,
Solitude alarms and troubles my mind.
I'd be less afraid, as I've already told you,
If I was hoping to fascinate you
Through a little bit of jealousy;
The fear of losing me would arouse longing,
The desire to keep me.
Say it's madness, if you like,
But to each his own, and most assuredly,
You'll find love in this idiosyncrasy
At least as much as in the fervor of the feeling
Your lips express so vigorously.
ATTALIDE. (*Somewhat bitter.*)
Ah! Here I see more flirtatiousness
Than sentiments designed to charm me, Azélis.
You hide it very skillfully,
But it shows, and reveals your inclinations.
Leave this deceit to those with cold hearts;
When you're sensitive, and love your husband,

You bring him to his knees
By feelings and not jealousy.
AZÉLIS. (*Lowering her eyes.*)
You're going to scold me. I'm not saying a word, Attalide.
You say you like to have the truth.
It likewise pleases me. The truth alone is my guide,
But as soon as my sincerity
Makes me accused of treachery,
I prefer silence, oh, yes, the strictest silence,
Than to see my feelings suspected.
(*The animals reappear.*)
ATTALIDE. (*Having figured her out; in a slightly ironic tone of voice.*)
Oh! You're charming, and my elated soul
Sees nothing more in you than an adored lover
Whose honesty delights me.
These trivial errors of your mind
Must certainly be released from your heart;
Don't consider me a savage any more,
A being made to persecute you.
I renounce my hermitage,
And I'm going to take you
A short distance away from its lair.
Those animals you see grazing
On the sea rushes of that shore,
Will pay tribute to you at this very moment
If you come out to pet them.
However, dread their zeal.
The test I'm giving you is cruel perhaps,
But, I think, with you, it's necessary.
Besides, it shouldn't frighten me because
Of the loyalty you promised me.
(*Cleverly.*) Am I wrong?
AZÉLIS. (*Shyly.*) Certainly not.
My lord, I hear you but I don't understand you.
What kind of test will help you?
Tell me what must be done.

ATTALIDE. (*Taking her hand and leading her toward the animals.*)
Touch that panther without fear,
Kiss that tiger, or caress that bear,
And with the breath of love
You'll bring about a metamorphosis
Like in a rose
When the wind causes it to open.
AZÉLIS. (*Very childishly.*)
Ah! No, no, really. I don't dare.
No, no, I'm seized with fear.
ATTALIDE. (*Shrewdly coaxing her.*)
Don't be afraid. Pet them with confidence.
Do you doubt your power?
Is it up to me to reveal it?
If you have to resemble the gods, they say,
To imitate their knowledge,
Risk everything without suspicion.
A single glance from your eyes
Will be their match!
AZÉLIS. (*She runs childishly after a lion that's running away.*)
Hey, this one's trying to get away!
(*She touches a tiger that immediately changes into a fifteen-year-old young man.*)
And this one is changing. Oh! Good heavens! It's a man!
Tell me what to call him.
He's very young and very handsome.
ATTALIDE. (*Looking at him.*)
Because of his age, he's called Lili.
AZÉLIS. (*She touches a panther who likewise transforms.*)
Let's take a look at this other one . . .
What? The same thing?
(*Throwing herself into ATTALIDE's arms.*)
Ah! My beloved prince, I love you
Much more now than ever.
ATTALIDE. (*To himself.*)
The shrewd creature. What art, without affectation!
AZÉLIS. (*Completely innocent.*)

Then tell me how I happen to be
Creating men now?
ATTALIDE. (*Very shrewdly.*) In these surroundings,
It's one of the rights of beauty.
Does it please you?
AZÉLIS. (*Blushing.*) Why not?
ATTALIDE. Ah! I'm enchanted.
AZÉLIS. (*Again running wildly towards the beasts.*)
I want to use my talent again.
(*She touches a leopard and the magic turns out the same. As soon as this third boy appears, the orchestra is heard, and the three boys dance around AZÉLIS. ATTALIDE does not stop looking at her. When the dance is over, the young men withdraw upstage, without leaving the stage. AZÉLIS has fallen into a deep reverie; the animals have disappeared.*)
ATTALIDE. (*After a pause, and looking attentively at AZÉLIS.*)
Well! Are you satisfied
With this benevolence?
Can I return them now
To their initial existence without regret?
AZÉLIS. (*Alarmed.*)
What? You're going to change them back into beasts?
Why, for heaven's sake?
ATTALIDE. (*Subtly pretending, and smiling, his hand on his forehead.*)
All heads like that are feared;
The slightest thing inflames them and subdues them.
AZÉLIS. (*Vivacity, finesse, and gaiety.*)
Good! You're jealous, and I'm enchanted by it!
We both gain by this event:
You earn love, most certainly.
Me . . . pride! Seeing that your troubled soul
Was afraid to lose me for a moment.
But you'd distress me if you thought
I was so easy to inflame.
No, no, to you alone belongs the glory
Of captivating and charming me.
Ah! Don't lower the price of the victory

By not knowing how to love better.
You were going to weaken it
By thinking I was a coquette,
And prevent yourself from assessing
The value of your conquest.
If I really have any charms,
Why wouldn't you want
To let them be adored by others?
Are their eyes like yours?
Do they offer any trivial tributes
To these features?
Well! It seems to me that's a triumph besides.
Forgive me this exaggeration,
But the more ardent the worship,
The more it seems to me that the idol
Should be dear to its worshiper.
ATTALIDE. (*Mixing bitterness with his sarcasm.*)
That's too much the way of the world,
But it's, nonetheless, rather pleasing.
I agree with you. When a person really is in love,
All suspicion should be abolished.
AZÉLIS. (*The most bashful audacity.*)
Well! To convince me, summon Lili to me.
You're growing pale.
Oh, what outrageous childishness!
Really, what vulnerability!
I don't know any more what I have to do
To prove my sincerity;
And you hear something mysterious
In the most trivial eccentricity of my frivolousness.
ATTALIDE. (*Hardly controlling himself.*)
Then that child was pleasing to you?
AZÉLIS. (*Somewhat restrained, and blushing.*)
Not a word! What a figment of your imagination!
Nothing pleases me but you.
You alone are what I want.
I thought he had pretty hair.
I wanted to see it. What a harsh expression!

(*Seeing that he's getting angry, she proceeds to wheedle him with candor and naïveté.*)
No, wait! Let's make up.
Whatever's making you angry,
I promise I won't do it anymore.
ATTALIDE. (*Shaking himself free of her arms.*)
Ah! That's too much! I can keep quiet no longer.
I understand your heart at last.
Now experience my anger:
The fatal moment has arrived.
(*During this speech, the young dancers have disappeared and the entire island is filled with savage beasts.*)
I leave you to yourself,
You certainly deserve it.
Is this then the way that people love?
What you call frivolousness
Is the most complete and best contrived
Refinement of coquettishness
I've ever seen in my life!
(*Indicating the beasts to her.*)
Wear out its features on these wretched beasts.
I hand them over to your artifice,
And leave you with them.
Completely astonished, I swear to you,
To discover that the hand of Love
Could place inside a being full of the bloom of youth,
So much beauty along with so much deceit. (*He leaves.*)
(*The sky becomes overcast; lightning flashes, and gradually claps of thunder are heard in the distance. The sea becomes restless, the wind makes the waves swell, and smashes them violently against the shore. The background begins to be filled more and more with ferocious beasts whose howling is terrifying. The entire delivery of this monologue is interrupted by sound effects that depict the various stages of the storm, the howling of the beasts, the blowing of the wind, and the bellowing of the tide.*)
AZÉLIS. (*Alone.*) Ah! How easily he gets angry!
I didn't think a lover
Took offense so quickly.

God! Now what is my fate?
He leaves me in this wild desert
With some animals who are now
Going to devour me in their rage.
(*She wanders upstage. Storm.*)
Maybe it's possible, however,
To protect myself from their cruel injuries
By stroking them like before.
(*She tries and trembles.*)
No, I don't dare.
Ah, if they turned into men
I'd be much less afraid of their rage.
(*The animals surround her; she trembles.*)
Whatever you may be, beasts, gnomes,
Pity my distress, and don't eat me.
That's all I'm afraid of.
(Storm. She looks at her companions.)
Those poor girls who are sleeping
Run even greater risks.
(*Storm. A thick cloud is overhead; claps of thunder become frequent, and the lightning becomes sharper and more frequent as well. It begins to hail, and the sea swells tremendously.*)
What horrible storms are gathering!
What dreadful weather!
(*The sun is setting. Calm.*)
Night is coming. I'm dying. Ah! Cruel day!
Now, I see all hope is far away!
(*Pandemonium. She goes near one of her sleeping companions; she shakes one of her arms without being able to wake her up.*)
Zéphirine. You're sleeping . . . luckier than I,
You won't be afraid of that moment of horror!
(*For a moment, she sits beside her companion; the thunderclaps are becoming very violent. A great clap of thunder. She gets up.*)
What did I do to deserve so much misery!
And why has God's inauspicious hand
Destined me for such a wretched life!

(*The stage is in total darkness. The setting is lit only by the multitude of lightning flashes, and the fire started by the lighting when it occasionally strikes a tree. The trees burning brightly add to the horror of the situation. The falling hail is terrifying as well. Claps of thunder.*)
Heavens! Here I am in the darkness!
I see only the ominous features
Of lightning flashing through the sky;
And nature, violently unleashed,
Seems to take a perverse delight
In exhausting its efforts
Above abandoned Azélis
To convince her of her miserable mistakes.
(*In tears, she leans against a rock. Animal cries. Thunder and lightning continue.*)
Oh, happy abode of innocence!
Gardens so dear to my childhood!
Charming places, you are lost!
Since my feeble existence is almost at an end,
My sad eyes will never see you again.
(*The sound of waves. A bolt of lightning falls with a crash. The lightning bolt falls beside her; she utters a cry, and throws herself to her knees.*)
Stop, vengeful God! Your thunderbolt enlightens me at last.
Attalide. Attalide, ah! Yes, I deceived you.
Kissing the dust, I realize my mistake.
At least condescend to hear my regrets!
(*She gets up. Groans.*)
What to do in this situation?
If I call the Fairy, Almanzor will appear;
And I only want the presence
Of the husband I offended by my behavior
A little while ago.
(*General disturbance. A bolt of lightning falls. A terrifying cry. After a long pause.*)
Good heavens! I'm breathing.
(*Gradually coming to her senses.*)
Ah! I'm still breathing.
By sparing me, the gods,

Yes, the gods whom I implore,
Are undoubtedly saving me for greater calamities
To overwhelm me with every misfortune. *(She weeps.)*
(*It seems as if nature is turning upside down. The ground shakes, the rocks fall down, the trees are smashed to pieces; the ocean waves, driven as high as the clouds by the storm, fall back into dreadful chasms with a horrible noise. AZÉLIS flees; she runs; she stops. If she escapes from one danger, she encounters another. She goes completely out of her mind.*)
(*Screaming.*) Oh, mother . . . mother . . .
Oh, for pity's sake, help me!
(*She turns toward the dawn, raising her arms as the FAIRY said. At this point, the storm is in its final stages and the striking bolts of lightning seem to follow her everywhere.*)
(*Continuing, with the same cries.*) Help me, help me, mother.
I'm dying of regret even more than fright.
(*An azure chair, drawn by swans, appears in the air. It belongs to the FAIRY. A sweet and melodic music replaces the sound effects of the storm. Gradually, the weather grows calm: the winds abate, the sea becomes quiet again, and the animals disappear. All the same, the stage is still in darkness.*)
FAIRY. (*She speaks the first four lines coming down from her chair.*)
Cease, restless winds! Flee, savage beasts.
With the stillness, I bring her heart tranquility.
At my command, let the clouds disappear.
Let us finally make good fortune shine!
(*When the chair is on the ground, the FAIRY steps off of it. The chair flies up again, and AZÉLIS proceeds to bow down at the feet of the FAIRY who continues.*)
Enlightened by your experience, Azélis,
Will you stop believing in coquettishness,
The deceitful allurement you were foisting on him?
AZÉLIS. (*In tears, at the FAIRY's feet.*)
Ah! I detest forevermore
The false ideas I had.
Because of my faults, I lost the affection
Of the wise and decent husband you gave me.
I missed that lesson in my youth.

Give him back to me, if he was meant for me.
I want to consecrate my life to him,
And make amends for the careless mistake
That justifiably alarmed him.
FAIRY. (*Lifting her up.*)
Yes, my power will restore him to you.
I am moved by your tears.
Soon, your husband will reappear
Before your very eyes.
(*She goes to touch AZÉLIS's companions with her wand, speaking the following three lines in such a way that all three of them regain the use of their senses only by the last word of the speech.*)
And you, young beauties, led astray by her words,
Like her, equally educated by misfortune,
Come, share her privilege.
(*Then, at the very edge of the stage, AZÉLIS and her companions fall at the FAIRY's feet in choreographed postures in order to create a pleasing picture, with the FAIRY in the middle holding the four of them, so to speak, under her wing.*)
Oh, my children, flee from error,
Shun its enchanting cup.
In a few moments, it deceives
And captivates our hearts
Through its intoxication.
The attacks of misfortune occur;
The days arrive when old age
Pays, at last, through misery,
For the false pleasures of youth!
The beauty that caresses us
Fades like a flower,
And as soon as its freshness is gone,
We're spurned and abandoned;
Our happiness disappears.
Our sex, born for tears,
Sensitive and sweet, weak and subdued,
Languishes in fear from the moment of our birth;
And from that moment feels downcast and demoralized.
But, starting with childhood, if duty is under control,

And our sex can find its charms in that duty
To recover, in due time, everything it has lost,
Our sex will find in duty two invincible weapons:
Innocence and virtue.
(*She strikes her wand. The scene changes and reveals a gorgeous living room, lit up for a party. At the back is a marble throne. PRINCE ATTALIDE and his three courtiers are leaning against the columns of the throne. As soon as they see the FAIRY and her children, each flies to meet his own: ATTALIDE to AZÉLIS, LILI to ROSÉIDE.*)
AZÉLIS. *(Anticipating ATTALIDE, throwing herself at his feet.)*
We meet again, sensible and tender man,
We meet again, and this time I'm worthy of you.
But, before giving me back the heart I long for,
Allow me, on my knees, to lament its loss.
ATTALIDE. (*Lifting her up, with tenderness.*)
I'm the one who should be on his knees, lovely creature,
A lover is only unforgivable
When his beloved is in tears.
Ah! Like you, whoever can make up for his mistakes
Rarely makes them again!
FAIRY. (*Uniting all eight of them, and in the center.*)
Pleasures and feasts, you take the place of sorrow.
Oh, god of love, let us complete the conquest,
Let us unite our powers at this sacred moment
To make the gifts of this happy celebration
As unique as they are dazzling.
Until the last day that fate prepares for them,
Let these married couples always be lovers.
(*The three young princes and some of the women of the Blissful Island perform a very brief ballet which will end the act. No men other than ATTALIDE's three favorites should appear in the ballet since they don't exist on the Fairy's island.*)

END OF THE PUNISHED COQUETTE

CONTINUATION OF THE MARRIAGE OF THE ARTS

(Mr. Desclapon's study is restored and the backstage scenes continue.)
BELVAL. At last we have succeeded, lovely Émilie. The scoundrel is unmasked, and soon I'm going to convince your father how much that man was unworthy of you. But be calm. He's back in his own house now, which I think is a lot better than being with you.
ÉMILIE. Oh, heavens! What have you done? My father will never forgive you.
VERCEUIL. Ah! I'm really counting on his gratitude rather than his resentment.
DESCLAPON. (*Very disturbed.*) Ah! Sir, what have I just heard? What does this bizarre behavior mean? My friend leaves. His marriage broken off.
VERCEUIL. (*Spiritedly.*) That man, sir, wasn't meant to claim your daughter's hand. Do you know him?
DESCLAPON. Perfectly.
VERCEUIL. I don't think so. Cast your eyes over these documents, sir. (*He presents a wad of papers that MR. DESCLAPON examines.*) They will prove to you that Mr. Vieuxblanc was only an adventurer, a swindler. And the property he boasted to you about never existed, except in his imagination. Fallen at last beneath the rule of justice, he is certainly going to be punished for his frauds. He's the one I portrayed for you in *The Dangerous Man*. I put the torch of conviction before his eyes; he preferred to run away rather than defend himself. You'll never see him again.
DESCLAPON. Ah! I don't doubt that these documents are authentic. Oh! How all of this surprises me! But, sir, who are you to claim my daughter's hand?
VERCEUIL. Disguised under the name of Belval to make things clearer for you, my real name is Count Verceuil. Rich, honest, and the most loving of men: those are my titles! Find

someone who embodies them more than I do, and I'll surrender my rights to him.

DESCLAPON. But what about that wretched man? What did you do with him? Where was he taken?

VERCEUIL. Everyone can tell you that he left in his own coach. I'm satisfied to have enlightened him. And now he's at home.

DESCLAPON. Sir, sir, I think all of this can be called very irregular behavior.

VERCEUIL. (*Presenting ÉMILIE to her father.*) I agree, sir. But here's my excuse: my advocate, *(Again showing the documents.)* and my evidence.

ÉMILIE. Oh, father, at your knees, I crave my life's happiness.

DESCLAPON. (*Preventing his daughter from moving.*) So that was the objective of all those scenes: to train me and to charm her with your examples. (*To MARTON.*) Here's one creature who's served you well, I think, throughout this entire game. She's the most scheming, the most mischievous . . .

COUNT VERCEUIL. (*Interrupting quickly.*) Easy, easy! I want you to be kind to her. I'm paying her a commission of a thousand crowns[42] for getting me married, sir. That would be well below her value, if I had to pay for her ability.

MARTON. (*To the Count.*) Oh, sir!

DESCLAPON. (*To ÉMILIE.*) In a word, daughter, you want him? I consent. Sir, I give her to you since she loves you, and I beg you always to consider me a second father.

ÉMILIE. Oh, tender and respectable father!

COUNT VERCEUIL. Ah! Sir, you'll soon judge my gratitude by my love. I want neither one of them to have any boundaries but my life.

DESCLAPON. (*Taking their hands.*) I'm counting on it. (*To the audience.*) But you, fathers of families, when you have daughters to be married, believe me, don't put on a play!

---

[42] A crown was worth about $24.00 in 2012 US currency.

Couplets

Tune: "From Top to Bottom."

DESCLAPON. A little bit of everything!
See how a lover takes advantage of
A little bit of everything
To drag a confession out of us.
Everything serves him to cover his cunning,
Ah! Be afraid of love when it uses
A little bit of everything.
VERCEUIL. A little bit of everything
In this perilous affair,
A little bit of everything
To possess the object of my desire;
If I thought I needed to be careful,
It's because to win a father, you have to have
A little bit of everything.
ÉMILIE. (*To the audience.*) A little bit of everything
That's the maxim of the true wise man.
A little bit of everything
But keep a happy medium!
For you have to fear disaster
When you intend to use
A little bit of everything.
MARTON. (*To the audience.*) A little bit of everything.
We'll often go to the theatre[43]
For a little bit of everything;
To hear the happy art of play
Mixing together with the sweets of life,
The charming philosophy:
A little bit of everything.

COUNT VERCEUIL. Up until now, sir, my dancers have had little opportunity to display their talents. Allow them, I beg you, to perform for you in something a bit more significant.

DESCLAPON. Very gladly, sir. What will be the subject of this spectacle?

---

[43] Sade's manuscript reads: *Thalia's House*. In Greek mythology, Thalia was the Muse who presided over comedy.

COUNT VERCEUIL. It's dictated by the hearts of all Frenchmen, sir. Respect, love, and gratitude have drawn it forth from mine. Heir to the name, titles, and property of a father fortunate enough to have earned, from his services, so much gratitude on the part of the sovereign whom we all cherish, I've been waiting for the opportunity to distinguish myself, and have done nothing yet to make myself worthy of possessing so many blessings so soon. What you're going to see will, therefore, celebrate, simultaneously, my wedding and the beloved master whose favors are mine to claim. Pitying the weakness of my abilities to make this tribute worthy of the one to whom it is offered, you will at least share the feeling that gave birth to the idea. Let's find our seats, sir, and let the glimmer of genius that happened to inspire me, electrify you as well. We ennoble ourselves by celebrating a hero.
DESCLAPON. Ah! All the tributes he's been given are sensual delights for a French heart.

(*The actors of the backstage scenes exit and the curtain rises.*)

THE SPECTACLE

The stage represents a forest of laurel trees consecrated to the god Mars. Trophies of arms and flags, on which are inscribed some of the Emperor's[44] great military victories, are placed on these trees. At the back of this grove, the temple of Glory is seen on a hill. The nine Muses are gathered on the colonnade of the temple. In front of the temple is placed the bust of the hero, resting on a pedestal of laurels, from which it seems to emerge. In the distance is seen the Temple of Janus whose doors are open. A warlike music is heard. People from the four corners of the earth, gathered into four groups composed of men and women dressed in their native costumes, fill both sides and the back of the forest, but in a semi-circle, in such a way that the bust is in the middle of them.

After the overture, each group of people, a mixture of men and women, files on to the proscenium in order of rank. Leaving, each group proceeds to return to its original place. And during this movement, the head of each group, always representing a warrior from the dominant nation of that group, places a crown of laurels on the bust. From the moment they begin their procession, to the sound of music indigenous to their locales, they sing in chorus the verse that is indicated for each of them, in the following order:

VERSE OF THE EUROPEANS

Let us sing, and in the forest of the god Mars,
Let us crown the beloved child with victory,
So that he may receive from all sides,
The sacred tributes that are due his glory.

---

[44] Napoleon.

VERSE OF THE ASIANS

From the Hindu shores to the Tartar sands,
May he see men at his feet as well.
Among civilized people or barbarians,
His brow will always be crowned with laurels.

VERSE OF THE AFRICANS

In the midst of the burning deserts of Africa,
His famous name aroused our love;
And his lofty deeds, his heroic valor
Have struck us like the morning star.

VERSE OF THE AMERICANS

From one pole to the other, he will see the hemisphere
United by Columbus to the rest of the world
Bring him both the homage and tribute
That we owe his valor, that we owe his virtue.

Once this ceremony is finished and each national group finds itself back in its original position, a leader from each group comes forward, with an olive branch in hand. Together they proceed to weave them into the laurels, which form the pedestal of the bust, and to place them in such a way that they shade it by intersecting and meeting in the shape of a crown whose top part seems to be ready for two other busts. During their movement, they sing the following verse whose music is a combination of the other four.

VERSE
(*Of the united people, and which all should repeat in chorus.*)

Before his altars, let the earth and the ocean
Fall with respect, as if at the feet of their gods;
If those they adore could create the world,
Napoleon, far greater, can make them happy.

The leaders return to their places at the head of their respective nations. Now, in the midst of the sweetest melody, the Graces carry in the busts of the Empress[45] *and the King of Rome*[46] *which they join to the bust of the Emperor by the garlands of myrtle and roses with which the pedestal is likewise adorned. Then they retire toward the Temple of Janus whose doors they close, grouping themselves afterwards on the steps of the temple.*

Three famous women in chariots, drawn by spread eagles, then lift up the three busts and proceed to place them on the steps of the Temple of Glory where they are received by the Nine Muses and the God of Marriage. A host of little Cupids take them away in order to place them on a platform designed to hold them, which should create the nicest picture.

Once this unveiling is completed, the Cupids gather around the chariots of the famous women and fly with them to the sky.

At that moment, the God of Marriage, the Muses and the Graces join with the groups of the various nations in a general ballet.

THE END

[45] Marie Louise of Austria.

[46] This designation is confusing since the Holy Roman Empire was dissolved in 1806, four years before the final manuscript of this play. Napoleon was king of Italy from 1805 to 1814, so the title, "King of Rome," may well refer to him. Even though he prided himself to be anti-religious, Sade may also have meant the leader of the Papal States, i.e., the pope. In that case, the designation would refer to Count Barnaba Niccolò Marìa Luigi Chiaramonti, Pope Pius VII.

The Festival of Friendship

Introduction

All of Sade's biographers and critics attribute *The Festival of Friendship* to his period of incarceration at Charenton between 1803 and 1814 and agree that the play was written in honor of the asylum's director, François Simonet de Coulmier who appears in the play as "Meilcour," the administrator of a mental aylum. The editors of Sade's plays note that the play bears the same title as an ode written by Sade for Cardinal Maury who visited the asylum on 6 October 1812, and that the manuscript is in the hand of the copyist at Charenton who produced the final drafts of *Oxtiern* and *The Shyster*. Annetta Foster argues that *The Festival of Friendship* was the last new play Sade wrote, his other dramatic activity being "restricted solely to revisions of his former works," while Geoffrey Gorer, Gilbert Lély and Maurice Lever simply regard it as the only surviving example of a number of plays Sade wrote for the theatre at Charenton. Although Lever suggests that the play was written between 1810 and 1812, the most peaceful of times between Sade and Coulmier, Dr. Iwan Bloch cites a letter from Royer Collard, Chief Doctor of the Hospital at Charenton, dated 2 August 1808, that refers to an "allegorical piece" written in Coulmier's honor. While it is conceivable that Sade wrote many such works at Charenton, it is likely that *The Festival of Friendship* was written as early as 1808, a year filled with theatrical activity at the asylum.

Sade's years at Charenton might well have been his most fulfilling theatrically. Coulmier approved of theatrical activity as proper treatment for the inmates at the asylum, as the following unpublished document suggests:

> We searched for ways to create diversions by means of innocent games, concerts, dancing, and plays in which the roles were filled by patients, which created a real rivalry between them . . . to get as much applause as their companions in misfortune. These occupations kept them active and warded off melancholy ideas, an all too common source of madness. . . . This moral treatment, approved by the most respectable people, by outsiders who eagerly sought tickets to see for themselves the influence of the arts on the moral as well as the physical, succeeded in establishing Charenton's reputation.[47]

It is not difficult to understand why Coulmier and Sade might have joined forces. A playwright, amateur actor, and director, Sade was the perfect choice of "artistic director" of the asylum theatre, a post he held from 1805 when theatrical performances began to 1813 when the theatre was officially closed.

A letter from Sade to his cousin Madame Bimard on 4 May 1811 provides us with a description of the theatre, evidently designed to Sade's specifications. Built over the woman's ward, the stage was fully equipped with dressing rooms, wing space and an orchestra pit. Across from the stage and above the audience was a special box reserved for Coulmier and his guests. On either side of this box were tiers of seats, twenty for men on one side, twenty for women on the other. These were reserved for the least violent of the hospital inmates. Sade's own "Sensible," Madame Quesnet was given a box of her own with seven seats and two hundred spectators were accommodated in the pit. A letter from Sade to Coulmier dated 1810 provides us with a typical audience breakdown, with the greatest number of seats (as many as 90) going to invited guests. Employees of the asylum were given 36 seats and the inmates 60 for a total of 186 (not counting Coulmier and his guests). It is unknown why the number of patients' seats was reduced to 40 the following year (as suggested by Sade's letter to Madame Bimard). Perhaps the warnings voiced by Doctor Royer Collard in 1808 regarding the harmful effects of theatre upon the patients were at last being heeded, or perhaps there were simply fewer patients in residence at the asylum. At any rate, among the celebrities in attendance were Madame Cochelet, a lady-in-waiting to the Queen of Holland (see

[47] Cited by Maurice Lever in his biography, *Donatien Alphones François, marquis de Sade.*

the letter dated 23 May 1810 below), the mayors of Charenton and Carrières, and an anonymous Irish physician.

Before long, Sade's lunatic theatre aroused considerable interest among Parisian intellectuals who vied for invitations to attend the operas, comedies or dramas staged once a month at the asylum. On holidays, the plays were even followed by a display of fireworks. That the reputation grew to international proportions is clear from a letter Sade sent to Louise Cochelet, a lady-in-waiting to Queen Hortense of Holland, dated 23 May 1810:

> The interest you've taken in the dramatic presentations of the *pensionnaires* of my house makes me want to offer you tickets to each of their productions. Spectators such as you, Madame, are such a good influence on their self-confidence, that they find, merely in the hope of holding your attention and pleasing you, everything that excites their imagination and nourishes their talent. Next Monday, the twenty-eighth, they're performing *The Spirit of Contradiction*, *Marton and Frontin*, and *The Two Savoyards*. I await your orders to send you the tickets you desire, and I beseech you to present my respects to the ladies in the court of her majesty the Queen of Holland.

Sade's use of the term *pensionnaire* is significant in that the Comédie-Française used the term to represent actors who worked on salary, as opposed to the *sociétaires*, who were sharing members of the troupe. It is clear that Sade was imagining himself a legitimate theatrical producer here when he refers to the theatre as "my house." *The Spirit of Contradiction* was a one-act comedy in prose by Charles, sieur de La Dufresny, produced originally in 1700. *Marton and Frontin; or, The Assault of the Servants* was a one-act comedy in prose by Jean-Baptiste Dubois, originally produced in 1804. *The Two Savoyards* was a one-act opera by Nicholas d'Alayrac (Dalayrac) with a libretto by Benoît Joseph Marsolier des Vivetières, originally produced in 1789.

While many of the roles in Sade's company were performed by inmates of the asylum, occasionally stars came from Paris to act the leads. In his biography, *The Marquis de Sade*, Donald Thomas argues against the theory that most of the roles were played by inmates of the asylum, suggesting rather that contemporary accounts of the productions prove that the acting was done primarily by professionals with inmates playing only minor roles. He concludes that for "most of the patients, therapy consisted in watching drama rather than in taking part." His argument, however, is at odds with Labouisse-Rochefort's account of the Marquis himself playing the lead role in *The Impertinent Man* on 5 July 1805 and the fact that only 40-60 seats were reserved for patients in the auditorium. Sade always directed with a help of Madame Saint-Aubin, the "diamond" of the Opéra-Comique company. Her presence often attracted the participation of young actors and actresses who felt that their association with her at Charenton might help further their careers. One such novice was Miss Flore whose *Memoires* provide an appealing account of the Marquis at Charenton:

> He had a handsome head, rather long, an aquiline nose, open nostrils, a narrow mouth, and a protruding lower lip. The corners of his mouth turned down with a disdainful smile. His eyes, small but shining, were hidden beneath thick, bushy eyebrows. His creased eyelids covered the corners of his eyes like those of a cat's. . . . He wore his hair tucked up in the style of Louis XV, slightly curled up on the sides, and all of it perfectly powdered. . . . His figure was erect and tall, his noble bearing was that of a high-society gentleman.

Sade did not only function as director and sometime author of the plays produced at Charenton. When required, he acted as prompter, stage-manager, scene-painter, and actor. The poet, August de Labouisse-Rochefort, provides us with an account of Sade's performance on 5 July 1805 of the title role in Joseph-François Edouard Corsembleu Desmahis's one-act comedy *The Impertinent Man*:

> He had nothing of the easy tone and grace

That the pit applauded in Fleury.[48]
I was tempted to cry out from my seat:
"Mister Damis, for heaven's sake, keep quiet;
Take elsewhere your insipid delivery,
Your shifty appearance, your sparkling costume,
And all your frozen gestures."
That actor is very big, very fat, very cold, very heavy;
He's a large mass, a vulgar, short man,
Whose head looks like a shameful ruin!
And yet, many a stupid spectator
Clapped their hands with too much enthusiasm for him,
Though often, the applause was short!

Whether or not critics are correct in dismissing the account as merely a caricature of the proceedings, it seems clear that the Marquis, a plump man now in his sixties, was more suited to off-stage endeavors, not the least of which were the dinner parties held in his rooms for the actresses from Paris, as well as other invited guests after the performances. There his beloved Madame Quesnet would act as hostess, while Sade would act the role of the theatrical entrepreneur, the part he most wanted to play all his life.

Since Miss Flore describes Sade in her *Memoirs* as the author of the "diversion and songs for Mr. Coulmier's birthday," and since a reference is made to an "allegorical" entertainment in Doctor Collard's indictment against the theatre at Charenton, it seems clear that *The Festival of Friendship* was produced at the asylum. Whether Sade himself participated as an actor in the production, or whether or not it was repeated annually for the director's birthday, is a matter of speculation.

---

[48] Abraham-Joseph Bénard, called Fleury (1750–1822). Doyen of the Comédie-Française until his retirement in 1818, he was considered the greatest comic actor of his age, and noted especially for his portrayal of Alceste in Moliére's *The Misanthrope*.

THE FESTIVAL OF FRIENDSHIP
Prologue
including
THE TOKEN OF APPRECIATION

Vaudeville in one act

CHARACTERS

Mr. Meilcour (Honeycourt), *owner of the land where the festival is taking place, and the guest of honor*
Mr. Blinval, *a society actor*
Mr. Dubosquet and Mr. Villebrun, *friends of Blinval, sharing the same interests*
Mr. Thierville, *another of Blinval's friends, given the role of Briserein (Breaknothing), the troupe's porter, in the prologue*
Madame Blinval, *Blinval's wife, and a participant in his dramatic entertainments*
Augustus, *their son, who also participates in the entertainments*
Adèle, *Mr. Meilcour's godchild.*
Two young village girls, *living on Mr. Meilcour's lands.*
A crowd of young village girls.
Several supernumeraries, *belonging to the Blinval troupe.*

The setting is Mr. Meilcour's garden, decorated for a festival.

PROLOGUE

(*When the curtain rises, several young girls are seen picking flowers from the trees in the garden.*)

Tune: "Rondo" from the opera, The Queen of Golconde[49]
ADÈLE. (*Alone.*) Everywhere, a day to celebrate . . .
CHORUS. Everywhere, a day to celebrate . . .
ADÈLE. Everywhere, a day to celebrate
Is a day of pleasure.
Yes, let this day of celebration
Be a day of pleasure.
CHORUS. To celebrate the festival,
Let's banish all sadness.
Our hearts are festive;
That's the surest
Of our pleasures.
It's the refrain
Of our pleasures.
The refrain
Of our pleasures,
The refrain
Of our pleasures,
It's the refrain,
The refrain
Of our pleasures.
Of our pleasures . . .
It's the refrain
Of our pleasures,
It's the refrain
Of our pleasures.
(*The orchestra plays a roundelay.*)
ADÈLE. (*Alone.*) Let's go, dear companions,
To enliven those fields
With our laughter and our songs.
Our songs express . . .
Our songs express
Our feelings.

[49] Composed by Pierre-Alexandre Monsigny with a libretto by Michel-Jean Sedaine.

CHORUS. Why, yes, truly,
Why, yes, truly,
Let's banish all sadness.
Why, yes, truly,
Why, yes, truly,
Let's banish all sadness.
Listen to the echo,
The echo is about to say
That sadness must flee.
ADÈLE. Everywhere, a day to celebrate
Is a day of pleasure.
Ah! Let the day of celebration
Be a day of pleasure!
CHORUS. To celebrate the festival,
Banish all sadness.
The chorus belongs to the festival,
Here's our refrain:
Of our pleasures
It's the refrain.
It's the refrain
Of our pleasures,
It's the refrain
Of our pleasures,
It's the refrain
Of our pleasures,
It's the refrain
Of our pleasures.
(*After the rondo, all the young girls go off and form groups to their right at the rear of the stage. There, they appear to talk among themselves and show one another the bouquets they've gathered. Then, from the left, enter BLINVAL, VILLEBRUN, and DUBOSQUET who leisurely walk down to the front of the stage. ADÈLE and her two companions are still with the other girls, until after the conversation between the three men.)*
VILLEBRUN. What are those children doing?
And what's the reason behind their charming efforts?
BLINVAL. It seems to me that everyone's getting ready
To praise the master of this place.

DUBOSQUET. Yes, truly, it's a day of celebration!
BLINVAL. Then we must take advantage of it for a wonderful outing.
DUBOSQUET. What are you considering?
BLINVAL. (*With a little thought*.)
Yes, we should get some fun out of our walking.
Looking for a good time, we used to go,
You know, with our companions
Not far from this district,
To one of our friends' houses, to spend a day merrily
Singing and dancing and acting a play.
What do you say? Let's not go any farther.
DUBOSQUET. Really, this seems like a very nice idea.
Let's hurry up and do it.
BLINVAL. And to make it even more enjoyable,
Let's introduce ourselves without embarrassment
As actors who travel the countryside
And who are everywhere accompanied by pleasure.
A person can act what he's not
When, so often, he's not what he acts.
Go, Dubosquet. Go at once
And reveal our plans and try to get them approved.
(*Detaining VILLEBRUN*.)
Let's both of us go and set things up.
(*Running after DUBOSQUET who was already going out*.)
Above all, you'll have to return immediately.
Let's approach them with all of our people.
(*DUBOSQUET exits*.) Don't be nervous.
Let's do all we can
So the deception
Can succeed to our liking.
(*Here, the three young ladies draw nearer; the others find new places beneath the trees and busy themselves in such a way as to be seen and heard when they proceed to repeat in chorus the last two lines of the couplets that are about to be sung*.)
ADÈLE. (*Coming forward*.) What do these gentlemen want?
BLINVAL. Excuse us, Miss,
We're traveling in this delightful and clear setting

Without anything recalling to our minds
The name given to this attractive place.
Admiring its thick, lush groves,
A person would think he was close to the groves of Amahonte,
For here he discovers everything that's been said
About that island where Venus used to attract mortal men.
The Graces are close to her altars.
ONE OF THE VILLAGE GIRLS. (*Lightly.*)
Enough of this small talk, gentlemen.
We don't at all deserve so much sweet talk.
What do you want from us? Say it simply.
VILLEBRUN. Would you kindly tell us where we are?
THE OTHER VILLAGE GIRL. First, you must begin by understanding
That no one worships Venus here.
Our religion is purer: it's based on virtues.
This blessed sanctuary is their temple
And we take as their example,
The generous mortal whom we're celebrating today.
ADÈLE. In me, you see his godchild,
And these flowers, these fruit that we're picking,
Are the feeble gifts of our hearts.
BLINVAL. According to what we hear you say about him,
Since the virtuous mortal is so rightly deified,
Undoubtedly, it's a god you're worshiping here.
ADÈLE. (*Sings. To the tune of "I love you so much, I love you so much."*)
The one who governs this place,
Who pleases and inspires us,
Is not yet in a class with the gods;
But he is as wise as they are,
And like them, he deserves the worship
That we owe to the masters of the earth.
He calls us his children,
And we love him like a father.
(*The last two lines of this song, and the first two lines that follow, are repeated softly, and in such a way as to imitate an echo in the forest.*)

ONE OF THE VILLAGE GIRLS. Every day, his latest act of kindness,
Charming our sensitive souls,
Attaches us to him forever
With indestructible bonds.
Then we foolishly think ourselves
Unable to increase our veneration;
But the next day, seeing him,
We love him even more.
THE OTHER VILLAGE GIRL. With this deep emotion
That tenderness requires of us,
We want to entwine roses
With the virtues that adorn his brow.
Ah! You know that, instead of these flowers
We're giving him for the celebration,
His crown should be made
With our hearts.
ONE OF THE VILLAGE GIRLS. (*Immediately.*)
Stay here with these gentlemen, Adèle,
For a moment. Don't be afraid.
You know that duty calls us;
When it is inspired by your heart,
All of your happiness lies in fulfilling it. (*She exits with her companions.*)
BLINVAL. (*To ADÈLE.*) We are impressed by your example
Of passionate enthusiasm,
But it makes us want to know the person
Who inspires it and whom you're celebrating.
ADÈLE. Stay with us; you'll see him soon.
From that moment on, you'll love him.
I'll bet you'll treasure him.
I beg you, tell me, while you're waiting,
What brings you here on this occasion?
In a word, what do you do?
BLINVAL. You want to know?
ADÈLE. Yes, I beseech you.
VILLEBRUN. (*To BLINVAL.*) Answer the question.
(*To ADÈLE.*) If the business hasn't got a great reputation,

It's at least very pleasant,
And most often preferable
To every other occupation.
ADÈLE. Well . . .
BLINVAL. Since we have to tell you . . .
We're strolling players
Who roam the countryside every day
Entertaining and instructing
Both the city and the simple folk.
ADÈLE. (*With a little disdain.*) That profession . . .
BLINVAL. (*Energetically.*) Of course it seems frivolous to you,
But it should be the school of virtue.
Virtue ought to be felt in the depths of the heart
When someone pretends to inspire it onstage.
Can anyone produce a sublime emotion
Without knowing it, without experiencing it?
Can the actor in the role of Titus
Portray it for you if he doesn't have his virtues?
Will he awaken them in the breasts of the audience
If, lying to his public, he's even belying history?
In short, I maintain that the student of Thalia
If he expects to be successful
Must be a respectable man,
And in him, a moment of deception is only excused
When it is true to nature.
ADÈLE. (*Moved.*) You've convinced me with this argument.
Truly, if I had the talent
To follow that career,
I'd join up with you.
VILLEBRUN. Really, you couldn't be better at it!
Come on, be brave. Join us.
ADÈLE. Well, stay for the celebration
We're putting together today.
Let your talents be presented to him
For whom, you see, we're preparing
A feeble token of respect, alas . . . but deeply felt!
From this moment, until it becomes
A problem to me, may your wish be granted!

BLINVAL. Without any hesitation, we accept.
VILLEBRUN. Look! We have exactly what we need.
It's a tribute we've already produced
For one of our friends, the most virtuous of men.
Oh! That's your man, word for word!
BLINVAL. We call it *The Token of Appreciation*.
That little opera is not without its charms
And would be appropriate in this situation.
You'll have to learn it quickly.
ADÈLE. Do you think I'm so arrogant to think
That I could learn the entire Lover's role
In an instant?
BLINVAL. (*Heartily*.) Ah! You'll learn it all, and enthusiastically!
And I'll vouch for your intelligence
When you have gratitude,
A powerful incentive in the heart.
Now, it's up to you to tell us, after all,
The name of the person who, on this day,
Affects you and inspires in you
These reactions of tenderness and love.
ADÈLE. It's Lord Meilcour.
To name him is to praise him.
BLINVAL. (*Very passionately*.)
Meilcour! Ah, yes . . . yes, he's an angel!
Who knows that better than I?
(*To VILLEBRUN*.) It's hard to put into words;
Alas, everything would be too trivial
To describe what I owe him,
But it's all in my heart and in my appreciation.
Could anyone ever forget
The being to whom he owes his existence?
ADÈLE. (*Very passionately*.)
I adore the effects of those kind sentiments.
Ah! How I'd love to see you experience my ecstasy:
I think that we love better when everyone is eager
To participate in our virtuous inclinations.
BLINVAL. Let's go. Let's not waste any time.
Most of all, keep quiet about this.

Don't do anything foolish.
Since he hasn't seen me for such a long time,
It'll only be after my sorry talents
Have entertained him for a few minutes
That I'll risk making him aware
Of the one who glorifies his existence
By loving him dearly until his dying day.
Villebrun, go find our people
And tell them . . . but here's my wife.
How pleased she'll be
When I tell her what's happening!
She's coming with Dubosquet,
The one who plays our old codgers and peasants
With so much natural ability! Ah!
You'll love his face. It adapts to every feeling!
DUBOSQUET. What the devil have you been doing here for so long?
We've been waiting for you for a whole hour.
Does a fellow earn his living standing around, gabbing?
You're making the carriage driver swear!
Don't you know we've got a lot of roads
To travel before nightfall?
You can't neglect your duties in this way!
BLINVAL. (*To his wife, very passionately.*)
Those duties are sacred . . . but soon you'll see
That the holiest duty of all is the one that invigorates me.
I'm sure your heart will handle it like mine.
Does there exist a law
That has more power over a man
Than the sweet gratitude
For kindness he's received?
MRS. BLINVAL. Alas, I've never heard of it!
But what's going on? Tell us about it, quickly!
BLINVAL. (*Rapidly.*)
Ah! Good heavens! When my heart is fluttering
And identifying with great virtues,
I'm so filled with feelings, alas,
I can feel nothing more.

Guess where we are?
At the home of the most virtuous of men,
In a word, at the home of that kind Mr. Meilcour.
MRS. BLINVAL. (*Eagerly.*)
Oh, God! How can we show him our love?
How can we acknowledge
All the friendship and tenderness
He has created in our hearts?
(*To her son who has entered with her.*)
Ah! My child, my beloved child,
You owe him much more than you do your own mother.
In a word, everything he could do for us,
My friends, I tell you, everything, great gods!
He did it.
(*She sings.*) For us he was a second father,
The consoler of our hardships,
A benign god and guardian
Who preserved us from misfortune.
Let us never leave him again, I pray you,
Let us stay near him forever.
We will improve our lives
Just by devoting all of our days to him.
THE CHILD. (*Sings, to the tune of "The moment he sets up house."*)
Ah! Mama, how I share in
That delightful sentiment!
A person doesn't talk much at my age,
But he experiences things deeply.
Take me to this kind father,
So that I might tell him ecstatically:
In making my mother happy,
You bind me to you until I die.
DUBOSQUET. (*Sings, to the tune of "One day Guillot found Lisette."*)
This scene is touching.
Even for me whose element is laughter.
Seeing that everyone's lamenting
I'm going to cry as well.
Blinval, is it a comedy

We're playing tonight
Or a tragedy instead?
BLINVAL. (*Finishing the song.*) Why, no. Really, it's a duty.
(*Speaking.*) Yes, we're fulfilling an obligation,
Very dear, alas, to nature,
Since chance has given us
The opportunity, sweet to my heart,
Of presenting to our benefactor
Our talents, and those of my wife.
My friends, support our plans here
With all your hearts.
DUBOSQUET. (*Softly.*) And what are they? Give us the facts.
Is everything changed then?
BLINVAL. No, really, nothing's changed.
DUBOSQUET. Well, then, we're always ready to serve you.
BLINVAL. How can we show you our appreciation?
ADÈLE. Ah! My heart can't keep quiet!
You know that. And I was the one
You were going to please here.
If you only knew what I owe:
Everything I'd eventually like to do,
And everything my heart forces me to do here.
DUBOSQUET. (*Staring at ADÈLE, and to BLINVAL*)
That girl is lovely and speaks with ease.
Who is she, my dear?
BLINVAL. I don't know where she comes from,
But I see a charming feature in her:
To show her appreciation,
She was about to become an actress.
DUBOSQUET. (Sings, *to the tune of "Wake up..."*)
I value her all the more for it.
This self-sacrifice does her honor.
But a person willingly gets involved in everything
When it involves a benefactor.
DUBOSQUET. (*Seeing them enter.*)
The rest of the company is coming here to fetch us.
Let's go. Let's not make them wait any longer.
(*To BLINVAL.*) We have to rehearse, my friend.

BRISEREIN. (*Entering. Slightly drunk.*)
Well, gentlemen, I believe, God forgive me,
That you want to sleep here.
Making me lie around like this
You're having a little laugh at my expense.
But it is time,
If you want to appear in Melun[50] tonight,
To leave this company
And go where your comedy
Calls you at the moment.
VILLEBRUN. My friend, we're staying here;
You see, we've got other things on our minds.
BRISEREIN. Very well. But, I say,
Are you making any money in this delightful place?
BLINVAL. We're performing out of duty
And that's worth more than money;
We're performing out of gratitude.
Whether we have gold or not, we're always happy
When virtue is our reward.
BRISEREIN. That's very well said, but that doesn't pay
For either your trouble or my salary.
Really, I'll grow very fat in this trade!
Am I so rich—me—to be put on the spot
With two horses at sixty francs for the pair
And my arms crossed with nothing to do?
All the same, you're wrong. I say it to each of you:
You'd make a hundred francs at Melun.
Mr. Gueulard and all his studies,
Mr. Daniere and all his students,
Mr. Pigeon with his pastry cooks,
Mr. Prelude, the organist,
Madame Egrillard, the prude,
John Giles Lescarpin with his cobblers,
Mr. Sirop, the druggist,
And Mr. Griffon, the notary—
All of these will have made more money in a day
Than you'll certainly earn in this place.
MRS. BLINVAL. Briserein, we repeat

[50] A village in France, located in the south-eastern suburbs of Paris.

We're performing here for love,
For the sake of our hearts.
And when we celebrate the birthday of a good friend,
Aren't we always very happy?
Go lie down, drink heartily, be peaceful, joyful . . .
Tomorrow, we'll sing on the way,
And we'll pay you well, my friend.
Nothing costs too much when a person's contented!
BRISEREIN. Well, you'll be equally content with me.
Besides, everyone around me assures me
That gentleman whom you're celebrating,
Whom you love, whom you're singing about,
Knows how to pay back, with interest,
What everyone has done for him.
I swear, his praise was everywhere today.
One was saying, "He's my father."
Another said, "He's mine."
Honor him then, you'll be doing well,
For, in truth, an honest man
Is a gift of nature.
(Here the chorus of the rondo is repeated. The village girls enlarge the circle and everyone sings in chorus. BRISEREIN and his companions have gone.)

"To Celebrate the Festival"

Let us banish all sadness,
Our hearts belong to the celebration,
That's the surest
Of our pleasures.
It's the refrain
Of our pleasures,
It's the refrain
Of our pleasures.
It's the refrain,
The refrain
Of our pleasures,
It's the refrain

Of our pleasures,
It's the refrain
Of our pleasures!
(*They exit, and the play that was announced is performed as follows.*)

THE TOKEN OF APPRECIATION

Birthday present – Vaudeville

A person is the very image of the gods
When he works for the happiness of mankind.
The Token of Appreciation

CHARACTERS

Hylas, *Hercules's companion, imprisoned by the nymphs from the gardens of Momus*
Lycus, *soldier in Hylas's company, imprisoned with him*
Momus[51]
Lincus, *a young Greek, in love with Orphanis*
Orphanis, *an Athenian girl, in love with Lincus*
Nais, Nereid, Oreade, Aspasia, Nymphea, Naiad, *six nymphs*
Four Cupids.

The action takes place near Athens, in the gardens of Momus, bearing fruit and flowers.

LYCUS. What a life we lead in these delightful groves in the midst of all these women, Hylas! You can say what you want, but this way of life pleases me more than where your attachment to Hercules drags you . . . always into battle.
HYLAS. Yes, but always to triumph! And I'd much rather the laurels I gather with Alcides than the dangerous perfume of the flowers with which the nymphs intoxicate me and hold me here in the most effeminate captivity.
LYCUS. They all claim the good fortune of capturing you. It's at least as cruel business as the one to which you're condemned. These women will bury you here. The honor of defeating all the

[51] In Greek mythology, the god of censure, ridicule, and satire.

monsters and captivating all the beautiful women belongs to Hercules alone, and you're not Hercules!

HYLAS. I'm jealous of his valor, not of his flirtations. Still, I have to submit. Ah! Lycus, do you have any idea of my fate? Only by earning the heart of one of the nymphs will I be able to return, one day, to the outside world. My chains will be broken only at that price. Momus, himself, Momus, the master of these regions, confirmed it again to me a little while ago.

LYCUS. Oh! But isn't there a better way of deciding on one of them than courting all of them?

HYLAS. It's the best way, my dear Lycus.

(Sings, to the tune of "The Ballad of Gulnare.")

To captivate a beauty forever,
And to hold her, alas, to excite her,
It's enough that, near to her, we use
The art of pleasing . . . and not of loving.
Know this then about that charming sex:
To bind us to it is its sweetest pleasure,
And without concern for our tender fears,
As soon as it triumphs, it laughs at our sighs.
And in turn, let us attempt to use
The alluring features
With which it likes to be assured,
And to conquer it, let's all have the courage
Of seducing it, rather than loving it.

LYCUS. Ah! My dear Hylas, whatever you may say about it:

(*Sings, to the same tune.*)

You can be sure, we defy it in vain.
We think we have conquered it,
But it subdues us,
And if, by chance, it becomes our slave,
In yielding to us, it alone is the one that's leading.

HYLAS. Be that as it may, Lycus, the route that I'm taking is better. By not committing myself, by behaving in the same way toward all these women, I'll soon excite the jealousy in their hearts. Then, inevitably, one will make up her mind. I'll offer no resistance. I might love her then, in turn—at least I'll let her think so—and my liberty will become the price of my success. I'll

return to Laomedon's[52] realms; I'll find my beloved Alcides again, and we'll go on fighting, instead of loving.
LYCUS. I don't like that plan very much. I'm very comfortable here, and I'd rather spend my life with women rather than soldiers.
HYLAS. Ah! You weren't made to serve a warrior like Hylas!
LYCUS. Well, leave me in these groves. I'm happy here.
HYLAS. Go away, you effeminate man! By the way, tell me, I beseech you, which one of the six nymphs we see the most frequently here would please you the most?
LYCUS. I'd be very much at a loss to decide. Naiad and Nymphea are still only hinting at the attractions Venus will bestow upon them some day. Nais has something alluring about her—a lovely figure. Nereid, a cheerful expression in her eyes that enchants me. Oreade is built like Hebe. And Aspasia has a certain *je ne sais quoi* about her which is highly esteemed by some lovers.
HYLAS. Well, here I am, after your description, in exactly the same place I was before! More decisive than you, I'll admit, my dear Lycus, that Nais is the one I prefer, and that she upsets, a little bit, my balanced judgment, which I want to keep in all things. I also believe that she'll be the one who'll decide most quickly in my favor. But, Lycus, do you know what they're coming to do in the gardens? Do you know why they're assembling today?
LYCUS. No.
HYLAS. I'm going to tell you. They're about to fulfill a sacred duty. Momus who reigns in these regions has more than one retreat on earth. At the head of one of these retreats located near Athens, several miles away, is a man of rare merit, a philanthropist, a friend of the poor, a supporter of the unfortunate—a sensitive man, precious among those men whose type, in a word, is so little known today, that they must be loved when they are recognized.
LYCUS. Well?
HYLAS. You know that tomorrow is the restoration of the Athenian era. They want to celebrate that period, and Momus wants to have the flowers and fruit from his gardens presented to

[52] King of Troy and Priam's father.

that person, beloved by his countrymen. "Those who sometimes are affected by my wretched influences," he said, "experience such benevolent assistance from him and his household. The pains he takes with them are so paternal and so tender, that it's up to me to repay him. Carry him," he continued, "all the most pleasing products of this garden. It's up to the Graces to praise the friend, the comforter of those who too often mislay their charms. For, don't be deceived," Momus added. "The extravagant worship that some of these unfortunate people give to love, the violent passions of some, the extreme sensitivity of others . . . these are the only causes of their madness, and these motives make them only a thousand times more interesting in the eyes of reason."

(*He sings.*) The spirit would be but a trifle
Without the happy disorder of the heart,
The trouble that this causes
Is the delirium of happiness;
The trouble that that causes
Is the delirium of happiness.
When he is near his love,
The lover doesn't always hear;
When he is near his love,
The lover doesn't always hear
The soft lepers' bells of madness
Joined with the arrows of love;
The soft lepers' bells of madness
Joined with the arrows of love.

LYCUS. Ah! How true this is, my dear Hylas!

HYLAS. Human errors, my friend, are ridiculed only by fools. The true philosopher pities them, reforms them, consoles those who are immersed in them, and deserves, because of that alone, the universal respect of his time. That's the occupation—every moment of the day—of the man to whom the gifts from these gardens are about to be presented. And such is the duty our nymphs are about to fulfill with as much gaiety as haste. (*Here, the introduction to the tune "Young lovers pick some flowers" is heard. HYLAS continues.*) Do you hear them? They're coming. As I myself am moved to tears, I don't want to disturb the ceremonies they're about to perform. Love is a virtue, I know, but charity is

a blessing more precious still. Oh, Lycus! Hercules's friend must know how to honor merit. He wouldn't be worthy of his master, if he did not imitate his virtues as well as his valor. (*They exit.*)
(*The ritornello of the tune mentioned above is heard. Six nymphs proceed to fill the stage and pick flowers from the garden, singing the following verses, to the tune of "Young lovers pick some flowers."*)
Let's share merrily between us
The cares of the entertainment we're preparing
For the generous and sweet mortal
Whose birthday we're celebrating.
The touching homage of these gifts
Is for us a labor very dear,
Since the business at hand
Is praising a tender father.
It's up to us to offer these tributes,
And when some charitable souls
Receive their rewards for virtuous behavior,
It is from our tender hands.
(*They lift their hands to the sky.*)
Oh, you, who give birth to the flowers,
You, who can beautify the earth,
Shower us with your blessings
So that we may honor our father.
Far away from us, seductive love,
Our hearts both flee you and renounce you
For no longer fulfilling, on this day,
The only duties required by nature.
Can the kind and deceptive gentleness
That you cause to reign at Cythera
Be equal to the happiness
Of honoring, of adoring one's father?
NEREID. Hylas has fled. He didn't want to disturb us.
ASPASIA. He could have joined us, and we would have willingly made wreaths from the flowers his hands had picked for us.
NAIS. Ah! You know that he has no less a share in our work. Although I enjoy his passion as much as you, to be fair to him, I think that his heart is as sensitive to love as it is to friendship. It will not have smothered feelings that are so precious to him.

NYMPHEA. He has to share all of ours.
NAIAD. He shares them well besides.
OREADE. Did you say that you knew something?
NAIAD. Oh! I know nothing. My dear, I only predict the future.
NEREID. You ought to have nothing to predict at your age!
NAIS. She's old enough to understand his heart! But here comes Momus. Let's go to him.
MOMUS. Well, have you collected flowers for the friend of all mankind?
ALL THE NYMPHS. (*Showing him what they've just picked.*) You see, Momus.
MOMUS. (*Sings, to the tune of "Filial devotion."*)
Strip all these bushes
To honor so good a father,
And believe that this day full of promise
Will be one of the most glorious days of your life.
These gifts that Flora displays for you,
Presented by your blessed hands
Are positive proofs
Of filial devotion.
We're content, we're happy,
Yielding to the ecstasy
Of the feeling
That a virtuous man
Inspires in us.
Seeing him, the heart produces
A sweet and divine impulse,
The exquisite delight
Of filial devotion.
NEREID. Yes, Momus, you have conveyed to our hearts the feelings that move you. Compassion does away with your high-spirited personality. That's the story of all good hearts. In them, madness doesn't alter the tenderness of their souls.
NAIS. But tell us about that kind man. We could never hear too much about the qualities that single him out.
MOMUS. (*Sings, to the tune of "Minuet of Exaudet."*)
The more one wants,
The less one can

Describe him to you.
The best way
To present him to you
Would be to imitate him
And attain his perfection.
When the gods
Created him,
Each gave him
Voluntarily
What he needed
To carry out
His existence.
One gave him his wisdom,
The other his tenderness;
For the gods,
In whose precincts
We find ourselves,
Wanted him to be able
Like themselves,
To make mankind
A little happier.
He did it.
His spirit,
His discretion,
His benevolence
And his tenderness,
His soul, his frankness,
Charm men's existence.
In misfortune,
His noble heart
Sets an example.
All the virtues in him,
Today, erect their temple.

(*Spoken*.) Besides, like I was saying, you have to read in his heart what my mouth expresses so poorly. Virtue is like the gods. You adore it but you don't describe it.

NAIS. Momus, you've convinced us. Expressions of truth are on your lips, and we're all happy to see that your tendency to joke around doesn't prevent you from being emotional and sincere when the time comes.

MOMUS. Don't you know that one day I scolded Vulcan for not having made a little window in the heart of the man he had created in order to see his most secret thoughts? The observation should convince you that I used to love to study that interesting creature. If I wish to point out his faults, I can appreciate his virtues and honor them accordingly, when they strike me, with a tone that's appropriately honest and true. Go, my friends, go prepare everything that's needed for the holy act we have in mind. (*Sings, to the tune of "Filial devotion."*)

May the oak and the olive tree
Rest upon his head,
And may what our hearts
Are about to proclaim
Echo everywhere.
Ah! With pleasure one expresses
This delightful feeling,
The most precious virtue to the gods,
And filial devotion.

THE SIX NYMPHS and MOMUS. (*Sing, to the same tune.*)

THE NYMPHS. Yes, we go passionately . . .

MOMUS. Fly, fly, passionately . . .

ALL. To fulfill a duty that honors us;
How sweet it is to present a flower
To the person everyone adores!
No other joy can equal
The one created
By so sweet a feeling.
Happiness is only part
Of filial devotion. (*The NYMPHS exit.*)

MOMUS. (*Alone.*) Oh! How charming the women are when virtue graces them! It's the make-up that makes them beautiful. But what does this young man want? His appearance interests me. Could he bear some relation to me?

LINCUS. Kind God of Madness, allow me to implore you. I was one of your victims in the past! Alas! I must have been, since I was a victim of love. The two of you are so much alike!

MOMUS. I'll listen to him. He supports my authority!
LINCUS. (*Passionately.*) I'm an example of what you're talking about. Be so good as to hear me out. I loved a young Athenian girl whose name was Orphanis. I loved her. Ah! Momus! With that passion people use your features to describe, when they want to express violence. I thought I was loved in return. I did everything I could to be, but I had a rival. I thought she preferred him, and the sudden disappearance of my beloved made me think I had been abandoned. I searched for Orphanis in vain. All of Greece reverberated with my cries and saw my tears flow. I never again found the one I loved. I lost the use of my senses. Disjointed words came out of my mouth. I could no longer articulate anything but love and Orphanis. To me they meant the same thing. A terrible illness weakened my spirit. They took me to the home of this famous man for whom, I know, you're preparing a celebration today. There, thank heaven! How precious and touching was the care! I had lost my father; I found him again in him. There I found everything that could bring me back to my senses and the hope of happiness that I thought had disappeared. "Go," that generous man said to me after several months, "you're completely healed, and the liberty, which had been deprived you to insure the success of your treatment, is restored to you with your health." And I cried, filled with tender feelings. "I'm happier than you," continued that model of humanity, "since I've made you happy. Contributing to the happiness of others is the only happiness I know."
MOMUS. What a decent, honest man!
LINCUS. (*Continuing quickly.*) But it's that he says the same thing to all the others. If they were there, if they heard me, I'm sure they'd all agree with me. Free, I hastened to you when I learned that your nymphs were going to honor him. I beg your permission to join them. I'll put my hand on my heart and say to them: "Here. Here's where you should place your offerings. For here he is, the one who is close to the gods, and who must, as a result, become the idol of men."
MOMUS. (*Aside.*) This child has compassion. I have to reward him. (*To LINCUS.*) Young man, do you still love the one who disturbed your senses?

LINCUS. (*Very quickly.*) Ah! Those senses, that soul, that love, it all belongs to her. Everything is hers. She's the mistress of it all. Let her disturb me. Let her upset me. Rather than the soundest wisdom, I prefer the disorder into which she plunges my senses. (*Sings, to the tune of "I love you so much," with the utmost passion.*)
How to describe for you the love
That inflames me and devours me:
Could I exist a single day
Without swearing to her that I love her?
My soul loses itself in her.
What keeps me alive? Her soul.
It is the one that answers
When I question my own.

She is in the flower that I smell,
She is in the star that I admire,
She's in my heart, in my blood
She's in the air I breathe.
If, for a moment, I implore the gods,
My homage is for her alone.
And in spite of myself, my soul and vows
No longer fly but to her image.

Ah! Momus, be so kind as to listen to me,
And return to me the one I love.
Though you're a god, please imitate
The man whom you are honoring.
You know him. Like the gods
He has no desires, no ambitions,
But the power to make happy
Those who come to him and surround him.

MOMUS. (*Calling.*) Aspasia! (*She enters.*) Bring here that young lady you and your companions found the other day near the forests that shade my home.

ASPASIA. I go to carry out your orders.

MOMUS. (*To LINCUS.*) You're going to see the one you love again. But, for the purpose of finding out what she thinks, stay out of sight for a moment. I'll call you when it's time.

LINCUS. (*About to hide under a nearby tree.*) All right. But don't restrain my love too long or soon it might break the harness you put on it.

(*ASPASIA leads in ORPHANIS and then goes out.*)

MOMUS. (*To ORPHANIS.*) As I was forced to return to Olympus yesterday, I was unable to hear the conclusion of your adventures. A few reasons make them even more interesting to me today. The threats that had been made to you regarding the young man whom you preferred over the one you were presented by the hand of greed, impaired your health to the point of being placed in that asylum in Athens where those kinds of illnesses are treated so successfully?

ORPHANIS. I stayed there for three months, and the kind comforter I found there, treated me with sensible methods that affected me mentally rather than physically. My health was immediately restored. Ah! I can't express to you everything my heart feels for him. (*Sings, to the tune of "When in an obscure tower."*)

Everything gets mixed up in me
When I think of the kindness
He's showered on me.
Alas! Scarcely out of childhood,
I knew little about my situation,
But by questioning myself
With frankness
And without equivocation,
I recognized that when a person is in love,
Friendship looks like love.

The virtues that heaven collects
Characterize his inclinations;
To love him, I had to gather together
All my feelings,
But to whom should they be given?
They electrified me one by one,
Then I saw that in a tender heart,
Friendship looks like love.

MOMUS. Precious and attractive child, were you unaware then that your lover was nearby?

ORPHANIS. That house, you know, contains individuals of both sexes, but during the course of the treatments, they neither see nor become acquainted with each other. Ah! Nothing that decency requires escapes the vigilant eye of that administrator. If when they are on the road to recovery, his kindness permits them to be together to speed it along, these rare and modest reunions take place under the clear and strict supervision of the sensible guardians who share his opinions. The moral purpose behind these gatherings is to allow the patients to enjoy together those honest pleasures which always benefit their recovery. Dances, an entertainment produced by the patients themselves, strolls . . . that's the unruliness that perfects the cures, and that brings us to the state you see me in.

MOMUS. But, Orphanis, the cause of your troubles has not been destroyed in you.

ORPHANIS. You can cure the sad effects of love, but you can never extinguish the fires it ignited in us, and especially those of a first love. (*Sings, to the tune of "The mind is a mere trifle."*)

Ah! My heart entirely belongs to Lincus,
I exist now only for him.
If he didn't trouble my thoughts,
Would my breast be beating today?
It would be easier to extinguish,
To blot out the sun,
Than to weaken or restrain
The sensation of my love.
Ah! No, no, I'll never forget him.

(*To the tune of "Oh, my Delia," with a great deal of expression.*)

Alas! Within the boundaries of life,
His name used to console my sorrow.
His image, always precious,
Used to calm my heart.
I saw his image always following me,
And I knew at that moment
That one could cease to live
Without ceasing to love her lover;

That one could cease to live
Without ceasing to love her lover.
(LINCUS, hurrying to his mistress's feet.)
LINCUS. (*Sings, to the same tune.*)
Ah! That lover for whom Orphanis mourns
Still burns for her attentions;
Every moment, heavens! Every hour,
He wanted to fly into her arms.
Join my soul with yours.
Let yourself love constantly.
When two people have suffered for one another,
Should they ever be separated?
ORPHANIS. (*Lifting him up, and along with him.*)
Ah! When two people have suffered for one another,
Should they ever be separated?
MOMUS. (*Joining them together.*) No, my children, no. You'll no longer be apart, and it is at the feet of the one who saved the day for you that you will promise to love each other forever. Instrumental in making you happy, he ought to be the one to make your happiness eternal. I know his soul; the more such delights are prepared for it, the happier it is. Go, my friends. You'll return with the nymphs, and you'll share with them the tribute they're about to present.
(*The young people exit.*)
HYLAS. I'm coming, my dear Momus, to call upon you to keep your word. My freedom, you said, had to do with the effect I will have on one of your nymphs: I'm free if I inflame her, captive forever, if I'm unsuccessful. I've tackled them all, and contrary to what I'm used to, I've encountered resistance in almost all of them. Nevertheless, there's one who loves me. I'm bringing her here so that you can question her, and so that you can keep your promise, if I've been successful.
(*NAIS bursts with laughter.*)
MOMUS. (*To HYLAS.*) Those inclinations don't seem too much in your favor. No matter. Nais, respond.
NAIS. Well, Hylas, since you need proof of my feelings for you, let me tell you that all I did was amuse myself at your expense.

My companions did the same thing, and you'll never see in me feelings that are different than theirs.

MOMUS. (*To HYLAS.*) If she isn't in love, at least she's honest!

HYLAS. Look at me, fooled again! Oh, women! Women!

NAIS. You'd stop complaining about them if you always treated them well.

HYLAS. (*Tenderly, to NAIS.*) Ah! I wouldn't complain about them if they resembled you.

NAIS. You know, Momus, these moments are devoted entirely to those efforts that cannot suffer any distraction. (*To HYLAS. Sings, to the tune of "I had dared to defy love."*)

For the one whom we all love,
Let us create crowns of roses,
In the midst of moments so sweet,
Can we do anything else?
Don't disturb the enjoyment
Of these delightful moments,
Today, alas! All my vows
Must belong to appreciation.

HYLAS. *(Sings.)* Ah! What could take the place
Of so gratifying an effort for our souls?
Would it be that feeble god
Who inflames us with his passions?
No, no, love and its favors
Could never do it;
The principal need of our hearts
Is to honor a sensible man.

NAIS. You've spoken in vain, my dear Hylas.
(*Sings, to the tune of "Sensible woman."*)
It is so sweet to worship the one you love,
To shower him with offerings and vows.
Ah! It's celebrating, cherishing virtue itself
When you pay homage to a virtuous man.
But I especially owe him so much respect
For the goodness with which he surrounded me;
I love him so much
That the heart which gives me life,
Becomes the altar where he must be adored.

HYLAS. It seems to me that all that could have been arranged. No one honors more than I the person we're talking about. His virtues, celebrated by all of Greece, did not come to my attention without exciting my admiration. But we can reconcile all these things.

(*Sings, to the tune of "Woman, will you try?")*

Today, you love a lover,
And tomorrow, you caress a friend.
The more the heart practices loving,
The more tenderness it has.
To whatever object it may be linked,
Let us always yield to its murmuring.
Love is, just like friendship,
A gift of nature.

NAIS. Ah! How far I am from your opinion.

(*Sings, the same tune.*)

With love, a person always is
Afraid or delirious,
Almost every moment of the day
You tremble about it,
Or you long for it;
And soon repentance
Will pay for a few weak attractions.
I'd rather live without pleasures
Than exist on the brink of tears.

But with tender friendship,
We don't feel any pain,
And if our heart is bound to it,
It doesn't complain about its bonds.
Peaceful and divine feeling,
It's with you that a poor soul
Offers an innocent sacrifice
On nature's altars.

(NYMPHEA, running in.)

NYMPHEA. Everything's ready, Momus. My companions await your orders.

(*Sings, to the tune of "With the games in the village.")*

We're burning to offer our praises
To our charming protector;
Our gifts are but weak indications
Of what causes our passion.
But there is nothing better
Than the heart's sweet offering.
That kind man is pleased more
With pure vows than with flowers.

The one we love and respect
Because of his godlike qualities
Should be arriving soon.
At the height of our prosperity,
Let's be content in offering him ourselves.
That's the sweetest thing for him.
He who succeeds in making others happy
Is always happy in his own heart.
(NAIAD enters.)
NAIAD. Hurry up, Nymphea, and tell us what Momus said. Ah! There he is, in person. Well, should we get started?
MOMUS. How your eagerness pleases me, my children! Yes, yes, you're about to leave. You're about to take to that virtuous man, on my behalf, all the feelings that he inspires in me. Have you prepared something to say to him, my dear Naiad, while you're surrounding him with your garland?
NAIAD. Nothing is prepared when your heart is speaking, that would be like using your mind. What do you need it for when feeling alone reigns? I'll just say to him quite simply:
(*Sings, to the tune of "Why am I not the fern?"*)
My duty is to please you,
My happiness is to love you,
One always knows how to express
What she thinks of her father.
You are to our youth
What the sun is to the flowers,
Your virtues show the influence
Of all your claims upon our hearts.
(OREADE enters.)

OREADE. (*To MOMUS.*) Ah! I certainly knew that we'd never get any news by sending these children to you. Very well. We'll be leaving.
MOMUS. We're rehearsing our songs, lovely Oreade. You've undoubtedly composed one.
OREADE. I don't know how to write verses.
HYLAS. (*To OREADE, tenderly.*) With so much grace in your face and your figure, you must have all the talent there is!
OREADE. Right! That's what he says to all the girls.
HYLAS. (*Softly to OREADE.*) But he's only thinking of you.
MOMUS. (*To OREADE.*) Go, on. Act as if you were there. Imagine that you're looking at the one you're celebrating.
OREADE. (*Sings, to the tune of "Hippolytus."*)
Why then this illusion?
Do we need so much skill
To recall the impression
Of the friend who inspires us,
Endowed with such appealing qualities?
It would be wrong to pretend
Since, at every moment, nature
Paints his qualities inside of us.
(Enter NEREID and ASPASIA.)
NEREID. Ah! I see why no one's returned (*To HYLAS.*) since the gentleman is here.
MOMUS. Always wicked, Nereid.
NEREID. But always true!
MOMUS. Ah! You rascal, you're in love!
NEREID. With him?
HYLAS. Why not?
NEREID. Why, you're too fickle to keep a woman!
HYLAS. (*Softly to NEREID, and tenderly.*) Nereid, your eyes would have to correct me of that fault.
NEREID. (*To the women.*) Well, you heard him! I bet he said the same thing to you just now.
MOMUS. Forget about all that. What will you sing today, Nereid?
NEREID. You know I can't sing.
MOMUS. Isn't the one we're honoring able to perform miracles?

NEREID. Oh, yes! Well: (*Sings, to the tune of "Oh, my tender bagpipe."*)
Without fear I'll show
The precious marble
Where Minerva painted
All his glorious features;
No words spoken,
My hand will touch my heart,
And that will teach it
Everything that is engraved there.
MOMUS. And you, Aspasia?
ASPASIA. (*Sings, to the tune of "To love you well."*)
Alas, alas, I lack eloquence;
My heart's so full, it can only melt.
He'll really have to forgive my silence,
One speaks little when she feels so deeply.
MOMUS. But you'll have to say something to him.
ASPASIA. I'll say to him: "Wise, and virtuous father,
It would take talent to sing for you,
And I have nothing but a sincere soul;
But what it offers is purer than songs.
Live happily, tender and faithful friend,
Heaven owes you long and peaceful days.
A person is the very image of the gods
When he works for the happiness of mankind."
MOMUS. Let's go, my friends. We're all assembled. (*To the wings.*) Let the cupids lead in the lovers. All these tender feelings suit a sensitive soul. They must all be presented to him.
(*Here the cupids appear holding the two lovers in their midst. The orchestra plays the ritornello to "Suitable Husbands." The two lovers take their places at the rear of the stage in the custody of one of the cupids. The three others dance to the same tune that the nymphs are about to sing, and give them the garlands it is their duty to present. HYLAS and LYCUS retire to the rear of the stage, near the group of lovers.*)
THE NYMPHS. (*Sing, along with the two lovers, to the tune of "We need suitable husbands."*)
What a divine and cherished task

We're about to perform together!
Is there anything more sacred
Than the duty that gathers us together?
Tenderness, respect, sweet desire,
All are united in our hearts,
How dear is the feeling
That friendship inspires and demands.

One day, our flowers will fade,
That sad destiny threatens them.
But the tokens of our love,
Ah! Never will anything erase them.
As long as his virtues
Live in the temple of memory,
Our sweet tributes will be seen there,
Entwined beside his glory.

What he has done will never die.
The hand of appreciation
Will engrave all of his good deeds
On the landmarks of life.
And we'll see posterity,
Recalling the age in which we live,
Pass them down through eternity
In the hearts of all mankind.

END OF THE TOKEN OF APPRECIATION

(*As soon as the vaudeville is finished, one of the nymphs, seeing MR. MEILCOUR come onstage, runs to him and leads him in, saying:)*
Ah! Here is the god among men! Here's that kind Mr. Meilcour whom we've just sung about. Let him receive in person, yes, in person and without allegory, all the tributes that we owe him.
(*MEILCOUR finds himself in the middle of the stage, surrounded by all the nymphs.*)
ONE OF THE NYMPHS. Ah, please accept
What we so foolishly attempted here
To entertain and amuse you.
Oh, my father,
Do not scold us for the feeling:
It is so tender to honor the person we love,
That, indeed, we got caught up
In its sweetness.
Promise us that your heart,
That heart so good, so sensitive, and so tender,
Will always agree to listen to
The language of friendship;
And since the signs of our affection
Are joined to you forever,
Promise that you'll always lavish upon us
These blessed gifts, like today.
For our part, we will swear to you
To always zealously imitate
The virtues of which your soul is such a fine model.
MEILCOUR. All my days will be devoted
To loving you and cherishing you always.
(*To everyone surrounding him.*)
My friends, what a happy moment!
But tell me, I want to know,
Whose idea was this interesting birthday present?
It wouldn't be right to keep it a secret now.
(*At that moment, the nymphs who were close to MEILCOUR set him apart by moving a little to the right or left. Then ADÈLE, who has just performed the role of ORPHANIS, runs to find the BLINVAL family, and leading them to MR. MEILCOUR, she speaks with a great deal of passion.*)

ADÈLE. Oh, highly respected and sensitive man, here are those in whom your good deeds have aroused the idea. Your heart, alas, will not be offended by it. Recall their cherished features.
MEILCOUR. (*In joyful ecstasy, and holding them next to his heart.*) What! It's you, oh, my beloved friends!
MRS. BLINVAL. Yes, it's us, whose affection and appreciation
Present to you the tributes of our tender hearts,
And who place with excitement
The crown of virtues on that radiant brow.
(*Here, the husband and wife place a crown on MR. MEILCOUR's head.*)
BLINVAL. (*Passionately.*) Here are the wife and child, my father,
For whom you saved the day.
In a moment so sweet and so prosperous for them,
Receive their tokens of love.
Under the disguise of a strolling player,
I got involved in the play that was being prepared for you.
And my friends, and my beloved wife,
All wanted to honor you like them. *(Indicating the group.)*
But now, everyone has to know
What attaches me to you so deeply.
Let me express it here in front of you,
Let me say it, my father!
(*During the last lines above, BLINVAL, his son, and two of the nymphs stand to MR. MEILCOUR's right, and the two other nymphs and ADÈLE stand to his left. Discovering himself in the middle as a result, MEILCOUR says nobly:*)
MEILCOUR. Silence. Alas! If I've been able to do
Something or other which has pleased you,
Oh, my friends, I no longer recall.
The man who has occasionally enjoyed the glory
Of drying, for a moment, tears of sadness,
Shouldn't keep the memory of it alive
Except to double the amount of good fortune.
You and your companions, settle here on my estate.
I want to live here with you forever.
(*Everyone bows.*) Here we'll build a theatre;
Like you, I was born to worship that art,

And I'll share your inclinations.
But, my good friends, I insist,
That as long as it exits,
On the proscenium shall be engraved:
GRATITUDE CONSTRUCTS IT,
FRIENDSHIP WILL MAKE IT ETERNAL.
(*The two last lines appear on the proscenium, by means of a transparent screen, and the curtain falls.*)

POEMS FOR THE DINNERS AT SAINTE-PÉLAGIE (1801)

I

The Society of the Dinners
to
The Opposition Party
Tune: "Spouses have to match."

Since a similar fate unites us,
Far from aggravating our troubles here,
Ah! Let's sow some flowers over our chains
In this little cubbyhole instead.
Mount Parnassus[53] has more than one laurel
For our brows, eager for glory;
The Nine Sisters[54] lead to the Temple of Memory
By more than one path.

You portray our wrongs in your songs,
Among us, our less demanding minds
Seek only your approval
And the sweetest means of pleasing.
In this poetic dispute,
To your verses, let us join our own;
But they only manage to sparkle
From borrowing your brilliance.

---

[53] In Greek mythology, Mount Parnassus was sacred to Apollo, and the home of the nine Muses.

[54] The nine Muses. The society of Dinners at Saint-Pélagie numbered nine members.

Friends, let us serve the God of Poetry,
With clamor, without anger, without alarm;
And the wishes offered by our hearts
Will be more charming in his eyes.
You will be led by the Graces
To make him accept these gifts,
But those that we will offer
We will glean from your footsteps.

II

Verses on a Picture of Diogenes

The muse Clio[55] *presented the Society with a superb painting depicting Diogenes, the cynic, his lantern in hand. The president of the Society*[56] *spoke the following verses:*

Looking for a man, Diogenes
Wanted to find virtues and talents in him;
And among the Greeks, who are famous
Less for their morals than for their true philosophers,
That combination was not too easy to find.
My dear friends, what do you say?
Let us imagine our France
Somewhat more fertile in this regard;
Would it pay him tribute?
I don't know, but at least I assert to the Institute
That the good philosopher might have lowered his lantern
And that his search might have reached its goal
If his auspicious country had given birth to Saint-P.[57]

---

[55] Clio's domain was history. Each member of the society took the name of a Muse. Clio likely represented Saint-Perne, the honoree of Sade's poem.

[56] Probably the Marquis de Sade himself.

[57] Saint-Perne, one of the members of the Society.

III

To my Rose

Tune: "About the Stormy Evening."

Lovely rose, queen of flowers,
Come, if you can, and soften
The extreme harshness of my miseries
By painting the beauties I love.

Charming Rose, gazing at you,
I see the freshness of Helen,
And my mouth, inhaling you,
Thinks it's inhaling her sweet breath.

Those tears, which every spring
Through the hands of the tender dawn
Drench your nascent buds,
To cool them, to make them flower;
Dear Helen, if you wanted
To become inflamed with the passion that troubles me,
I know, indeed, where I would see your nascent buds,
When your heart is beating next to mine.

My rose also offers modesty
With which your brow often becomes incensed.
If I wanted to pull the petals off the flower,
The thorn is there to prevent me;
Do not use greater efforts;
Pleasure is your reward,
And set against my sweet raptures
Only a thorn for your defense.

If I want to open wide its bosom,
Yours appears before my eyes;
Its pleasing outline shows
An altar, created by the hand of a god;

But my rose is likewise
The sad image of your love;
It blossoms and dies in a day;
Have you sighed longer?

IV

Whimsy

Tune: "About the Baroness."

At Pélagie,
You spend your days so gaily,
That it would be utterly stupid
For you to leave right away
From Pélagie.

At Pélagie,
For those who will come to see you,
Without arousing envy, you can give
A few concerts in the parlor
At Pélagie.

At Pélagie,
When one likes pleasures so much,
It's truly madness
Not to limit his desires
To Pélagie.

At Pélagie,
The music must delight
More than that of *Iphigenia*,[58]
And to hear it, you have to stay
At Pélagie.

At Pélagie,
When one joins the battalion,

[58] *Iphigenia in Tauris,* composed by Chistoph Willibald Gluck in 1778 with a libretto by Nicholas-François Guillard. This opera marked Gluck's final triumph at the Paris Opera.

Parents, liberty, are all left behind;
And one has no other stimulus
But Pélagie.

At Pélagie,
Seeing the fat S.[59] as a sapper,[60]
Behaving like a child…
Alas! Who could be afraid
Of Pélagie.

At Pélagie,
When M***[61] appears as a sultan,
Whose wife wouldn't want
To spend a moment
At Pélagie.

At Pélagie,
When D***[62] writes poems,
Quite easily one forgets
The bolts and latches
Of Pélagie.

At Pélagie,
Since so many charms exist,
Let's sing about love and madness,
We may owe it to ourselves to never leave
Pélagic.

---

59 Sade.

60 A soldier, usually in a military unit of engineers.

61 A.P.F. Ménégault, one of the members who had previously plagiarized Sade's *Aline and Valcour* under the title, *Valmer and Lydia.* Sade complained about this to the *Journal de Paris* on 5 December 1798.

62 Probably Hurard Saint-Désiré, an amateur poet, and one of the three inmates who founded the Society.

VERSES

Which were sung to His Eminence
Monseigneur Cardinal Maury,[63]
Archbishop of Paris
6 October 1812,
at the mental asylum
near Charenton.

To the tune: "Since My Childhood."

Like the son of the Almighty,
With a goodness that's rare,
Under the appearance of a mortal,
Coming to console the unfortunate,
Your soul, full of grandeur,
Always steady, always fair,
Beneath the pontifical purple
Does not scorn misfortune.

---

[63] Jean-Sifrein Maury (June 26, 1746 – May 10, 1817), a prelate of great wit and eloquence, and a staunch supporter of Louis XVI and the papacy during the French Revolution. He held the position of Archbishop of Paris from 1810 to 1817.

A Select Bibliography

Bloch, Dr. Iwan. *Marquis de Sade: His Life and Work.* Translated by James Bruce. N.p.: Brittany Press, 1948.

Bremmer, Jan, ed. *From Sappho to De Sade: Moments* in *the History of Sexuality.* London and New York: Routledge, 1991.

Cleugh, James. *The Marquis and The Chevalier.* New York: Duell, Sloan and Pearce; Boston: Little, Brown and Company, 1952.

Dawes, C.R. *The Marquis de Sade: His Biography and Writings.* New Yor*k:* The Macauly Co., 1927.

Dictionnaire Dramatique, Contenant L'Histoire des Théâtres, les Règles du genre Dramatique, les Observations des Maîtres les plus célèbres, et des Réflexions nouvelles sur les Spectacles, sur le génie et Ia conduite de tous les genres, avec les Notices des meilleures Pièces, le Catalogue de tous les Drames, et celui des Auteurs Dramatiques. Three volumes. Paris, 1776; reprint, Geneva: Slatkine Reprints, 1967.

Du Plessix Gray, Francine. *At Home with the Marquis de Sade: A Life.* New York: Simon and Schuster, 1998.

Endore, Guy. *Satan's Saint.* London: W.H. Allen and Company, 1966.

Foster, Annetta. "The Place of Theatre and Drama in the Life of the Marquis de Sade, *homme de lettres extraordinaire.*" Ph.D. diss., University of California, 1975.

Gorer, Geoffrey. *The Devil's Disciple: The Revolutionary Theories of the Marquis de Sade.* Paris: Collection "Le Ballet Des Muses," 1933.

_______. *The Life and Ideas of the Marquis de Sade.* New York: W.W. Norton and Company, 1963.

Hartman, Janine Cey. "The Politics of Decadence: The Political and Social Ideas of Sade, Gautier, Baudelaire, and Flaubert." Ph.D. diss., University of Illinois at Chicago, 1986.

Hayes, Julia Candler. "The Representation of the Self in the Theater of La Chausée, Diderot, and Sade." Ph.D. diss., Northwestern University, 1982.

Horace. *Satires, Epistles, Ars Poetica.* Translated by H.R. Fairclough. Cambridge, Massachusetts and London: Harvard University Press, 1991.

Howarth, William D., ed. *French Theatre in the Neoclassical Era, 1550-1789*. Cambridge: Cambridge University Press, 1997.

Kennedy, Emmet. *A Cultural History of the French Revolution.* New Haven and London: Yale University Press, 1989.

Laborde, Alice M. *Correspondances du Marquis de Sade et de ses proches enrichies de documents, notes et commentaries*. 27 vols. Geneva: Editions Slatkine, 1997.

Le Brun, Annie. *Sade: A Sudden Abyss.* Translated by Camile Naish. San Francisco: City Light Books, 1990.

Lély, Gilbert. *Vie du marquis de Sade.* Paris: Mercure de France, 1989.

Lernig, Walter. *Portrait of de Sade: An illustrated Biography.* Translated by Sarah Twohig. New York: Herder and Herder, 1971.

Lever, Maurice. *Donatien Alphonse François, marquis de Sade.* Paris: Fayard, 1991.

Manceron, Claude. *Age of the French Revolution.* 5 vols. Translated by Patricia Wolf. New York: Simon and Schuster, A Touchstone Book, 1989.

Marchand, Henry L. *The French Pornographers: Including a History of French Erotic Literature.* New York: Book Awards, 1965.

Nodier, Charles. *Souvenirs, épisodes et portraits; pour servir a l'histoire de la révolution et de l'empire*. Brussels: L. Hauman, 1931.

Pauvert, Jean-Jacques. *Sade Vivant*. 3 vols. Paris: Editions Robert Laffont, 1986.

Rodmell, Graham F. *French Drama of the Revolutionary Years.* London: Routledge, 1990.

Sade, Donatien Alphonse François, Marquis de. *Lettres inédites et documents retrouvé par Jean-Louis Debauve.* With a preface by Annie Le Brun. Paris: Editions Rams*ey, Jean-Jacques Pauvert, 1990.*

______. *Oeuvres complètes.* 16 vols. in 8. Paris: Cerde du livre précieux, 1966–1967.

______. *Oeuvres complètes*. Vols. 32-35 Théâtre. With a Preface by Jean-Jacques Brochier. Paris: Jean-Jacques Pauvert, 1970.

______. *Selected Letters.* With a preface by Gilbert Lély. Translated by W.J. Strachan. Edited and with a new introduction by Margaret Crosland and with an afterward by Jeremy Reed. London: Peter Owen, 1965.

Schaeffer, Neil. *The Marquis de Sade.* New York: Alfred A, Knopf, 1999.

Schama, Simon. *Citizens: A Chronicle of the French Revolution.* New York: Alfred A. Knopf, 1989.

Smith, Daniel T. Jr. "Libertine dramaturgy: Reading obscene closet drama in eighteenth-century France." Ph.D. diss., Northwestern University, 2010.

Thomas, Donald. *The Marquis de Sade.* New York: Citadel Press, 1992.

Toepfer, Karl. *Theatre, Aristocracy, and Pornocracy* New York: PAJ Publications, 1991.

Wilson, Colin. *The Misfits: A Study of Sexual Outsiders.* New York: Carroll and Graf Publishers, Inc., 1988.

www.ingramcontent.com/pod-product-compliance
Lightning Source LLC
LaVergne TN
LVHW020534100826
845148LV00010B/1459

* 9 7 8 1 5 9 3 9 3 7 4 1 6 *